ENSURING TEACHERS MATTER

Where to Focus First So STUDENTS Matter Most

SHELLY WILFONG RYAN DONLAN

Solution Tree | Press

Copyright © 2024 by Solution Tree Press

Materials appearing here are copyrighted. With one exception, all rights are reserved. Readers may reproduce only those pages marked "Reproducible." Otherwise, no part of this book may be reproduced or transmitted in any form or by any means (electronic, photocopying, recording, or otherwise) without prior written permission of the publisher.

555 North Morton Street
Bloomington, IN 47404
800.733.6786 (toll free) / 812.336.7700
FAX: 812.336.7790

email: info@SolutionTree.com
SolutionTree.com

Visit **go.SolutionTree.com/teacherefficacy** to download the free reproducibles in this book.

Printed in the United States of America

Library of Congress Cataloging-in-Publication Data

Names: Wilfong, Shelly, author. | Donlan, Ryan A., 1967- author.
Title: Ensuring teachers matter : where to focus first so students matter
  most / Shelly Wilfong and Ryan Donlan.
Description: Bloomington, IN : Solution Tree Press, [2024] | Includes
  bibliographical references and index.
Identifiers: LCCN 2023038756 (print) | LCCN 2023038757 (ebook) | ISBN
  9781954631915 (paperback) | ISBN 9781954631922 (ebook)
Subjects: LCSH: Teachers--Professional relationships. | Teachers--Mental
  Health. | Educational psychology. | Teacher-student relationships. |
  Professional learning communities.
Classification: LCC LB1775 .W5143 2024 (print) | LCC LB1775 (ebook) | DDC
  371.102/3--dc23/eng/20230914
LC record available at https://lccn.loc.gov/2023038756
LC ebook record available at https://lccn.loc.gov/2023038757

Solution Tree
Jeffrey C. Jones, CEO
Edmund M. Ackerman, President

Solution Tree Press
President and Publisher: Douglas M. Rife
Associate Publishers: Todd Brakke and Kendra Slayton
Editorial Director: Laurel Hecker
Art Director: Rian Anderson
Copy Chief: Jessi Finn
Production Editor: Miranda Addonizio
Copy Editor: Evie Madsen
Proofreader: Charlotte Jones
Text and Cover Designer: Fabiana Cochran
Acquisitions Editor: Hilary Goff
Assistant Acquisitions Editor: Elijah Oates
Content Development Specialist: Amy Rubenstein
Associate Editor: Sarah Ludwig
Editorial Assistant: Anne Marie Watkins

Acknowledgments

I have such gratitude for leaders—especially those I worked with during my most formative years as a teacher—including Jim Kirkton and Dr. Robert Duell. Thanks to Dr. David Hoffert and Dr. Steve Troyer for continuing to support my growth as a district leader. I also need to acknowledge my coauthor, Dr. Ryan Donlan; this book would not have been possible without your guidance.

—*Shelly Wilfong*

Many thanks to the incredible educators who contributed notably to my mattering as a teacher, including Elice Howard, Rick Wiles, Jim Winkworth, Mark Lancaster, Rex Bufe, and Jim "Chef" Daunter. Our principal, Bob Doctor, had teacher mattering down pat! With profound influences on my lifelong mattering, I acknowledge my favorite teacher, mentor, and best man, Dr. William A. Halls. Please know you all helped me build from the inside what others have received from me on the outside, putting me first so I could be about others most.

—*Ryan Donlan*

With deep appreciation for his generous contributions of time, encouragement, interest, and expertise, we would like to offer sincere thanks to Dr. Steve Gruenert, who was not only an invaluable scientific resource in the factor analysis that led to the discovery of the foundational elements of mattering but also an invaluable thought partner, dissertation committee member, colleague, and friend.

—*Shelly Wilfong and Ryan Donlan*

Solution Tree Press would like to thank the following reviewers:

Taylor Bronowicz
Math Teacher
Sparkman Middle School
Toney, Alabama

Amber Gareri
Instructional Specialist, Innovation and Development
Pasadena ISD
Pasadena Texas

Kelly Hilliard
Math Teacher
McQueen High School
Reno, Nevada

Jose "JoJo" Reyes
Chief Administration Officer
Parlier Unified School District
Parlier, California

Rachel Swearengin
Fifth-Grade Teacher
Manchester Park Elementary School
Olathe, Kansas

Allison Zamarripa
Reading & Language Arts Curriculum & Instructional Specialist
Pasadena Independent School District
Pasadena, Texas

Visit **go.SolutionTree.com/teacherefficacy** to download the free reproducibles in this book.

Table of Contents

Reproducibles are in italics.

About the Authors ix
Introduction 1
    What Is *Mattering*? 2
    Contemporary Challenges for Teachers 7
    Foundational Elements of Mattering for K–12 Teachers 9
    The Role of Teachers in Mattering 11
    The Obligation of School Leaders in Mattering 12
    About This Book 14

CHAPTER 1
Celebrating the Team, Not Just the Score: *Community* 19
    Getting Started With Community 21
    Implications for Teachers 28
    Implications for School Leaders 30
    Conclusion 34
        Next Steps: Chapter 1 Recap Activity 36
        Your Personal Professional Development:
           Thought Experiment—Community 37

CHAPTER 2
Embracing What You See, and That's a Whole Lot of Me: *Authenticity* 39
    Getting Started With Authenticity 41
    Implications for Teachers 46
    Implications for School Leaders 48
    Conclusion 50
        Next Steps: Chapter 2 Recap Activity 52
        Your Personal Professional Development:
           Thought Experiment—Authenticity 53

CHAPTER 3
Getting Lost in the Moment, With a Good Crowd Around: *Flow* 55

    Getting Started With Flow 57

    Implications for Teachers 64

    Implications for School Leaders 65

    Conclusion 67

        Next Steps: Chapter 3 Recap Activity 69

        Your Personal Professional Development:
        Thought Experiment—Flow 70

CHAPTER 4
Staying the Course, En Route to My Why: *Purpose* 73

    Getting Started With Purpose 76

    Implications for Teachers 80

    Implications for School Leaders 83

    Conclusion 85

        Next Steps: Chapter 4 Recap Activity 87

        Your Personal Professional Development:
        Thought Experiment—Purpose 88

CHAPTER 5
Seeing the Downside as a Necessary Upside: *Assimilation* 91

    Getting Started With Assimilation 95

    Implications for Teachers 100

    Implications for School Leaders 102

    Conclusion 104

        Next Steps: Chapter 5 Recap Activity 106

        Your Personal Professional Development:
        Thought Experiment—Assimilation 107

CHAPTER 6
Getting Real With How Educators Stack Up: *Compensation* 109

    Getting Started With Compensation 112

    Implications for Teachers 118

    Implications for School Leaders 120

    Conclusion 122

        Next Steps: Chapter 6 Recap Activity 124

        Your Personal Professional Development:
        Thought Experiment—Compensation 125

CHAPTER 7
Taking Care to Take Care: *Stability* 127
    Getting Started With Stability 129
    Implications for Teachers 135
    Implications for School Leaders 136
    Conclusion 137
        Next Steps: Chapter 7 Recap Activity 139
        Your Personal Professional Development:
          Thought Experiment—Stability 140

CHAPTER 8
Letting Things Be Loose or Tight: *Job Crafting* 143
    Getting Started With Job Crafting 146
    Implications for Teachers 152
    Implications for School Leaders 154
    Conclusion 155
        Next Steps: Chapter 8 Recap Activity 158
        Your Personal Professional Development:
          Thought Experiment—Job Crafting 159

CHAPTER 9
Putting It All Together: Smarter Stuff That Matters 161
    Getting Started on Putting It All Together 162
    Foundational Elements of Mattering Survey for K–12 Teachers 162
    Teacher Reflection Tool: What Is Most Important to Me? 166
    Teacher Reflection Tool: My Area of Focus Matrix 166
    Teacher Reflection Tool: The Ideal State of Mattering 167
    Teacher Action Plan 168
    Principal Action Plan 170
        Foundational Elements of Mattering Survey for K–12 Teachers .. 172
        Teacher Reflection Tool: What Is Most Important to Me? 175
        Teacher Reflection Tool: My Area of Focus Matrix 176
        Teacher Reflection Tool: The Ideal State of Mattering 177
        Teacher Action Plan 178
        Principal Action Plan 179

Epilogue 181
References and Resources 183
Index 199

About the Authors

Shelly Wilfong, PhD, is assistant superintendent of Wawasee Community School Corporation in Syracuse, Indiana. She has been an educational professional for thirty years, with nineteen years as a classroom teacher. Dr. Wilfong's main responsibilities include all aspects of curriculum, instruction, and assessment. She also enjoys working with educational professionals as an adjunct for Indiana State University. Prior to her current role, Dr. Wilfong served as a district chief analytics officer. Her main responsibilities included assessment and data analysis, support to staff in understanding and interpreting data, program evaluation, and leading initiatives to improve student achievement.

Throughout her career, Dr. Wilfong has presented at multiple national and international conferences, including for ASCD, International Baccalaureate Americas, and Indiana Association of School Principals. Dr. Wilfong became a National Board Certified Teacher in 2000. While a teacher, she was a guest panelist for National Public Radio's *Talk of the Nation* on the topics of teaching students about the presidential election (2000) and student reaction to the Iraq war (2003).

Dr. Wilfong earned a bachelor's degree in history and education from Huntington University in Indiana, a master's degree in curriculum and instruction from Indiana Wesleyan University, and a doctorate from Indiana State University.

To learn more about Dr. Wilfong's work, visit https://matteringk12.com or follow @shellywilfong on X (Twitter).

Ryan Donlan, EdD, is a professor in the Department of Educational Leadership at the Bayh College of Education at Indiana State University. Dr. Donlan served for twenty years in traditional and charter schools in K–12 education—as a teacher as well as a school building and district leader. He taught for years at the college and university levels in the areas of leadership, communication, and education. Dr. Donlan conducts and offers school program reviews, a variety of training opportunities, consulting services, and professional presentations for educators, stakeholder groups, and organizational leaders.

A member of various professional organizations, Dr. Donlan enjoys robust teaching, scholarship, and service and received the Holmstedt Distinguished Professorship and Faculty Distinguished Service awards. Dr. Donlan has presented throughout the United States and abroad on adaptive communication, leadership agility, and leveraging relationships for professional and personal success. He has served on numerous boards, committees, and task forces and is a frequent faculty sponsor for doctoral dissertations.

Dr. Donlan pens articles for a variety of magazines and professional journals, and his books include *Minds Unleashed: How Principals Can Lead the Right-Brained Way*, *The Hero Maker: How Superintendents Can Get Their School Boards to Do the Right Thing*, *The School Board Member's Guidebook: Becoming a Difference Maker for Your District*, and *All Other Duties as Assigned: The Assistant Principal's Critical Role in Supporting Schools Inside and Out*.

Dr. Donlan earned a bachelor's degree in social sciences and English from the University of Michigan–Flint, a master's degree in curriculum design and classroom teaching from Michigan State University, and an educational specialist's degree and a doctorate from Central Michigan University.

To learn more about Dr. Donlan's work, visit https://ryandonlan.com or follow @RyanDonlan on X (Twitter).

To book Shelly Wilfong or Ryan Donlan for professional development, contact pd@SolutionTree.com.

Introduction
A Blinding Flash of the Obvious: The **What** and **Why** of Mattering

Before the start of every commercial flight, you hear the familiar phrase, *In case of a cabin pressure emergency and the oxygen masks deploy, please put on your own mask first before assisting others.* You listen to these words and often don't give them a second thought—but you should. One sentence stated thousands of times each day to millions of travelers every year has far deeper relevance.

Self-sacrifice and selflessness are admirable traits, or so people think. Movies and television shows exaggerate these traits. Protagonists give *all* in service to others, with heroic efforts to save the world. All too often, life imitates art with dire consequences. Education is replete with such examples. Teachers believe they need to perform heroic acts on a daily basis, year after year. While you are called to heroism and embrace your calling, much of what others ask you to do is unsustainable, leading to untenable professional circumstances.

Teachers are critical to the success of students. Educational researcher and author Robert J. Marzano (2007) states, "The single most influential component of an effective school is the individual teachers within that school" (p. 1). There's no doubt: effective teachers have a powerful impact on student achievement. New Zealand education academic and professor John Hattie (2003) reminds educators, "We should focus on the greatest source of variance that can make the difference—the teacher. We need to ensure that this greatest influence is optimised to have powerful and sensationally positive effects on the learner" (p. 3).

In their desire to put students first, have educators forgotten this is not a zero-sum game? Focusing on student needs does not mean educators cannot or should not focus on teachers' needs. An in-vogue phrase when helping students is *Maslow before Bloom*. That is, educators should attend to students' basic human needs that American psychologist Abraham H. Maslow (1943) defines before expecting them to take on the challenges of academic work Benjamin S. Bloom (1956) lays out in his taxonomy. The same should be said for teachers. Teachers, like those in dicey commercial aviation situations, must have their oxygen masks on before they can help others. And not just during an emergency; they must have those oxygen masks in place each day.

Since around 2016, educational thought leaders placed more emphasis on teacher wellness and self-care. Educator and author Timothy D. Kanold's (2017, 2021) *HEART! Fully Forming Your Professional Life as a Teacher and Leader* and *SOUL! Fulfilling the Promise of Your Professional Life as a Teacher and Leader* help teachers reflect and refresh as professionals. Kanold collaborated with educator advocate Tina H. Boogren (2022), whose body of work includes numerous practical wellness resources for educators, to write *Educator Wellness: A Guide for Sustaining Physical, Mental, Emotional, and Social Well-Being*, as well as create the Wellness Solutions for Educators framework. We also recommend Boogren's (2019) *180 Days of Self-Care for Busy Educators* and elementary educator and teacher well-being expert Morgane Michael's (2022) *From Burnt Out to Fired Up: Reigniting Your Passion for Teaching*.

These talented authors are addressing long-overdue teacher needs. However, a root-cause analysis would also serve educators, as systemic changes in the profession demand more be done to prevent so many teachers from needing additional help with mental health and wellness. We come by the notion of *root cause* both literally and symbolically. Consider a tree whose roots represent the importance of a solid, strong foundation that largely goes unseen yet gives a tree life. The tree itself—including branches, leaves, and all that grows upon it—represents the interaction of all that goes on in a school and the lasting impact teachers have on students' lives. There must be a similar foundation provided in schools. We believe that foundation is teacher mattering. Teachers need to matter to students, parents, leaders, and community members but especially to *one another*. Almost all else grows out of this. In the following sections, we define and discuss the research-based concept of *mattering*, highlight the challenges teachers face, and identify the eight elements of mattering for K–12 teachers.

What Is *Mattering*?

To understand how mattering relates to teachers, educators need a basic understanding of the concept of mattering. *Mattering* is the feeling that your actions, thoughts, and desires are significant to others, and others would miss you if you were gone (Flett, 2018; Rayle, 2006; Rosenberg & McCullough, 1981). *Mattering* is also the "perception that, to some degree and in a variety of ways, we are a significant part of the world around us" (Elliott, Kao, & Grant, 2004, p. 339). *Mattering* is "central to our sense of who we are and

where we fit in to be able to say that others think about us . . . , seek our advice, or would care about what happens to us" (Elliott et al., 2004, p. 339).

To help illustrate how mattering (or *not* mattering) can make a difference in teachers' lives, we begin with a real-life scenario, though we've changed the names and some of the details. Each chapter will have a short vignette, some real and others fictional, that many readers will relate to throughout their teaching career.

> Susan was a fifteen-year veteran teacher who taught at the same school her entire career. She would often spend time outside school learning new skills and honing her craft. Susan saw many ups and downs in the school during her tenure but continued to stay positive throughout most of the changes. Others considered Susan an effective teacher, and many novice teachers went to her for advice when they had issues in their own classrooms. Susan believed it was important to support new teachers and welcomed the additional work as part of advancing the profession. The district and school leaders would often tap her to work on extra projects and take on additional duties. Susan jumped at the chance to do so whenever possible. She loved her school. She enjoyed working with her colleagues and most particularly, she loved the most challenging students. Many people commented on how loyal she was to the district over the years, and she said she never wanted to leave the school she loved so much. Susan found herself in numerous teacher leadership positions. Although this meant additional work for no additional compensation, she loved it. For Susan, her work was about moving the school forward and improving teacher practice to help all students achieve.
>
> When the longtime principal retired, Susan found herself trying to navigate new unknowns with a new principal. She quickly found herself excluded from school leadership meetings she once attended. Instead of being part of making decisions, Susan received edicts handed down with no input. The district decided to create a new teacher leadership program that would compensate

a teacher for doing the things Susan had been doing in the years prior without any compensation. The new position would allow an experienced teacher to mentor other teachers, help them with difficult students, offer guidance on effective teaching strategies, and more. Many of the teaching staff were reluctant to support the new program, but Susan reassured them it would help the school improve.

Ultimately, the position went to a teacher who never showed any interest in helping mentor teachers in previous years. Once the district implemented the program, teachers stopped collaborating with one another; the school's culture became more about compliance rather than growth. Evaluations focused on compliance and competition, rather than improvement.

Later, Susan asked for an explanation of why she did not get the job. She was frustrated, yet she wanted to improve so she could assume other leadership positions. In a frank conversation, the assistant superintendent told her, "Not everyone has the skill and ability to make it to the big leagues." Upon reflection, Susan knew this was the beginning of the end of her career in that district.

So, after fifteen years as an effective teacher committed to her craft, Susan began looking for careers outside teaching. As Susan examined other professions, nothing seemed as if it could replace her passion for teaching. She discussed different paths with others and, despite her dissatisfaction and disillusionment, she wanted to stay in education. At the same time, Susan knew she couldn't stay because she was miserable. Her health and happiness were suffering. She was miserable and knew her career there wasn't sustainable.

What makes someone who has an obvious love and passion for education turn to other careers? What was missing? Is there something Susan or someone else could have done to prevent this from happening? By now, you can guess what our answer is: Susan didn't feel she mattered to other educators in her school, and her leaders did nothing to help her.

While mattering is essential to a person's well-being, education researchers have, for the most part, ignored it (Flett, 2018). We believe researchers disregard mattering largely because there is an almost complete lack of awareness of the term. Many preK–12 researchers may not know mattering exists, so researchers do not know to research it. Further, if teachers don't know about mattering, how can they realize it has benefits or focus on improving it? A cognitive bias called *frequency illusion* is a phenomenon that occurs once someone becomes aware of something. People have a tendency to notice something more once they hear about or experience it (Benisek, 2022). Imagine buying a car when all of the sudden you notice (after driving it off the lot) how many people have bought the exact same car. Once you become familiar with the term *mattering* and the elements that lead to teacher mattering, the more you will recognize its presence (or absence). Growing your vocabulary, in this case, grows your knowledge. If employers want to increase employee job satisfaction and retention, they must evaluate mattering and design ways to increase it (Jung, 2015).

Sometimes, people are familiar with the term but in a more general sense, tantamount to being aware of the existence of others (Elliott et al., 2004). Researchers and coauthors Login S. George and Crystal L. Park (2016) discuss *mattering* in existential terms, focusing on the perception that people feel their lives are of profound and lasting importance through time. Using this definition, teachers might feel they matter to students when they focus on the lasting impact they have in students' lives. This sense of mattering, however, is still limited in the scope of career satisfaction in teaching. Because of the ways teachers interact with others—students, parents, colleagues, and so on—teachers' sense of mattering is complex and essential. Teachers who have a strong sense of mattering feel they make a difference—not just to students but also to their fellow educators. In this book, we focus on adult-to-adult relationships in schools.

A common question we get when we discuss mattering is whether mattering is simply a synonym for *belonging* or *significance*. Mattering is often mistaken for belonging, but it has several distinguishing characteristics (Flett, 2018). *Belonging* is about feeling connected to a group, but *mattering* is distinct because it captures the impact others have on you and reflects your need for the people in your life to value you—not simply that you and others are connected. "Mattering also reflects core questions that people ask themselves, such as 'Who really cares about me?' and 'Who would miss me if I was not around?' and 'Do people realize how much they matter to me?'" (Flett, 2018, p. 5).

Similarly, mattering is not just another term for having significance. Mattering is more complex than significance; mattering necessitates a certain degree of *meaningful* significance. Figure I.1 (page 6) illustrates how *significance* differs from *mattering*.

The person is significant to another   The person matters to another

Source: © Wilfong, 2021. Adapted with permission.

FIGURE I.1: Distinctions between significance and mattering.

With significance, all the pieces need to be present to complete the box, but the order makes no difference. Mattering is having the exact pieces in their exact places. The number 2 piece cannot fit into the puzzle in any other way; if you remove or replace the piece with a different shape, the puzzle is incomplete (see figure I.1). For example, a cashier is significant to a store customer, but any cashier can fill in for one who is absent; the individual cashier doesn't truly *matter* to the customer. Significance can be transactional; it does not need to go beyond the reciprocal impact of the moment. Mattering is transformational; people who matter to others make a difference in their lives. You might replace people who matter to others, but they would be missed. For example, when a colleague leaves for another position, someone takes that colleague's place. The new addition might be equally talented and skilled, but the team dynamic is still not the same. There was a uniqueness the person who left brought to the group that made a difference to the group as a whole.

Mattering is more complex than significance; mattering necessitates a certain degree of *meaningful* significance.

According to Morris Rosenberg and B. Claire McCullough (1981), developers of the notion of mattering we explore in this book, *mattering* consists of three main feelings.

1. **Attention:** The feeling others are interested in or notice you
2. **Importance:** The feeling of being important to others or subjects of their concern
3. **Reliance:** The feeling that others depend on you for any reason

The rubber meets the road with the interpersonal aspect of these feelings, especially of importance and reliance (Elliott et al., 2004). Teachers need to feel they matter to other adults. University of Miami professor and author Isaac Prilleltensky (2014), who considers *mattering* what makes life worth living, identifies two components of mattering.

> **1.** When people recognize "what we have to say has meaning and that we are acknowledged in the room, in our family, at work, and in the community" (Prilleltensky, 2014, p. 151)
> **2.** When people sense what they are doing has an impact

For readers familiar with response to intervention (RTI), think of mattering as teachers' Tier 1 (prevention). Self-help books and resources on reducing stress are Tier 2 (intervention). And as author, speaker, and practitioner Mike Mattos (2022) notes, if most people are in Tier 2, you don't have a Tier 2 problem, you have a Tier 1 problem. You have a *what are we doing all day, each day* problem.

Educators must address this tiered, adult-level issue not individually, but collectively as schools, districts, and a profession. The burden of staying well cannot and should not be on individual teachers. Educators cannot ignore their own responsibilities for wellness and passion for teaching, yet a larger collective is in play. Management thinker W. Edwards Deming says, "A bad system will beat a good person every time" (as cited in Hunter, 2015). If educators want the work of Kanold (2017, 2021), Boogren (2019, 2021), Michael (2022), and others to stick, we must improve how teachers feel in the system.

Contemporary Challenges for Teachers

If school leaders, key stakeholders, and teachers understand the foundations of *how* and *why* teachers feel they matter, this may lead to more positive work environments, which in turn lead to higher job retention and success. Understanding mattering is useful when examining some common problems educators face, including high stress levels, job dissatisfaction, the pressures of public opinion, and the lack of a sustainable wage. Without adult-to-adult support, the work environment can be a thankless landscape at times. We will discuss how mattering can help alleviate those issues in much more detail throughout this book, but first, we believe it's important to briefly highlight the teacher shortage and how dire the situation is becoming.

In the narrowest of terms, *teacher shortage* refers to "insufficient production of new teachers, given the size of student enrollments and teacher retirements" (Sutcher, Darling-Hammond, & Carver-Thomas, 2019, p. 4). Teacher shortages are not a new phenomenon; staffing difficulties have been present in the United States since the mid-1930s (Behrstock-Sherratt, 2016). However, since the 1990s, the number of teachers has continued to dwindle while the demand has continued to grow (Darling-Hammond, Furger, Shields, & Sutcher, 2016). The Great Recession not only hurt immediate teacher salaries but also made the profession less desirable. Teacher retention and recruitment continue to be challenges and have yet to return to early 2007 (pre-recession) teacher levels (Allegretto & Mishel, 2016). In 2016, estimates show the U.S. teacher shortage would increase to 112,000 teachers by 2018 (Sutcher et al., 2019). In reality, the teacher shortage was much more serious; a

September 2019 Bureau of Labor Statistics report shows the *teacher employment gap*—the gap between actual education employment and the employment needed to keep up with growth—increased far beyond the 2016 estimate (Gould, 2019). The trend has only worsened in the post-COVID-19 pandemic era. Coauthors Tuan Nguyen, Chanh B. Lam, and Paul Bruno (2022) from Brown University conservatively estimate over 36,000 vacant positions, and underqualified teachers hold 163,000 positions. According to another study from Education Resource Strategies (2023), post-pandemic turnover increased 4 percent and beginning teacher attrition increased 6 percent from pre-pandemic years. A survey of members of the American Federation of Teachers finds teachers are more dissatisfied and feel conditions are worse than before the pandemic (Hart Research Associates, 2022).

Linda Darling-Hammond, Roberta Furger, Patrick Shields, and Leib Sutcher (2016) of the Learning Policy Institute identify several factors besides salary that impact the number of people entering the teaching profession. Budget cuts lead to layoffs, deteriorating working conditions, and increased class sizes—all of which contribute to a dwindling pool of candidates. Not surprisingly, the number of people entering teacher education is insufficient to sustain current and future education needs. Between 2010 and 2014, the number of college-bound high school seniors interested in pursuing a career in education decreased by 16 percent (Darling-Hammond et al., 2016). In 2006, the number of newly licensed teachers was 22 percent of total college graduates, and by 2020, only 11 percent of college graduates (Peetz, 2022).

Beyond recruiting new teachers, Sutcher and colleagues (2019) argue teacher staffing problems include other factors, such as teacher turnover and school district location, making it harder to attract and retain teachers in some areas of the United States than in others. Numerous frustrated teachers are leaving the profession before retirement age; they are burning out. Almost half (46 percent) of new teachers move to positions outside the classroom or resign within five years (Aragon, 2016). The most cited reasons for teachers leaving the profession include overall job dissatisfaction, loss of autonomy, and lack of feedback from supervisors (Aragon, 2016). In 2023, a *Chalkbeat* article examined data from multiple states and determined the mass exodus of teachers worsened in 2022 after the pandemic (Barnum, 2023).

As a whole, society has become progressively more critical of teachers' classroom performance, demanding better results with fewer resources (Leachman, 2017). Among the demands are lower-level knowledge-performance scores on standardized tests rather than the complex skills of collaboration, creativity, and ingenuity that will improve society. The reality is schools can do, and are doing, so much more—but standardized tests do not measure those critical points of pride. Schools often take on the role of the parent, assuming responsibilities educational institutions were never designed to support. The integral role schools play in communities became clearer when states and provinces began to shut down school buildings during the COVID-19 pandemic, starting in March 2020. In addition to imparting an education, schools were to "provide indispensable student-welfare services,

like free meals, health care, and even dentistry. They care for children while parents work" (Sawchuk, 2020). A shortage of teachers affects more than just students' education.

Retaining high-quality teachers is extremely important for any school district. A tremendous amount of time and money goes to recruitment and onboarding due to high teacher turnover. U.S. districts note shortages in key areas, a trend likely to continue (Aragon, 2016). Exploring ways to retain high-quality teachers is critical for any successful school system. But finding the key leverage points eludes most administrators.

Foundational Elements of Mattering for K–12 Teachers

As we previously discuss, research on mattering in education is scant. It wasn't our plan to research it. As the late artist, instructor, and television host Bob Ross (1983–1994) might say, *it was a happy little accident*. Eager to solve U.S. teacher-retention problems, we pondered how we—a doctoral student sharing passion and purpose for a topic with her dissertation chair—could make progress because a lack of retention is a problem of practice that puts a costly strain on the substitute teaching system.

If teachers are the most important element in the classroom, as Marzano (2007), Hattie (2003), and many others show, then when they miss school, a natural result is students lose out, correct? After all, a teacher missing a day of school means students in the class miss valuable instruction—important stuff only the teacher can provide. We thought having a teacher in the classroom has to matter; otherwise, why would there be certified teachers at all? Don't teachers know their presence in the classroom matters?

In front of a whiteboard filled with words, phrases, arrows, and drawings, we worked to map out a niche for a doctoral dissertation. After repeatedly probing into the *why* behind the complexities of the problem, what finally materialized was the notion of mattering.

As we traded drafts of a literature review and enjoyed learning from others we consider giants of thought, we realized new research efforts—*our research efforts*—could lead to valuable and important insight not only on curbing teacher absenteeism but also on increasing career satisfaction and longevity, while potentially reducing depression. We knew it instinctually and yearned for research affirmation: teachers need to feel like they matter. Teachers need to feel like what they do matters to their colleagues as well as their students.

To continue researching the impact of teachers feeling like they matter, the dissertation process let us take a step back and determine what invites teachers to feel like they matter. After an extensive literature review, a well-crafted survey gauged various things that matter (in a sense). A statistical factor analysis uncovered eight elements necessary for teachers to feel like they matter to colleagues (Wilfong, 2021). Follow-up research (Wilfong & Donlan, n.d.) extends and legitimizes these initial discoveries. We believe an understanding of these eight elements is essential to increasing teachers' career satisfaction. They are

critical to understanding *how* educational leaders and other key stakeholders can provide an atmosphere where teachers feel more satisfied and are less likely to leave the profession.

Figure I.2 visualizes and defines the eight foundational elements of mattering.

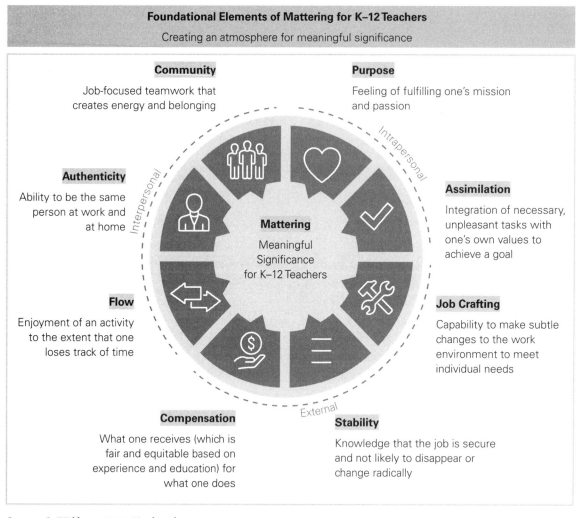

Source: © Wilfong, 2021. Used with permission.

FIGURE I.2: Foundational elements of mattering.

These eight elements are arranged in three different domains: (1) interpersonal, (2) intrapersonal, and (3) external. We will detail how each element fits into these domains in subsequent chapters.

After the original dissertation in which we discovered a mattering framework, we ran a follow-up study with thousands of teachers. That study shows mattering has a strong relationship with collective teacher efficacy, organizational health, individual efficacy, openness to change, and positive culture, all important elements linked to student success (Wilfong & Donlan, n.d.). Collective efficacy specifically is one of Hattie's top influences on student learning in his meta-analyses (as cited in Donohoo, Hattie, & Eells, 2018). We hoped one of these areas would relate to mattering and, to our delight, all did—an eye-popping and critical find for our profession!

The Role of Teachers in Mattering

As we talk to U.S. educators regarding our discovery pertaining to what *adults* need to thrive (not simply survive), we are convinced the topic for this original PhD dissertation is an invaluable addition to the education community. Often, teachers say something like, "Yes, this is exactly what I am feeling!" And then they look around, as if they shouldn't say it—at least not without permission amid the persistent *students-first* narrative in the education profession. Something nebulous or maybe even against the rules to say has come into focus, and teachers often seem so desperate to embrace it yet feel they shouldn't because of pressure from colleagues.

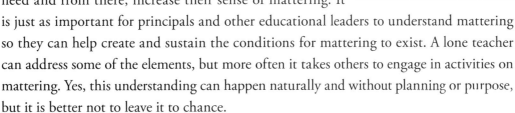

Mattering has a strong relationship to collective teacher efficacy, organizational health, individual efficacy, openness to change, and positive culture, all important elements linked to student success (Wilfong & Donlan, n.d.).

Teachers must understand mattering to identify areas of need and from there, increase their sense of mattering. It is just as important for principals and other educational leaders to understand mattering so they can help create and sustain the conditions for mattering to exist. A lone teacher can address some of the elements, but more often it takes others to engage in activities on mattering. Yes, this understanding can happen naturally and without planning or purpose, but it is better not to leave it to chance.

In every school building, there are teacher leaders often in proximity—through conversation, collaboration, or even conflict resolution—with most other teachers. Teacher leaders are those who know their game, can garner interest in the profession, have the respect and connection to colleagues, and typically do not have a desire to move into school administration anytime soon. It makes sense that a preponderance of the responsibility for ensuring teachers matter to other teachers rests with those in teacher leadership roles. This is a balancing act, with some responsibility for building a sense of mattering left to individual teachers, some with teacher leaders, and some with administrators. The amount of responsibility for any of these groups depends on the group dynamic itself.

Even in schools that haven't embraced the elements of mattering, teachers can be proactive in their trust circles to provide elements of mattering to one another. Trust circles have different forms and functions and can vary considerably; some exist in teachers' lounges, others in coffee klatches, and still others more formally in collaborative team conversations. Common among all healthy *trust circles* is an open, authentic atmosphere, with agency and the belief that participating individuals benefit from the collective community. As this whole notion of teacher mattering is relatively new to the conversation (as a product of research), we consider devoting a certain amount of time and energy to this correlation to collective efficacy well worth the time.

Here are some actions teachers can take.

- Teacher leaders can assess their own mattering using the eight elements to authentically model for their fellow teachers what teacher mattering looks like—and its positive influence on them while they go about their days. They must project the fact that *not mattering* is not an option; others then vicariously learn how mattering can have a positive effect on them too.

- Teachers can request each element of mattering as a whole-school discussion topic each month during the course of the school year and highlight both their needs and the successes they have experienced with that element. Leaders have the responsibility to allow this, but the teachers have a responsibility to ask for it. It may not occur to the principal to discuss these elements. Ideally, teachers should conduct these discussions near the beginning of schoolwide staff meetings. Take ten to fifteen minutes to celebrate the value of the adults in the building—for the sake of the adults and the profession.

- Teachers should ensure they check in on their *best friend at work* (see chapter 1, page 19) to see how things are going and try their best to offer an invitation for their best friend to matter, especially when the going gets tough, because it certainly does at times in the teaching profession. Have each other's backs and give your friend reason to live one of the eight elements as often as possible.

The Obligation of School Leaders in Mattering

School leaders must cut through the noise and understand the root causes of teacher dissatisfaction and stress if they are to make a real difference in how teachers view and experience their careers. Leaders must focus on ensuring the right conditions are present to help teachers feel satisfaction with their choice of profession. For teachers to experience satisfaction in providing education—with all of the daily complexities and difficulties the profession entails—they must feel significant and that their work matters to the people around them.

Saying the words "You matter" without action means nothing. Thus, saying "Teachers matter" really doesn't do a whole lot unless the people saying it engage in concrete actions to actually make individual teachers believe it. Billboards and public service announcements fall short.

A trusted member of the school leadership team (often an assistant principal, dean, or closely affiliated school counselor) should continually assess these eight foundational elements of mattering. It behooves leadership to indirectly choreograph mattering in the school as opposed to serving as direct conductors. In other words, school principals and others might consider what they can do by modeling to foster each of the eight elements.

Think of it as environmental stewardship. We learned through both research and practice that the best leaders gain teacher mattering as a natural by-product of quality leadership, and when leaders strive for effectiveness over justification, mattering prevails.

School leaders are also in a prime position to recognize respected and connected teacher leaders and check in with them about how things are going with the adults in the building (aside from what the students are doing or achieving). It pays dividends for leaders to be active in checking in with the levels of mattering present in their schools. Think of this as "chatting with the canary about the coal mine" or monitoring an early warning system. Mattering mindfulness shouldn't feel like it takes an inordinate amount of time. Teacher mattering is much of what leaders should be spending time on, whether they realize this or not. Mattering has huge potential in leveraging success in teaching and learning.

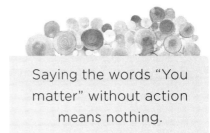

Saying the words "You matter" without action means nothing.

Consider how sad it is that leaders for many years have said, "It's not about us; it's about our students." This implies that *it must be one or the other*, and we simply don't believe that's true. Leaders can show genuine, individual, and frequent interest in the personal circumstances of teachers, including but not limited to their friends, families, hobbies, interests, and issues beyond their school performance and into the people they are. That's what matters!

Here are some actions leaders can take.

- Focus on one of the mattering elements each month in your leadership meetings and provide an honest appraisal of how each element impacts your school community and what you might do to authentically bolster its impact. The key is holding up a mirror and not thinking like an administrator. If you are a former teacher, consider what you would be thinking if you were on the front lines again, dealing with more complex issues than you faced when you were in the classroom.

- As you talk with others to gauge the levels of mattering in your school, if you learn an element within your control to improve needs addressing, do so quietly and without fanfare; don't advertise, even with your confidants. Just work on the problem and improve the lives of the adults under your care.

- Act on issues important to teachers and do something unrequested; this shows you know these personal issues and are also willing to spend time learning about and supporting teachers. Remember the names of teachers' family members and pets. Be curious about your teachers' lives beyond the classroom, extracurricular performances, and what they can do for you. Do something for them occasionally so teachers know you care.

In any workplace, employees need to feel a sense of value from both their supervisors and colleagues. Without this feeling, workers each feel like a commodity and become dissatisfied with the work (Chapman & White, 2019). Mattering positively correlates with mental health, suggesting mattering has the potential to alleviate various work-related stresses (Amundson, 1993). Psychologist Morris Rosenberg and mental health counselor B. Claire McCullough (1981) call *mattering* a "compelling social obligation and a powerful source of social integration" (p. 165). Leaders have an essential obligation to ensure teachers feel they matter.

About This Book

The first eight chapters of this book discuss each of the eight foundational elements of mattering and explain how teachers and leaders can use the mattering construct as a basis for improving the overall teaching profession. Each chapter opens with an *anticipatory set* (activities that align with student learning objectives) to help you visualize how you might conceive the chapter's topic, develop a belief system about it, and take action to embrace and accomplish it. Coauthors and speakers J. Stewart Black and Hal B. Gregersen (2002) and David Imonitie (2020) inspired us to offer conceiving, believing, and achieving as a way for you to *take your mark, get set, and matter.*

Chapters continue with an opening vignette that offers one person's professional experience with the chapter topic, sometimes through challenges and other times through productive struggles or successes. An explanation of the chapter topic, implications for teachers and leaders, and a short feature we call *Making [Topic] Matter* follow. Each chapter closes with a concluding portion of the opening vignette, reproducible tools that offer ways to reflect (including a conceive, believe, and achieve template), and a personal professional learning tool to help you move toward broader and deeper levels of understanding and confidence in taking charge of the power of mattering in your professional and personal life.

Here is a breakdown of the details in each chapter.

Chapter 1 addresses how a sense of community regarding mattering is different from *community* in a professional learning community (PLC), which is "an ongoing process in which educators work collaboratively in recurring cycles of collective inquiry and action research to achieve better results for the students they serve" (DuFour, DuFour, Eaker, & Many, 2016, p. 10). We discuss why it is important to have both congenial and collegial relationships with coworkers. The feeling of belonging in an organization is important in bringing about a sense of community.

Chapter 2 shares that teachers need to feel they can be their authentic selves at work. This chapter examines the code-switching of teachers (linguistically, culturally, and personally) in terms of their personalities. Balancing teachers' need for an environment that allows them to be their authentic selves while ensuring a diverse teaching population is important in building a cohesive team.

Chapter 3 notes the concept of flow, which has been around for years but is not always widely discussed in preK–12 education (Csikszentmihalyi, 2008). Most experienced teachers have had at least one lesson go perfectly as planned, with time seeming to fly. While most teachers focus on the elements of a lesson plan that create these conditions, other things that contribute to this phenomenon are within the control of teachers and school leaders.

Chapter 4 stresses teachers' need to identify their life purpose and determine if their purpose aligns with their school and district's mission, vision, and values. All too often the school and district's mission, vision, and values (*de jure*) are different from the lived version (*de facto*) within the collective or inside those individually responsible for carrying them out. It is important for teachers to reflect continually on their sense of purpose.

Chapter 5 expands on the concept of *assimilation*, which closely associates with the concept of integrated regulation in self-determination theory (Ryan & Deci, 2000). Many tasks extremely important for the functioning of the school or safety of the students and staff are simply unpleasant. Teachers must find a connection between their sense of purpose and these unpleasant tasks.

Chapter 6 discusses compensation in a way that transcends a paycheck. While increasing salaries is important to teachers' needs and administrators do need to address this element, more pay does not automatically remove stress and emotional fatigue; research shows more pay is not a satisfactory motivator for complex tasks or professions. At the same time, it is important to be aware of the *teacher pay penalty* (that is, the salary gap between teachers and other professionals) and how that impacts teacher career satisfaction.

Chapter 7 states *job stability* not only refers to a person's keeping a job but also a person's awareness of the job's expectations and responsibilities. Fair, equitable, and transparent evaluation systems must be in place. Factors such as changing teaching assignments multiple times, moving to other buildings often, and changing grade levels year after year (unless a teacher wants to) can adversely impact job stability.

Chapter 8 explains *job crafting* as the ability to make changes to the work environment to best meet individual preferences. It is the balance between teacher autonomy and district consistency. Leaders must accord teachers the latitude to act with agency, with respectful deference to their creativity, ingenuity, and ability to keep their eye on the ball, while playing the game of school—to a certain degree—their own way.

Chapter 9 includes the foundational elements of mattering survey and instructions on how to use it for individual teachers and teacher leaders. This chapter also includes self-reflection tools for teachers and teacher leaders to use as they address the sense of mattering in their schools and districts. The book closes with a brief epilogue.

We hope this book helps teachers understand the important role of mattering in the workplace. It is also for administrators, so they may become more versed in the concept of mattering for teachers. Administrators can be powerful in this discovery by not only bringing attention to the concept but also creating conditions for mattering to thrive. When teachers read the implications for school leaders, teachers can understand what and how administrators can help build teacher mattering and formulate discussion points to have with administrators. Conversely, when administrators read the implications for teachers, they can use that information to coach and mentor teachers who may be struggling with mattering.

Now that you have a little more background on the elements of mattering, we'll revisit Susan to see how deficits in these elements affected her professional life.

> Susan found herself missing several key elements of mattering. Although her official job title did not change, she was no longer able to mentor teachers and provide instructional support the way she had previously. This was part of her purpose—one of the elements of mattering. She no longer felt able to fulfill her mission and passion for helping other teachers the way she had in the past.
>
> The new evaluation system created animosity among the teachers, and the once-strong sense of community Susan felt was gone. Teachers became guarded when it came to sharing their best lesson plans and ideas. Individual teachers knew that only a select few would receive stipends and didn't want to risk giving away their best ideas.
>
> Although she knew her job was secure, Susan had reservations on how her job would look in the future based on the new school leader's previous comments. Her job stability, another element of mattering, was in question. Would the new leader move her to teaching a subject area she was uncomfortable with or did not want to teach? Would the new leader give her duties and responsibilities she previously did not have? Would she have opportunities to perform the additional responsibilities she once had under the previous principal?

Awareness and action related to the foundational elements of mattering can lead to a better understanding of how to invite teachers to feel more satisfied and fulfilled in their careers. If the essential elements making up their sense of mattering are lacking for teachers, then school leaders can focus on those elements to create an environment more hospitable to mattering. District and school leaders can use their knowledge to inform teachers of factors that cause dissatisfaction. For example, teachers might believe the school culture needs to change to bring more of them satisfaction when, in reality, the teachers need external validation or affirmation. It is essential for all parties to understand mattering and determine how it can impact the educational environment. We have observed many educational leaders who do not focus their energy on mattering. Clearly understanding how teachers come to feel a sense of mattering will prompt leaders to examine their practices in a new light. Given the numerous contemporary issues facing educators, it is critical to illuminate the important and mostly ignored concept of mattering.

With this book, teachers and school leaders who identify the foundational elements of mattering absent from their schools can target areas to help teachers feel more satisfied with their career. Additionally, teachers reading this book can focus on ensuring the right combinations of the elements of mattering are present to help them feel more satisfied with their choice of profession.

Since the 1990s, the education profession (with good intentions) has pounded *students first* into educators' heads; ultimately, educators are in this business to help students. Yet for students to matter *most*, educators must know where to focus *first*. If you want to keep students at the forefront of your care and concern, then you must do something in a slightly different and more proactive way to support teachers and allow them the energy to give of themselves. Teachers are the champions closest to students—the most important components in a classroom—and leaders must do what they can to ensure there is no question teachers matter to one another so their efforts can matter to students.

We hope by the time you finish this book, you will embrace a newfound look at your profession, the appropriateness of saying "You matter," a sense that you do come *first*, and permission to prioritize ongoing self-care to be the best version of yourself as a servant, professional, and person destined to help others. Remember the oxygen mask; you cannot help others if you need help. There is a difference between giving your all, giving your best, and being a martyr. In short, our wish for you is to celebrate your strength and confidence to expect you can and should matter, not only to the students and families you serve but also (and just as important) the adults you spend time with each day. Your time at school is special, valued, and appropriate; this is time you will not get back, so it's important to value this time while it occurs.

So, stop putting yourself and your colleagues in second or last place each day. You deserve better, and by expecting and providing for mattering, the students you went into this profession to serve will be better off because of a better you—a you who *matters*.

CHAPTER 1

Celebrating the Team, Not Just the Score: *Community*

Community falls into the interpersonal domain of mattering, which includes elements related to a person's relationship with others. The other two elements in this domain are authenticity and flow, which chapters 2 (page 39) and 3 (page 55) will address. The extent to which a person interacts with others is an important component of mattering for K–12 teachers. Community is the most obvious of the interpersonal characteristics, as it requires interaction with others. As members of a team or group, teachers feel a close connection to and responsibility for other members, professionally and personally.

The following vignette, a real-life scenario, begins to illustrate how vital community is to a sense of mattering.

> A long time ago, in a community a stone's throw away, two teachers worked at a juvenile detention center. They were such wonderful educators that students would intentionally recidivate to seek the safety and security of their classroom. This was, of course, a folktale, but the fact remained that these educators were so effective they received an opportunity to start a consortium-based school program with the

expressed purpose of educating students who had difficulties in their resident school districts. Students no longer had to be locked up to attend their school.

For more than two decades, the school enjoyed increased opportunities to operate autonomously (under state law) with a small yet powerful staff, each of whom wore too many hats to count. Community members touted the school as a difference maker, a model that citizens respected locally and renowned statewide. The school gained rapt attention on how students would beat the odds of what life presented them, not simply surviving but thriving. It was a really great place and continues as such.

A truly special relationship among adults materialized organically, allowing for an inviting, wonderful place for students—a vicarious by-product, it seemed, by the way adults worked together. The leaders, teachers, and staff were friends as well as colleagues; they made tough decisions through critical consensus and, at times, engaged in lively debates. They made sure to take care of one another first so they could be about students most. They were candid about issues, brutally honest about techniques and perspectives, and at times, behaved more like siblings than coworkers. Periodically, they sparred tooth and nail over their deep convictions (but only when the students weren't looking). When they struggled, they would have one another's backs, support one another, fail forward, and when appropriate, take one another down a peg or two when a refresh was overdue. In short, they had community.

Figure 1.1 provides an anticipatory set for the element of community. The reproducible "Next Steps: Chapter 1 Recap Activity" (page 36) gives you the opportunity to fill in your own ideas.

The Interpersonal Element of Community in Mattering
Job-focused teamwork that creates energy and belonging
One Way to Conceive:
Imagine each day's lesson plan for a room without walls and all colleagues within earshot, serving as invaluable complements to your teachable moments.
One Way to Believe:
Have intentional and ongoing discussions with your team members about taking time to be in one another's classrooms, along with the supervision and supports members provide one another to make it feasible. Encourage and expect leaders to support the endeavor.
One Way to Achieve:
Embrace satisfaction in knowing students consider it the norm when adults help one another, teaching congenially and assisting collegially through instructional challenges best addressed collaboratively.

FIGURE 1.1: The interpersonal element of community in mattering.

Community requires interaction with others; *community* means being a member of a team or group that one feels a close connection to and responsibility for professionally and personally. In this chapter, we start with community by celebrating the team, not just the score. A sense of community regarding mattering is different from community in a PLC, and we discuss why it is important to have both congenial and collegial relationships with coworkers. We present three components of community: (1) belonging, (2) friendship, and (3) professionalism. Following are implications for teachers and school leaders, the latter including the little and bigger things. We conclude with the reproducibles "Next Steps: Chapter 1 Recap Activity" (page 36) and "Your Personal Professional Development: Thought Experiment—Community" (page 37).

Getting Started With Community

You could define *community* in many ways, but in the context of mattering, we consider *community* job-focused teamwork that creates energy and belonging (Wilfong, 2021). It's important to keep in mind the different things *community* means to different people. The phrase *a community of teachers* could simply mean an organization or group of people in the teaching profession. According to the *Oxford English Dictionary*, *community* (n.d.) can also mean a person has a feeling of fellowship with others as a result of sharing common attitudes, interests, and goals. There are several elements to a sense of community: *membership*—the feeling you belong; *influence*—your ability to make an impact on the community; *fulfillment of needs*—the community can help you realize physical and psychological needs (*integration*); and *shared emotional connection*—identifying with and connecting to one another (Haim-Litevsky, Komemi, & Lipskaya-Velikovsky, 2023).

For a satisfactory way to describe *community* in the context of mattering, we draw from the work of educational consultant and author Roland S. Barth (2006) to identify the components of community. We also examine belonging, which community creates and nourishes, and discuss friendships and professionalism in a school community.

Components of Community

Barth (2006) describes four types of relationships among adults in a school: (1) parallel play, (2) adversarial, (3) congenial, and (4) collegial.

Parallel play, as the name implies, is teachers working independently of one another, side by side, with little to no meaningful interaction. Some often refer to this as *the teacher acting as an independent contractor*—heroic teachers standing on their own, succeeding with little help from others. Educator, author, and consultant Richard DuFour (2004) sometimes calls classrooms that operate in this way *silos*.

Adversarial relationships occur when competition or angst exists among staff members. Teachers are reluctant to share best practices. They see other teachers as competitors rather than teammates. Evaluation systems that rank teachers by evaluation scores and include performance pay based on those rankings have the unintended consequence of creating an adversarial environment. Outside stressors and pressures can create an environment where teachers end up at odds with one another. When so much that impacts a job is outside a teacher's locus of control, sometimes the most natural defense mechanism is to attack others.

We often see *congenial* relations among teachers or people who work together and generally enjoy one another's company. They help one another when one has a problem. They count on one another for support. One example would be coworkers who eat together during lunch break and have conversations on topics unrelated to education. They interact not because they are required to do so because of a meeting or planned activity but rather because they are interested in one another's ideas, opinions, and lives. A congenial setting is generally seen as a positive working environment.

The last type of relationship Barth (2006) identifies is the *collegial* relationship. This type of relationship occurs when teachers talk to one another about teaching, share their professional knowledge, actively observe one another while teaching, and generally wish success for one another (Barth, 2006). Collegial is the most elusive and hardest type of relationship to create in a school environment. The collegial relationship is what *community* means in a PLC, in which teachers work together in collaborative teams and focus on student learning, collective responsibility, and results (DuFour et al., 2016).

Do not assume just because a school or district practices the PLC process, it automatically has a strong sense of community. PLCs create many systems and structures to help teachers achieve the community of a PLC. While these are impactful and important, simply focusing on collegial relationships falls short of what is necessary to have community as it applies to mattering. A high-functioning PLC offers a good foundation for achieving the community aspect of mattering. However, schools that do not utilize the PLC process or are struggling to implement it *can* achieve a sense of community. Community will look different in different places. The key is to have a balance of collegial and congenial relationships, regardless of the other processes in place.

Community in mattering *combines* collegial and congenial relationships. Both are necessary for teachers to have a sense of mattering. If teachers solely rely on collegial relationships, they would get together only to collaborate on school-related classroom activities and student achievement.

Leaders put little emphasis on colleagues knowing about one another outside what is necessary to know regarding school business. Congenial relationships occur when the individuals care about one another and enjoy one another's company. While many of their conversations may be about education-related topics, they may find themselves discussing family vacations, likes and dislikes, hobbies, and other topics not related to work. Mattering is the feeling that your actions are significant (collegial) and would be missed if you were gone (congenial). Think of it like a mathematics equation: collegiality + congeniality = community.

One Natural Outgrowth of Community: Belonging

The combination of collegial and congenial relationships can create a sense of belonging. *Belonging* is the human need to be an accepted member of a group (Godin, 2008). Humans are social animals and need to feel part of a community, regardless of whether they are introverts or extroverts (Anderson, 2010). One might say the environmental and behavioral exchanges occurring in the workplace are essential to the development of a person's sense of mattering (Curry & Bickmore, 2012); however, the sense of belonging develops differently among the various members of groups. People will have their own perspectives. For some, a sense of belonging might come from raising a family, and others develop it participating in team sports. As organizations become places in which communities develop, employees crave a sense of belonging (WorkHuman Research Institute, 2017).

The feeling of belonging to a larger group doesn't just feel good, it is vital to people's survival. It is a basic human need. The quality of relationships with others in the community, mutual trust, and doing things for one another above and beyond typical social support impact a person's sense of belonging (Haim-Litevsky et al., 2023).

Individuals come together and bond when the group struggles together (Heath & Heath, 2017). Whether it is a connection to an idea or a bond made over some hardship or challenge, a sense of belonging among individuals is critical to the success of an organization and the individuals in it. Such groups do not need to belong to an official or structured organization. For example, in the Okinawan culture it is called *moai*, or an informal group of people with common interests who look out for one another (García & Miralles, 2017). *Moai* originated among rural farmers who gathered together to share ideas and best practices, as well as help one another during harvest seasons (García & Miralles, 2017).

Organizing Genius: The Secrets of Creative Collaboration discusses *great groups*, or teams of people who become more than the sum of their parts and create something better than any one member could as an individual (Bennis & Biederman, 2007; Robinson, 2009). When a school or district achieves community in mattering, the group creates energy. A member of a great group forms bonds with other community members. These bonds, in turn, lead to feelings of unity and validation (Heath & Heath, 2017). This creates a systemic strength. According to Deming, "a bad system will beat a good person every time" (as cited in Hunter, 2015). An organization is more significant than any one person and difficult to change. If people do not have a sense of belonging, they will either change to fit in, be miserable, or find a different organization.

Thus, a sense of belonging helps not only the organization but also the groups in it achieve greater goals than they would without a sense of belonging. Ken Robinson (2009), an internationally recognized leader in the development of creativity, innovation, and human potential, states, pulling together into these groups "provides inspiration and provocation to raise the bar on your own achievements. In every domain, members of a passionate community tend to drive each other to explore the real extent of their talents" (p. 118). Next, we'll dig into how to create belonging and how belonging can lead to workplace health.

CREATING BELONGING

It is possible to create an environment conducive to people connecting and developing a sense of belonging with one another. While leaders have a lot of influence, creating a sense of belonging is not solely their responsibility; organizational support also comes from coworkers as social networks grow in the work environment. *Organizational support* is the employees' "belief concerning the extent to which the organization values their contribution and cares about their well-being" (Hayton, Carnabuci, & Eisenberger, 2012, p. 235). When employees perceive organizational support to be strongly positive, such support will lead them to have stronger psychological well-being. Strong social networks in an organization shape and define that organization. As the management structure of an organization becomes less top-down and employees have more say, the importance of its social networks to the overall success of the organization and well-being of its employees increases (Hayton et al., 2012). Author Daniel H. Pink (2009), author of several books about business, work, creativity, and behavior, calls this concept *synchronization*.

The first principle of synchronizing is syncing with the boss. Best-selling coauthors Chip Heath and Dan Heath (2017) call this *creating a synchronized moment* for the people involved. The boss, someone who is separate from and typically above the group, sets the pace of work and change. The boss is an essential part of participants realizing a sense of belonging. The boss maintains standards for employees and focuses on the collective mind of the group. Leaders can attract people with their ideas. When a leader has a great idea, people "cannot resist the rush of belonging and the thrill of the new" (Godin, 2008, p. 3). After individuals synchronize with the boss, synchronization becomes the external standard that sets the pace of the work. Individuals then synchronize with one another (Pink, 2009), inviting one another to take part in a shared struggle (Heath & Heath, 2017). Synchronizing with one another requires firm connections (with a strong sense of congeniality and collegiality) in the community. This helps teachers feel good, and feeling good at work improves group productivity. Pink (2009) adds, "Working in harmony with others makes it more likely we will do good" (p. 199). Finally, synchronizing with the heart can occur; individuals connect their actions to a shared meaning (Heath & Heath, 2017; Pink, 2009). Thus, synchronization is essential to the development of people's sense of belonging.

Author and blogger Eric Barker (2017) observes that not everyone gains a sense of belonging from the same place or the same group of people; where some people feel they belong, others might not. People must seek out places where they feel they belong. Barker (2017) describes this as *choosing the right pond*—people must select the right environment to provide for their needs, and those environments differ from person to person.

FROM BELONGING TO WORKPLACE HEALTH IN ADULTS

A healthy work environment determines how much people enjoy their profession (Watson, 2015). However, the teaching profession ranks as one of the highest in terms of occupational stress (McCarthy, Blaydes, Weppner, & Lambert, 2022). University of York professor Chris Kyriacou (2011) defines *teacher stress* as the unpleasant and negative feelings that teachers have that stem from their profession; these can include anger, anxiety, tension, frustration, or depression. These emotions result from the perceived threat of the demands teachers face. Some common stressors for teachers include too much work (or being overworked), ambiguity of responsibilities, conflict among peers, little professional recognition, being left out of decision making, little communication with administrators, and student behavioral issues (Watson, Harper, Ratliff, & Singleton, 2010). During the COVID-19 pandemic, we heard many teachers say this was a great opportunity to re-envision and reimagine teaching and learning. Unfortunately and for the most part, post-pandemic teaching and learning seem to have stayed as they were pre-pandemic. However, teaching conditions worsened as teacher shortages, substitute teacher shortages, and challenging student behavior increased. The Institute of Education Sciences (2022) reports 80 percent of schools experience behavioral and emotional development issues. Discipline issues (such as tardiness and classroom disruptions) increased due to the pandemic (Institute of Education Sciences, 2022).

When teachers experience the accumulation of daily stress, which at times runs over the brim of their cup, as we say, there's often nowhere they can go to de-stress. There's simply nowhere to hide. Teachers are in their classrooms with students in their care, with students' eyes watching everything they do, every moment. Professional success demands teachers handle stress by bottling it up, bottling it deep, and bottling it quick. This can have repercussions, both short and long term, all with the required perma-smile, no matter how teachers feel inside.

> Professional success demands teachers handle stress by bottling it up, bottling it deep, and bottling it quick. This can have repercussions.

A strong sense of community, and the feeling of belonging community fosters, can alleviate these challenges. Relationship experts Gary Chapman and Paul White (2019) posit that a healthy work environment includes seven elements:

- Quality team members;
- Effective communication skills and procedures set to facilitate regular communication;
- Trusting relationships;
- Common vision and goals among team members;
- Standardized processes and procedures, including standards to be met and ongoing monitoring of performance;
- Healthy methods for correction and conflict resolution;
- Clear lines of responsibility, including accountability and rewards for results. (pp. 233–234)

A common thread among these elements is the connections with belonging.

Teachers are happier and healthier if they have meaningful connections with one another (Anderson, 2010). Over 50 percent of teachers completing *The OECD Teaching and Learning International Survey (TALIS)* report rarely or never engaging in team teaching with colleagues (Organisation for Economic Co-operation and Development, 2014). However, during a typical week, teachers spend almost half their waking hours in school, so it's crucial they feel accepted in that setting. Teaching relies on strong relationships. The more teachers feel a sense of belonging, the more likely they are to positively engage (Anderson, 2010). School leaders can begin to make that happen.

School leaders have significant impact on a teacher's sense of community, and a supportive, collegial environment is critical to teacher retention (Kirkhus, 2011). According to *Primary Sources 2012: America's Teachers on the Teaching Profession*, four of the top seven factors that affect teacher retention involve other school personnel (Scholastic, 2012). Teachers desire more time to collaborate with one another. There is a disparity between how much time teachers want to spend collaborating and the amount of time they actually do. Teachers' job satisfaction and feeling of belonging positively relate to feeling they share the prevailing norms and values of their school (Skaalvik & Skaalvik, 2015).

Teachers who enjoy their work and work environment are more likely to be productive and less likely to seek new employment or a new career (Rogerson, 2004). A lack of collegial support results in feelings of isolation, but collaboration among teachers encourages a sense of belonging (Rogerson, 2004). Team collaboration improves when team members truly feel they belong to the group (Wei, Corbett, Ray, & Wei, 2019). An active teacher community that takes collective responsibility for students can also have a positive effect on teacher retention and performance (Kirkhus, 2011).

MAKING *COMMUNITY* MATTER

Community is job-focused teamwork that creates energy and belonging, and teachers can get intentional about doing just that. Begin by determining when your colleagues should be in your classroom. While teachers' doors are often closed to abide by school safety rules, it does not mean your colleagues should not be in your classroom every day. Consider this a figurative as well as literal invitation. Get serious about focusing your teamwork. As with any event requiring mutually dependent parts, take stock of your talent. Create space in your spaces—teachers' lounge, work room, or staff commons area—to identify the talents you have as a team. Whether it's a word wall, photo gallery, or comment collage, post your names and boldly name one of your talents that helps with school success. One might be helping struggling readers. Another might be dealing with difficult students or helping de-escalate conflicts. It might even be helping challenge gifted and talented students, so they don't get bored. Whatever it is, articulate your talent

and stop being humble! If your colleagues are hesitant, post a talent you identify in them.

When you have problems or challenges at school, filter your solutions through this "talent wall." Ask yourselves, "Who has something that can help here?" Create ad-hoc groups to triage local practice issues. Leverage capacity, and as you notice new talents or shining stars emerge, post something new on the wall. You'll notice your community of options expanding because you're allowing community to create energy and belonging. Consider that when colleagues are nice to one another, they not only create belonging but also a more authentic and sustainable belonging because they accomplish something difficult together, as when they build energy and respect to help themselves through times when failure is possible and fun is absent.

The whole point here is to balance congeniality and collegiality, provide one another with stretch opportunities, and thus grow your community of resources. Even with the challenges of new approaches to school safety and what arguably could be a more separate and solitary approach to teaching, you're in one another's classrooms and community every day, envisioning how your colleagues might approach what you're experiencing with students. All this requires is intentional time spent in your actual, physical community space. You simply must make the decision to spend part of your individual planning time adding value to whatever conversations are taking place on your community resources (or talent) wall. It's really where true professionals can come together to discuss problems of practice and options for opportunity. Community comes from its participants making decisions that ensure community will be present in their schools.

Friendships and Professionalism

One issue that can arise when creating community in mattering lies in examining the different definitions of the word *friend*. According to Merriam-Webster's online dictionary, a *friend* (n.d.) can be someone who you are extremely close to or someone who is "not hostile" toward another. Between these two extreme definitions lies a host of other meanings. It is important to have a common understanding of what everyone means when using this term and discussing friendship in the context of work.

Facing high stress and time-consuming responsibilities at work while juggling family obligations, teachers may rightfully feel overwhelmed at adding to their plates the notion of making friends at work. Others may feel they spend so much time at work, they do not want to spend additional time with their coworkers outside the workday. While these sentiments are valid, it's important to remember the definition of *friend* in this collegial context of *community* in mattering. We're referring here specifically to *workplace friends*, so the time spent with one another occurs largely at work. Teachers can have friends at work but never go to the movies, shop, or hang out on weekends together. Time exists for those activities to be separate from work and home. Therefore, a helpful definition of *workplace friendships* is those that "involve mutual commitment, trust and shared values or interests between people at work, in ways that go beyond mere acquaintanceship but that exclude romance. These relations involve heightened norms of openness, informality, and inclusiveness" (Berman, West, & Richter, 2002, p. 217). Workplace friendships link to improving organizational outcomes such as productivity and performance, reducing employee turnover, garnering emotional support, and bettering the experience of tedious work (Rumens, 2017).

The ways to build workplace friendships are as varied and diverse as the individuals involved. Here are a few ideas to jump-start your thinking that will hopefully not overwhelm you. Administrators, meanwhile, can use this list to help consider how to create conditions for these ideas to occur—hopefully with creativity and flexibility in terms of how ideas might be more allowable than in the past.

- Make a conscious effort to eat lunch with colleagues at least once a week.
- Participate in work events, such as sitting in the staff section at a basketball game.
- Have a colleague check-in prompt at the beginning of grade-level or department planning meetings.
- Celebrate colleagues' birthdays and anniversaries.
- Have a brag board where teachers can share personal, family, or pet highlights.
- Keep a shared list of favorite snacks, drinks, and treats of every teacher so everyone knows what to give others for random acts of kindness days.
- Have a text message or private social media group to share highlights, jokes, or other issues related to the workplace friends' group.

> It is unlikely everyone in the school building will be friends with everyone, but it is important for everyone to be friends with someone.

Gallup research finds friendships add to workplace retention (Miller & Adkins, 2016; Rumens, 2017). Remember, in the context of mattering, people need to feel they would be missed if they were gone; this is something that can occur only when there are strong congenial relationships (that is, friendship) with colleagues. It is unlikely everyone in the school building will be friends with everyone, but it is important for everyone to be friends with someone. Not every group of coworkers will have a strong bond, but it is important they know and care about one another's success and well-being, both in and out of school.

Implications for Teachers

Teachers need to have a sense of community with those around them to feel connected with the school community. They must reimagine roles and intentionally balance collegial and congenial relationships during the workday. Each building has a unique climate and personality. Some teachers are sadly miserable in their jobs, not because they do not like teaching, but because they lack the sense of community in the group and have an unfulfilled need to belong. This is within their purview to reimagine. Administrators need to address the conditions to improve the situation for struggling teachers. Although teachers are ultimately responsible, it is the building leaders

who make community possible (or impossible). Teachers should not be afraid to seek and expect environments where they feel this sense of community. We find that some teachers are reluctant to seek other teaching jobs because they haven't identified lack of community as the issue; rather, they believe it is teaching itself they are dissatisfied with, leading them to leave the profession prematurely. They may need to choose a different pond (Barker, 2017). That's why teachers should hold up a mirror and reinvent their idea of where they need to be. Perhaps it was always your dream to teach in a particular building or community only to find the realities of that place are not conducive to your mattering. If so, you would change where you teach, rather than look for work outside the field of education.

One challenge teachers face in role acceptance is what the teaching profession prescribes for them. Given the prevalence of PLCs, an emphasis on working together collaboratively is present in education. Collegial relationships focus on talking with one another about practice, sharing knowledge of teaching, observing one another, and being excited for the success of colleagues (Barth, 2006). Most widely accept that teachers have these types of relationships in the school. In fact, the antithesis of this type of atmosphere would indicate a toxic culture. This perception creates a binary condition that leaves out half the necessary equation for community. Some overlook the positive role of congenial relationships or friendships. Considering the importance of community, this is problematic.

There are several actions teachers can take, and administrators should empower them to. It is important to remember that a lack of community is not solely an individual teacher problem to address. It takes the individual, the building leader, and the rest of the staff working together to accomplish the following to-dos.

- Embrace that your needs for adult community deserve a place at the forefront in schools, before almost everything else you do. Respectfully disagree with perspectives otherwise; they are out of date and incongruent with our research.

- Identify what you need in a community. It may be obvious; however, this initial step is important, as each person's community needs do differ. Be confident in sharing with those you trust, as this will build openness and mutual understanding.

- Plan for a certain amount of professional time each week to devote to the needs of other adults in your community. You don't need to formally schedule these times; they can be flexible. We realize how busy you are each day. With this said, there are simply some times when your colleagues need you. Spend this time (just a few moments) with your open door or employ an open mind during planning times, lunch, or even before or after school. Find a breakroom or coffee klatch niche where you can take time for your work friends at a time that works for you.

- Strive to see situations where you can serve as a model of both congeniality and collegiality. We suggest starting first with congeniality (if this is natural for you), as it paves the way for more of the critical conversations collegiality invites. However, if you are smack dab in the middle of a tough conversation, don't offer too much congeniality; it will appear inauthentic. Check in the next day (after a difficult day together) to connect with the person with a kind affirmation, nod, or thank-you for having the tough talk. The idea is to model both for others who struggle with congeniality or collegiality.

- Advocate for necessary and sufficient time with your principal and district leaders. Negotiating what your school day will look like, what your professional responsibilities will entail, and what time you will be compensated for (and whether that time is assignment oriented or duty free). Prioritize duty-free space for community to thrive. Don't apologize for saying you need a community of adults, as well as a community of learners, in your school.

Implications for School Leaders

School leaders can create conditions in the school that allow groups of teachers to work as a community both collegially and congenially. There are numerous resources for PLCs and collective teacher efficacy regarding their positive impact on student achievement (Donohoo et al., 2018; DuFour et al, 2016, Hattie, 2003, 2009). Yet, a focus on congenial relationships is often seen as extraneous and unimportant. In fact, there's a tacit, underlying idea that people should not have too much fun at work. What a drag, and how counterproductive!

In his book *Effortless: Make It Easier to Do What Matters Most*, sought-after speaker Greg McKeown (2021) discusses the false mindset people feel when they are not working hard enough, enjoy their job too much, or are not totally drained when they complete the job. The idea of making work enjoyable and—dare we say—fun is not new. Coauthors Stephen C. Lundin, Harry Paul, and John Christensen (2000) created a metaphor regarding employee morale. Their book, *Fish! A Proven Way to Boost Morale and Improve Results* identifies four key tenets to boost employee satisfaction (Lundin et al., 2000). One of these pillars is *play*, or *have fun*. In many professional organizations (including schools), the idea of playing or having fun is likely looked down on. Rarely, if ever, does an educational leader state, "I want my teachers to play." As educational leaders, giving teachers permission to enjoy one another's company, have fun while working, and generally feel a sense of camaraderie among colleagues will go far in creating a sense of community that leads to mattering.

Leaders must follow up words with action. It is relatively easy for a leader to get in front of the staff and say, "I want you to enjoy one another's company. I want you to go out and have fun with one another while you are working." Leaders must follow up with action; create an environment and atmosphere where teachers feel safe to have fun. This requires that you discuss with teachers activities they find enjoyable. Building principals will often use something like a jeans day to celebrate and allow teachers to dress more casually. Another approach is to create a *climate committee*, which typically includes teachers who want to focus on creating a positive school climate. Yet, we caution, these committees often miss the mark. While this committee can be beneficial in many ways, it often does little in the way of creating the sense of community we refer to. That's because leaders typically relegate climate committees to one-off events or special occasions with little direct tie-in to the actual job of teaching. While wearing matching T-shirts on a designated day may engender a sense of unity, it is typically surface-level unity akin to going to a football game and cheering alongside strangers. There's a connection because you are rooting for the same team and belong to the same group, but essentially you are still sitting by a stranger.

Although wearing jeans or matching T-shirts at school may make things a bit more relaxing, does it create a fun atmosphere? That depends on the individual building and the people who work in it. What a teaching staff determines as *fun* is as unique as the individual building culture. What teachers in one building may find fun, teachers in another building may find a burden or useless. Leaders must build a culture of community in deeper ways and not rely on superficial add-ons like jeans day. (Is that even a thing anymore?) A leader must know what teachers find fun and not rely on what other building leaders do. While some may find it fun to create an online lip sync about the latest education fad, others may find it stress inducing and see it as a waste of time.

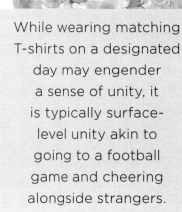

While wearing matching T-shirts on a designated day may engender a sense of unity, it is typically surface-level unity akin to going to a football game and cheering alongside strangers.

The Little Things

School leaders might create check-in questions to ask teachers prior to staff, department, or grade-level meetings. These questions could help teachers get to know one another, and they may find common interests about which to connect with one another. It is important to ensure teachers can answer your check-in questions relatively quickly and that the questions feel fun. Spend only a short time on check-in questions, as they are not the primary reason for the meeting. Also, individuals should feel confident that not answering is perfectly acceptable; let individuals skip answering questions that aren't their style. School leaders using lighthearted and connective measures to begin most typical meetings could become the norm.

School leaders can create coordinated activities to go along with school events to help create community—for example, organize a designated staff tailgate night at a high school football or basketball game. Creating a space where teachers and their families can commiserate before an extracurricular event is a great way for staff to get to know one another. School leaders should plan some casual pickup games, ensuring plenty of chairs for participants and an atmosphere conducive to conversation. Be careful not to create too much organization, as some of the best experiences are those that occur naturally. Additionally, people like to interact at gatherings in different ways, so it is important not to force people out of their comfort zone. Be cautious when saying things such as, "You cannot talk about work at the tailgate." For some, discussing work is an on-ramp for talking about other topics. If you are concerned about some conversations turning negative, pre-plan with some teacher leaders about how to casually change the conversations if necessary. This could be as simple as asking a few teachers to try to sway the conversation back positively if they hear a negative conversation. Of course, it's OK for people to use this as an opportunity to vent. Sometimes, a little bit of complaining is healthy! The trick is to know when venting becomes more harmful than helpful. There is also a difference between complaining and identifying what needs to change (solution focus). Occasionally poking a little bit of fun at the less-desirable aspects of the job is a stress reducer.

The Bigger Things

Teacher evaluation systems are one aspect of community educational leaders should address. Evaluation systems that rate teachers against one another or place teachers in competitions that impact pay rates can have a negative effect on community building. These evaluation systems are the antithesis of creating community and authenticity. School leaders must find ways to implement evaluation systems that create conditions for community. Doing so can have implications for both adults and students:

> Cultures of professional collaboration do not only characterize higher performing systems; they also outperform matched samples in which individualism prevails, and there is clear evidence that the trust they establish among adults has a prior influence on eventual outcomes in student learning results. (Hargreaves & O'Connor, 2017, p. 82)

Even the term *evaluation* can have negative connotations. The primary purpose of evaluation systems should be continual professional improvement. However, more often, school administrators see evaluations as only helpful for dealing with ineffective teachers. Evaluation models focus on highly effective teachers (by giving additional compensation to those who rank higher on the rubric) and create a sense of competition among colleagues. While the intention of these types of evaluation systems is ultimately to increase student achievement, the results show no impact (Glazerman & Seifullah, 2012; Hargreaves & O'Connor, 2017).

There is little evidence that competitive incentives for teachers are effective in improving education (Hargreaves & O'Connor, 2017). As Pink (2009) points out, competitive incentives are only effective with jobs consisting of low-skill and routine tasks. Extrinsic incentives for complex occupations that require professional judgment are damaging. The idea of rugged individualism as a redeeming characteristic is prevalent in "teacher as the superhero" movies but has little actual relevance in the classroom. Education thought leaders back this up: "Given the complex challenges facing schools, it is virtually impossible for an individual teacher, working alone, to successfully teach *all* . . . students" (DuFour, DuFour, Eaker, Mattos, & Muhammad, 2021, p. 125).

Educational leaders must ensure the evaluation system in place aligns with the core values of the organization. They must address unintended negative consequences of an evaluation system to ensure evaluations enhance the learning organization. Even the words evaluations use for the various categories have an impact on the teachers' perception of the rating. Evaluations that pit one teacher against another for pay bonuses hinder a collaborative environment. Evaluations may treat education as a finite game (with a definitive end and winners and losers) instead of an infinite game where there is no end point (Sinek, 2020).

Leaders should develop the system to encourage teacher growth and learning (even when it means teachers are not perfect when trying new teaching strategies). The system should encourage

teamwork and collaboration. Leaders must also recognize a rubric cannot possibly account for the complex nature of teaching. There are just some things a rubric cannot capture. Even the words leaders use are impactful. What if leaders change the rating categories from *highly effective, effective, needs improvement*, and *ineffective* to *strongest area, successful area, growth area*, and *needs improvement*, with the final rating either *effective* or *ineffective*? Teaching is too complex to differentiate (often to the tenths or hundredths of a decimal) if teachers are effective or highly effective. An evaluation system should not hinder the collaborative structure schools strive to achieve. Leaders must be explicit in their expectations. They should discuss the purpose and goals of the evaluation, and then back up what they say with action. In other words, if an educational leader states that collaboration is an important part of being an effective teacher, then the evaluation the leader uses must reflect that. Just as teachers identify power or essential standards, educational leaders must identify evaluation priorities.

School leaders can also take action on building community through hiring. Hiring staff with the lens of mattering in mind creates several opportunities for increased mattering in the school. If teachers are going to have a sense of community, they must be able to work together. Often teachers are involved in only the late stages of hiring new teachers or not at all. Consider that teachers spend more time with one another than administrators spend with them, so wouldn't it be prudent to directly involve teachers early in hiring processes? A sense of community does not mean a homogeneous group of people (by race, ethnicity, other identities, or opinions); leaders serve communities best when the staff includes diverse populations from many different backgrounds. By leveraging diversity, leaders can foster an inclusive community.

We often see leaders across the United States enact formal measures to build community. Many schools and districts implement the PLC process. PLCs take a variety of forms and are implemented differently across districts. How a school structures its PLC can have an impact on the teachers' sense of community. School leaders must develop PLCs in cooperation with teachers. Mandating rigid PLC structures can create an atmosphere not conducive to the goals of increased teacher collaboration. In *Learning by Doing: A Handbook for Professional Learning Communities at Work*, the coauthors describe a *loose-tight* structure (DuFour et al., 2016). Some areas are *tight* (not up for discussion), while other areas are *loose* (provide for flexibility). When leaders bureaucratically impose a PLC, they can undermine collegial trust (Hargreaves & O'Connor, 2017). If a PLC is so rigid it negatively affects collaboration, then it is not a true PLC.

School leaders can even build community through efforts beyond the school walls. Leaders also need to find ways to create more time during the school day for teachers to work together; working together toward a common goal builds community. School leaders must work with elected officials and policymakers to examine policies and mandates that detract from teachers' abilities to work together. For example, in 2019, an eight-page memo to Indiana school districts outlined mandatory training for teachers (Indiana Department of Education Office of Legislative Affairs, 2019). Many of the training mandates are annual. Although the topics the mandatory training addresses are important, there are alternative avenues to refresh teachers in a more efficient, timely manner. When the states give the leeway to do so, leaders should find creative ways to lessen the burden of these annual training mandates. Leaders can utilize some professional learning time to give teachers the ability to complete this training during contract time instead of making them complete the training on their own time. Streamline training for experienced teachers. Sometimes, less is more. Instead of using pre-scripted, generic training, customize the training to address current or past situations in the district, making the training more relevant.

By taking deliberate action, educational leaders can have a big impact on developing a community for mattering. Often, building leaders feel helpless in reducing the emotional labor of teachers. It is critical for leaders to acknowledge it and discuss ways to help.

- Ensure you value and promote time for community in a way that interfaces with the PLC process in your school. If you do not have formal methods to spend on community time, then support informal methods (such as when teachers need to connect with others and ask colleagues—or you—to cover their classes). Understand that each time one of your teachers needs a special favor, it is not really a precedent-setting incident. It is a real need that a member of the community can help meet.

- If teachers are saying, "Students must come first," applaud their altruism and commitment, but remind them of the oxygen mask scenario on anyone's airplane (see page 1). Give teachers permission to *be first* at times—to take time for themselves—because you want to authentically project that you value the needs of adults in your building too. Let them know it's much more efficient to be about themselves first and then get back to the needs of students quickly, if they *have* community.

- Implement deliberative hiring practices to enhance community. Ask candidates questions during the interview to determine if they can help promote community in your building and encourage the hiring team to consider their answers when making recommendations. Ensure those you hire wish for a positive adult community as much as, or more so, than those already working in the school. They might not tell you this (it's not typically what a candidate prepares to say in an interview), so read between the lines.

- Take one or two issues per year of key interest to teachers and make a decision regarding them based on consensus, rather than through a democratic vote or advisory recommendation. In other words, be thoughtful in your consideration to spend appropriate time getting all viewpoints in your community. Then, frame your decision as something *all can live with* together. This takes time. Honor that.

Conclusion

Now, we'll revisit the community school we highlighted at the beginning of the chapter.

> Years hence, one couldn't help noticing the retention rate in these educators, some having served many years in this small but special school, even despite other more financially lucrative opportunities in neighboring districts. At one point, amid a state economic calamity, the team made cuts to outside services through tough decisions, took on extra duties, and even cleaned their own building. School leaders assigned themselves the restrooms.
>
> The staff even banded together and agreed to freeze their own wages for a time, thus protecting one another from layoffs while precarious times befell other schools. All the while, this team kept things invisible from students, deeply enjoying each day's learning challenges and educational opportunities. Students observed the healthy functioning of adults in their building and responded similarly, even those students who came with resumes chock full of disciplinary infractions and bouts with the law. One thing was inherent in everything that went on interpersonally in this special place, the one thing that kept everyone together and hopeful during good times and bad: a sense of community.

Note what was really going on in the school from the vignette. Teachers and staff enjoyed coming to work each day. During tough times, they had one another's backs and leveraged the sum of their efforts to find solutions. Mutually respectful cohesion—that combination of collegiality and congeniality—created true job satisfaction that transcended levels in neighboring schools and school districts. Students benefited from teacher and staff longevity, and so did the school's budget, which saved professional induction and mentoring costs. In short, students benefited most because the adults took care of one another first. They did so in community.

All too often, teachers and leaders leave community building to chance. At best, they will partake in fun or isolated activities. To build a climate of job-focused teamwork that creates energy and belonging, actions must be purposeful.

In the next chapter, we'll discuss authenticity.

Next Steps: Chapter 1 Recap Activity

Fill in the following diagram from the chapter's beginning, this time with unique information pertinent to you and this foundational element in mattering.

The Interpersonal Element of Community in Mattering	
Job-focused teamwork that creates energy and belonging	
Your Way to Conceive:	
Your Way to Believe:	Community
Your Way to Achieve:	

Ensuring Teachers Matter © 2024 Solution Tree Press • SolutionTree.com
Visit **go.SolutionTree.com/teacherefficacy** to download this free reproducible.

Your Personal Professional Development: Thought Experiment—Community

The following thought experiment gives you an opportunity to imagine a different reality. Take time to visualize the scenario. You may want to revisit these questions several times to get a complete picture. It takes practice. Find your quiet space and consider the possibilities.

If the staff were *perfectly* collegial *and* congenial in your building:
What would it look like?
How would conversions among coworkers be different?
What could you do differently?
How would you feel?
What would change about the student experience?

Questions to ponder:

How important is the sense of community to you in your workplace?

What resonates most with you about community?

Do you see a sense of community in your building? If so, where?

How can you expand community in your building?

What is one small thing you can do to strengthen a sense of community?

Do you have a workplace best friend, and what does person this mean to you?

CHAPTER 2

Embracing What You See, and That's a Whole Lot of Me: *Authenticity*

Authenticity is the second of the three elements that fall into the interpersonal domain, which again pertains to people's relationships with others. *Authenticity* is when teachers do not have to shed who they are at the schoolhouse gate and can be themselves without pretense. This ties into relationships with others—teachers must feel safe to be themselves around the people they work with on a daily basis.

The following fictional story introduces a teacher struggling with a lack of authenticity.

> After his college graduation, Damon, a high school social studies teacher, took a position in an elementary school in a community where mainstream political, economic, and social beliefs contrasted with his own. He wanted to get involved in causes dear to him but would have faced pushback from other teachers, as well as potential rebuff from students' parents, who may have seen his postings on social media. Damon wished to expose his students to a wide plethora of social sciences perspectives available among news and media outlets; however, hot-button issues gave him a near-certain warning light to stay within established lanes when he arrived at

the schoolhouse gate each day. While school leaders had not explicitly stated what he was to teach or discuss, Damon had seen firsthand how the school district's board of education meetings had become town halls for negative conflict among interest groups and school administrators. More and more, the arguments were about what teachers were teaching, in part because of new state mandates and what teachers were exposing students to in terms of literature, dialogue, and conversation. Professionally and personally, Damon felt he must look and act a certain way to fit in, and for a time he wrote it off as a stretch opportunity to try new things. With colleagues, he found better connections through laughing at certain jokes and embracing the way things have been done for years, and of course, perspectives on the teaching profession. He struggled to embrace typical banter in the teachers' lounge about students and families as something representing his values or those he could buy into.

In short, it was getting harder and harder to be him . . . at least the him his colleagues, principal, and students' parents seemed to expect. He feared that over time, this would be how his students knew him, shared with others, and came to expect. Damon really didn't know how to marry two worlds—the world he preferred to live in and the one where he resided professionally. He feared that attempting to build a bridge would mean either living inauthentically in both realms or staying authentically on only one side or the other without making a daily commute across. As he watched reality television each week, he could relate to the characters who were living their veneer and risking each day being found out.

Figure 2.1 provides an anticipatory set for the element of authenticity. The reproducible "Next Steps: Chapter 2 Recap Activity" (page 52) gives you the opportunity to fill in your own ideas.

The Interpersonal Element of Authenticity in Mattering
Ability to be the same person at work and at home

One Way to Conceive: Imagine a drive to or from school in which you need only ponder with excitement what you'll say and do around students to be your most excellent teaching self, not worrying what you must say or do to justify who you are.	 **Authenticity**
One Way to Believe: Seek opportunities for staff, faculty, and administrators to discuss how everyone can *keep things real* with students without putting forth a company line in reaction to unrealistic pressure to avoid showing your true self.	
One Way to Achieve: Find your groove of confidence as a member of a diverse, inclusive professional mosaic, where you comparatively contextualize your opinions while valuing perspectives different from your own.	

FIGURE 2.1: The interpersonal element of authenticity in mattering.

Teachers should feel they can be their authentic selves at work. In this chapter, we start with authenticity by embracing what you see, and that's a whole lot of me (meaning *you*). We examine the code-switching or surface acting that occurs for teachers linguistically, culturally, and personally in terms of their personalities. *Code-switching* is a term from linguistics to explain how multilingual people can switch from one language to another. We use this term to also mean when people change their behaviors to conform to a group. This includes the way they speak, dress, and act. Many people code-switch to conform to a different norm than what they might authentically do at home or around friends. While some degree of code-switching between work and personal life is normal, too much can lead to exhaustion, mental fatigue, and distress. Balancing teachers' need for an environment that allows them to be their authentic selves while ensuring a diverse teaching population is something all educational leaders must take into thoughtful consideration when building a cohesive team. Along with code-switching, we discuss emotional dissonance, surface acting, and people's need for sensebreaking in this chapter. We find these concepts fascinating. Soon to follow are implications for teachers and educational leaders. We conclude the chapter with the reproducibles "Next Steps: Chapter 2 Recap Activity" (page 52) and "Your Personal Professional Development: Thought Experiment—Authenticity" (page 53).

Getting Started With Authenticity

Many who tune in to various reality television shows notice a profound difference between participants when they first present themselves and when their true selves come out later on. In some instances, the participants keep their true selves secret and live with the disparity for a time before being discovered after some significant event reveals the truer aspects of their personality, preference, or intent. In other instances, the participants are so immersed in projecting a certain image of themselves that they, along with others, believe that is who they are—until something more deeply emotional begins chipping away at the veneer to reveal different people. Then, these participants each begin holding up a mirror to the new *me* (actually, the old *me*) and give those around them a peek—or not. In either instance, these circumstances have consequences that lead toward interpersonal growth and better understanding. However, these circumstances are also replete with short- or mid-term consequences, especially if they deny what the participants' true selves are saying for a time. We've seen the same in teaching.

> The farther you get away from your authentic self in your organization, the more effort and energy it takes for you to be happy and comfortable in that environment—or in your professional skin.

Being your authentic self means you can be who you are and not be concerned with finding approval (or disapproval) in others. Mike Anderson (2010), author of the book *The Well-Balanced Teacher*, shares what you need to be accepted for who you really are. The more an organization aligns with your personal beliefs, goals, and values, the more authentic you feel working in that environment every day—and the more comfortable you are in your own skin. The farther you get away from your authentic self in your organization, the more effort and energy it takes for you to be happy and comfortable in that environment—or in your professional skin. Teachers must be able to be their authentic selves to the largest extent possible in school. Situations where teachers feel compelled to be different in their careers than what they are in their personal lives create internal conflicts that are difficult to reconcile.

Reconciling your personal and professional lives is not simply a nice thing to do, it is necessary. University of Edinburgh researchers Carolin Kreber, Monika Klampfleitner, Velda McCune, Sian Bayne, and Miesbeth Knottenbelt (2007) note:

> Authenticity is seen to make individuals more whole, more integrated, more fully human, more aware, more content with their personal and professional lives, their actions more clearly linked to purpose, empowered, better able to engage in community with others, and so forth. (p. 24)

Coauthors Blake E. Ashforth and Beth S. Schinoff (2016), in "Identity Under Construction: How Individuals Come to Define Themselves in Organizations," offer the question, "Who am I?" and state the extent to which a person internalizes an identity is the definition of *self*, as in the example, "I am a teacher" (p. 113). We pose that such identification influences what people think, how they act, and what they feel. When people say, "Being a teacher does not define me," it could be an indication of a healthy work-life balance or that they have a loose identification with the teaching profession and have trouble with feeling like their authentic selves when engaged in teaching. This latter might occur if their workplace doesn't allow them to be their authentic selves at school.

Whenever teachers need to hide their authentic selves to fit in, it takes additional energy. The larger the gap between the authentic self and workplace self, the more energy the individual expends. Teaching has always been an emotionally exhausting profession; it is exacerbated when individuals feel the need to placate others to fit in.

Whereas in *community*, as we note in chapter 1 (page 19), teachers come together and work as a team. Authenticity is about moving more into yourself and operating as an individual. It is about being *self-full*—taking elegant care of your own individual needs first, so you have the energy to provide your own contributions to the team and others. The notion of *self-fullness* derives from the work of psychologist Taibi Kahler (2008), creator of the Process Communication Model®, notes psychologist Nate Regier (2020), founding member of Next Element Consulting, and creator of the Compassion Mindset®. While the concepts of working as a team and being yourself may seem contradictory, they actually strengthen each other. The common and oversimplified saying, *There is no I in team*, leaves out an important tenet—when individuals bring their unique strengths through multiplicity of individual effort and contribution, they strengthen groups.

Why is a lack of authenticity so affecting? Without authenticity, teachers can struggle with emotional dissonance and an excess of *surface acting*, or putting on an act to fit in. *Authenticity* in the context of mattering means teachers can question themselves in healthy and fulfilling ways to change and grow, a process known as *sensebreaking*.

Emotional Dissonance and Surface Acting

Emotional dissonance, the difference between how people feel and what they display to others, has been the topic of much research. Lack of authenticity in your professional life leads to emotional dissonance. Coauthors Elaine O'Brien and Carol Linehan (2019), in "Problematizing the Authentic Self in Conceptualizations of Emotional Dissonance," note multiple studies showing "negative individual consequences including emotional exhaustion . . . ; burnout . . . ; . . . low job satisfaction and organisational withdrawal" (p. 1531). Coauthors Jared Kenworthy, Cara Fay, Mark Frame, and Robyn Petree (2014), in "A Meta-Analytic Review of the Relationship Between Emotional Dissonance and Emotional Exhaustion," state, "Because it is resource-consuming to display false emotions, doing so for extended periods will likely lead to emotional exhaustion (a chronic state of emotional and physical depletion)" (p. 97). While code-switching originated in linguistics and most often occurs when someone is multilingual or multicultural, surface acting can happen even when code-switching does not. *Surface acting* describes when people fake their feelings to fit the organizational norms without changing any of their true feelings. A disconnect from what they feel and what others around them expect can lead people to engage in surface acting.

Researchers Ute Hülsheger and Anna F. Schewe (2011), in their meta-analysis on the costs and benefits of emotional labor, note emotional dissonance and surface acting are detrimental to both well-being and performance outcomes. Thus, emotional dissonance often leads to emotional exhaustion, a key component of burnout. To find comfort in an organization, people feel they must conform to expectations on how they should act and what they should say at times. Yet, authenticity can only occur when people's values and actions are congruent. Teachers' personal values must match the values of their schools. If these values conflict or teachers feel disconnected from the school's values, it is difficult to feel authentic in the classroom.

Everyone participates to some degree in surface acting while at work. In fact, it's integral to high functioning. There are days when you're not feeling well or have a terrible headache, and yet you smile and greet someone nicely even though you would rather just sit and not talk at all. You have probably had difficult conversations with parents or students who get on your last nerve, yet instead of yelling and screaming (like your inner voice is), you address the students and their parents calmly and professionally on the surface.

When we discuss authenticity through the lens of mattering, we focus on the amount of surface acting that occurs between colleagues. As cowriters Alicia Grandey, Su Chuen Foo, Markus Groth, and Robyn E. Goodwin (2012) state in "Free to Be You and Me: A Climate of Authenticity Alleviates Burnout From Emotional Labor," "Given that employee burnout is linked to absences, turnover, and performance decrements, helping employees feel 'free to be you and me' in a work group can be a critical step in improving employee and organizational well-being" (p. 11).

Surface acting, though necessary, takes a lot of energy. People sometimes run out of energy, and the emotional dissonance becomes too great. They can no longer surface act when needed. It is extremely important for educators to understand and identify when these situations are brewing before they become inclined to unleash their less-professional inner selves. In these moments, if teachers feel psychologically safe in their organization, they can seek help from those around them before something drastic happens. Why? Because teachers know they matter to others around them who have their best interests at heart.

Psychological safety is the sense that you can express your thoughts and feelings without risk of embarrassment, reprimand, or negative repercussions. If you feel psychologically unsafe in an environment, you will resort to surface acting in an unsustainable way. Teachers in a psychologically safe environment will express themselves when they are feeling emotional dissonance and can talk through internal conflicts with colleagues without unnecessary risk.

Our Need for Sensebreaking in Authenticity

Finding and maintaining authenticity does not preclude the necessity of change. In fact, part of people's growth as humans occurs when they internally challenge their beliefs and expectations. Boston College professor Michael Pratt (2000) describes *sensebreaking* as questioning who you are when someone challenges your sense of self; it involves "the destruction or breaking down of meaning" (p. 464). The more teachers connect to teaching as part of who they are, the more sensebreaking is necessary for change to occur. This happens when teachers discover a new teaching method as "a must" to use over their preferred method. Sensebreaking occurs when teachers use stretch goals to get out of their comfort zones and take risks. When people start to question a deeply held belief, they may feel they are going against their authentic selves, but in reality, questioning their beliefs is part of growth and change to their authentic selves.

Simon Sinek (2020), noted author and inspirational speaker, refers to *education* as an infinite game—a game, if played optimally, without endings, wins, or losses necessary . . . just cycles and an opportunity for educators to participate. To be successful in an infinite game such as education, you must have *existential flexibility*—an ability to shift your beliefs once you discover new evidence (Sinek, 2020). When you come to a point in your career (or life) when you reach a sensebreaking moment, authenticity invites existential flexibility to change. You replace the old deeply held belief with a new belief that becomes part of your evolving, authentic self. Sensebreaking and existential flexibility help you create updated versions of your authentic self, while conversely, emotional dissonance and surface acting create a short-lived facade that will work against overall mattering.

MAKING *AUTHENTICITY* MATTER

Making authenticity matter is a bold step, and many are simply unwilling to take it because they think they cannot accomplish it with the lives they lead. Here is how: ensure you spend time each day being the best *you* that you can be. In other words, spend this time each day doing something for you (and nobody else), and do so without sacrificing sleep.

What this means, plainly and simply, is that you'll need to reallocate how you spend your own time, being not only what others need you to be for them but also (and especially) being what you need for yourself. We acknowledge that in some communities it may be difficult (even impossible) to be your authentic self. You need to acknowledge that the farther away you are from your authentic self at work, the more time you need to re-energize and refocus. For example, imagine that you're an introvert who finds that you must spend the day at a teacher workshop with people you do not know and where you will have lots of interaction with strangers. At the end of this day, you must give a presentation on a particular topic you just learned about. Compounding this is that you get nervous when you speak in front of adults, especially when you have not had time to rehearse. What this might demand of you is to surface act all day. You need to exude confidence and talk to everyone in the room. Deep down, you know you would rather just sit in the corner typing on your computer to prepare for your presentation. What you actually need is to reallocate time during the day—an intentional, self-full gift of solitude delivered at reasonable intervals. Instead of spending the whole lunch hour socializing and networking, might you politely excuse yourself after a twenty-minute chat at the lunch table to go take a call, make a call, or just pretend you're doing so?

Whether you use this time to work on your presentation is not really the point. The point is *you're doing something for you*. At larger workshops, you might spend one full breakout session by yourself in a quiet location reflecting on the topics you have already seen or heard in other sessions. Allowing for time spent authentically will bring a better you to those challenging situations. In this case, it could allow the best you possible to attend the conference during the day—your way—and deliver your presentation that evening.

While this may sound selfish or inconceivable to some, it is really more than just possible to do; it's necessary. You will find in approximately thirty days' time, if you leverage the time and space to be authentic (or act self-fully for you), the *you* who is of service to others and your profession will be a different and more productive, efficient, and authentic version. You will have more energy, you will begin noticing more passion in your calling. Even if your current professional position is incongruent with your dream

> job, preferred grade level or content area, or ideal assignment in terms of extra duties, you will bring a different perspective to those daily roles with more holistic, authentic attention to your true self.
>
> Take time for authenticity by being self-full and putting yourself on the clock, as you are the only one responsible for you during the one and only life you lead. You are worth it, and we hope you know that too, as you make authenticity matter.

Implications for Teachers

School districts with a clear mission and stated core values they practice on a daily basis can also help teacher candidates in the area of authenticity. When schools clearly state their own missions congruent with the direction of their district, teachers can determine whether they can be their authentic selves within that structure. As a teacher, it is important to transparently discuss with colleagues and leaders the areas in which their stated mission and core values do not align with their lived mission and core values. Teachers in schools that operate as PLCs understand the importance of the school mission and values to achieving the overall goals of the school. The mission typically focuses on student achievement. When teacher mattering connects to the school's mission, it also connects to student achievement.

When confronting the daily challenges in a school, it can be easy to unintentionally disregard the values the district or school has put in place. After all, much is on your plate! With the pace of what you're being requested to do, it's important to assume positive intent in your leaders. This does not mean teachers should ignore decisions that go against what they believe aligns with their own mission and core values but rather discuss their concerns. After all, if teachers feel leaders are not following through on the promises of the district, chances are other teachers are feeling that as well.

Code-switching and surface acting are also topics with implications for teachers. While teachers need to feel they can be authentic while at work, there will always be some element of social, cultural, or linguistic code-switching that occurs between teachers' private and professional lives. The amount of code-switching one does during the day can take a psychological toll on individuals (McCluney, Robotham, Lee, Smith, & Durkee, 2019). The same is true of surface acting. This balancing act takes energy because it has elements of remaining professional, relevant, politically correct, and inspirational, all at the same time. As such, teaching can be emotionally and physically draining.

This perceived need to code-switch could also be a reason it is difficult for schools to recruit historically underrepresented or minoritized teachers. Teachers may see the work environment of a school as a place where they cannot be their authentic selves. In schools or districts not already inclusive, attempts to recruit teachers of color met with skepticism of the school's motives (Simon, Johnson, & Reinhorn, 2015). Those in the majority may fail to understand that authenticity would best serve everyone; many do not have a minoritized experience and do not even understand code-switching or surface acting when they see it. Any disconnects present may be in leaders' blind spots, so teachers initiate redress of the drain on their energy. This must be a joint effort on the part of both teachers and leaders. There is also another way community can contribute to mattering; teachers with more privilege (whether that privilege comes from their identity, background, or their veteran status in the school) can speak up on behalf of their colleagues when they see an opportunity for authenticity to flourish.

If you are struggling with being your authentic self at work, discuss your concern with a trusted mentor or colleague. In limited cases, it could be your perception of others not accepting your authentic self is not the reality your mentor or colleague sees. It is important to discuss your feelings with others if your concern strikes at the heart of your authenticity. More often, it could be excessive code-switching is what you perceive others expect; others just simply do not realize the degree to which each day makes you feel uncomfortable or unwelcome. While not all teachers will be at risk of developing burnout and suffering from psychological health impairments due to emotional dissonance and surface acting, it may very well be you are at that point. With open discussion, you might discover some new strategies to use or even reframe strategies with the perspective of others and close the distance within your authentic self. The more you keep code-switching and surface acting to a minimum, the better off you will be.

Ultimately, if you are in an organization where you are in constant emotional dissonance and struggling to be your authentic self, the best outcome may be to seek out a different assignment within the organization. Often, those in proximity to you will change if you begin working in a different grade level or building. In rare circumstances, you may wish to seek opportunities in a different building within the same district or a different organization altogether. It should not be your burden to change the entire organization or people in it. The emotional or physical energy to do that would work against one's self-fullness and leave little behind to focus on students. Sometimes, you need to make a tough decision about where you wish to spend your professional life.

Some schools and districts live core values one person cannot change. Changing the culture of an organization takes years. Some people thrive in change and would relish the challenge of changing an organization so the stated and lived missions and core values are the same. That isn't for everyone, but for others, this kind of struggle and challenge are what help them achieve their authentic selves. Reiterating here: sometimes, you just have to find another pond (Barker, 2017).

Surface acting is physically and emotionally draining. It is important to understand and identify areas where surface acting is necessary and when you can be your authentic self. Understand that the more surface acting necessary, the more time you'll need for recovery. Here are some suggestions to deal with the surface-acting dilemma.

- Have the courage to recommit to your workplace more authentically (or consider something new if you cannot), knowing the real you is important to your success. Make a plan to leverage as much authenticity as you can while at work each day, even incrementally for a while, as this is important. Be cautious if the gap between the real you and *the you present at work* has been extreme. (If this has been the case, our inquiry suggests your job has been suboptimal or exhausting to perform.)

- Find environments in your school that require a minimal amount of code-switching, and earmark a certain amount of time to spend there each day, even if on your preparation period or during duty-free lunches, if available. Try to find time in these environments to discuss being your authentic selves with others who will do the same. Strive to affirm one another's individuality and identity.

- Sit down with colleagues and your principal and have an honest conversation about where you would like your professional assignment to be in three years. Be honest about your preferences, even if you feel vulnerable about sharing. It does not negate your present service or misidentify you as the right person for your students right now. It's an indication of healthy self-honesty. If you face rebuffs of any kind, you might wish to be around different adults in three years as well.

- Dedicate a section of your classroom to the theme of *you being you* if you have not done this already. Display pictures of what you do in your spare time—how you enjoy recreation and time being self-full. Be tactful in what you share, but don't hesitate to discuss with students if your sharing could augment a lesson or your positive relationship with students. While your sharing doesn't have to be an in-your-face stamp on a visitor's arrival, ensure your classroom has your personal signature to the casual onlooker.

Implications for School Leaders

Educational leaders should keep the district's core values at the forefront of decision-making processes. Schools must close the distance between their stated and lived missions and core values. Teachers in the district expect leaders to say what they will do. That's truth in advertising. Your stated mission and core values are what you advertise with a good housekeeping guarantee. No baits and switches allowed. Educational leaders should make it clear that anyone in the organization can identify those not aligning mission and core values, and call them out compassionately. If it's impossible to align behaviors with the school mission and values due to true divergence, then leaders may need to change the school's mission and core values. Key for leaders is facilitating open dialogue. Mission and core values must guide and direct the school or district's decisions.

Leaders should identify potential areas where emotional dissonance could occur and proactively discuss these issues openly. For example, more recent research may question a reading strategy that teachers have long believed is best practice. The district might desire to implement a new learning-to-read strategy that contradicts those long-held teacher beliefs on how students learn to read. In these instances, leaders must recognize that teachers aren't resistant to change or stuck in old ways, but rather are going through emotional dissonance at the heart of authenticity.

When looking at change through this lens, a common phrase (*They need the* why) is inadequate. Knowing the *why* is only partially the issue. Teachers need time to reconcile the emotional dissonance they are feeling. Teachers who strongly identify with teaching may understand the why, but emotionally it is still difficult. As Heath and Heath (2010) describe in the book *Switch: How to*

Change When Change Is Hard, change entails both a rational element (head) and an emotional element (heart). When change provokes your authenticity, the experience challenges both the rational and emotional elements within the very essence of *who you are*. Being able to identify and discuss these situations with others to whom you matter will help with your feelings of dissonance. Ultimately, teachers want to do the best job possible—as in the previous example about using best practices for teaching students to read. If teachers taught a certain way for many years and all of the sudden a purported better way comes along, do they feel their leaders discounted their work up to then? As a leader, you must assure teachers you haven't. Do the teachers understand where you are coming from? Leaders must be explicit with teachers and have conversations about how they might be feeling.

Leaders can also help with teacher authenticity by openly discussing sensitive topics as a staff. As your awareness of emotional dissonance (and the associated negative outcomes) increases, work with teachers to create a psychologically safe environment that balances students' needs with teachers' emotional experiences. Implementing a training program on how to communicate with colleagues can help mitigate emotional dissonance (Kenworthy et al., 2014). There are numerous reasons why people feel they can't be their authentic selves at work. Without effective leaders, generational, racial, economic, and social differences among a diverse staff can foster an environment where some do not feel comfortable as their authentic selves. It is important for leaders to identify and understand these differences and discuss them as a staff. Having a diverse faculty and staff can tremendously benefit the entire school environment. However, if individuals in the school do not understand differences or make false assumptions about them, those individuals can create unnecessary tension and discomfort. Having open discussions regarding differences among staff can help bridge understandings between individuals.

Having open discussions regarding differences among staff can help bridge understandings between individuals.

School leaders may not spend much time thinking about teachers being their authentic selves at work. Some who surface act the best are those who do it the most. It is often difficult to identify when someone is surface acting. It is important to be outwardly supportive of people and cultures who diverge from the majority.

- Ensure you provide a clear and coherent mission that the school lives out each day; do not simply promote the mission as a slogan hanging on the wall. Strive to center the school's core values on what you believe and what you practice so teachers and staff will see you living your mission as a leader and person. This provides a good role model and offers permission for others to do the same.

- Find peace by knowing in the best school buildings with the best leaders, teachers and staff do not have to shed their personal selves and lives at the schoolhouse gate. All educators have a story, and their values might not always align with yours. Do not define tacit compliance or, at times, resistance as necessarily obstinate or insubordinate. Instead, use these reactions as an opportunity for conversation.

- Look for *outliers* (those who don't seem to fit in or those whose performance might be lagging because of it) on your team of professionals. Put a keen eye on those who might be fitting in but doing so at the expense of their eventual retention and sustainability because fitting in is burning them out. Get curious. Have a tactful and sincere conversation. Figure out what these teachers might need to be more comfortable personally in their professional selves at school.
- Read research and listen to experts about *implicit bias* (that is, a form of bias that occurs automatically and unintentionally) and how you or your school may be unknowingly making it difficult for some staff members (and students).

Conclusion

As we note at the beginning of the chapter, Damon doesn't know how to bring his two worlds together. Let's see more of his story.

> Damon had both a need and an obligation. He had the need for mattering, which demanded authenticity. He also had a need to bring his true self to work, as much as he could each day, with psychological safety while charting the waters of sensebreaking, emotional dissonance, and surface acting. The distance between Damon's personal beliefs and those of his community could allow him to serve as a role model, empowered to expand the minds of those around him in a way that added value to already existing contemporary community standards and fostered respect. Of course, if it got to be too much for Damon, he could find another pond, as Barker (2017) suggests. However, we hope it didn't come to that. There were probably students in Damon's classes who saw something inspiring in both Damon and themselves they wouldn't otherwise see without him as their teacher. Fostering authenticity through mattering could hopefully keep this part of the school experience around more often than it drove it away.

Authenticity is an internal feeling. It relates to the level of comfort one has to be themselves around others. Although some level of surface acting is important, the amount and degree must be in balance to mitigate the negative effects. Teachers need to feel psychologically safe to express their feelings and emotions to their colleagues without reprimand or repercussions. When a teacher feels emotional dissonance, emotional regulation is important to utilize.

What stars of reality television shows sometimes experience in full view of an audience is similar to what occurs in schools—the world they prefer to live in, and the one where they currently reside, professionally. Teachers like Damon are good for students and the community and, in terms of mattering, to the other teachers, their colleagues.

In the next chapter, we share what is possible if you are so connected to something, you actually lose sense of time, as the clock is ticking.

Next Steps: Chapter 2 Recap Activity

Fill in the following diagram from the chapter's beginning, this time with unique information pertinent to you and this foundational element in mattering.

The Interpersonal Element of Authenticity in Mattering	
Ability to be the same person at work and at home	
Your Way to Conceive:	
Your Way to Believe:	Authenticity
Your Way to Achieve:	

Ensuring Teachers Matter © 2024 Solution Tree Press • SolutionTree.com
Visit **go.SolutionTree.com/teacherefficacy** to download this free reproducible.

Your Personal Professional Development: Thought Experiment—Authenticity

The following thought experiment gives you an opportunity to imagine a different reality. Take time to visualize the scenario. You may want to revisit these questions several times to get a complete picture. It takes practice. Find your quiet space and consider the possibilities.

If you could truly be your authentic self as a teacher:
What would be different?
How would conversations with colleagues change?
How would your relationships with students be different?
When you walk out of the building at the end of the day, how would you feel?
Would anything change for the student experience?
Think of a time when you experienced emotional dissonance. What was the cause?

Ensuring Teachers Matter © 2024 Solution Tree Press • SolutionTree.com
Visit **go.SolutionTree.com/teacherefficacy** to download this free reproducible.

How did it make you feel?

If you could go back to that time, what would you do differently?

Questions to ponder:

How important to you is authenticity in your workplace?

What resonates most with you about authenticity?

Do you see authenticity in your building? If so, where?

What is one small thing you can do to strengthen authenticity in yourself?

How can you expand authenticity for others?

CHAPTER 3

Getting Lost in the Moment, With a Good Crowd Around: *Flow*

Flow for teachers is when they get so enjoyably immersed in a teaching activity, they don't look at the clock or wish for the day to end. It's when you get lost in time. Sometimes, such as when doing a hobby, being alone helps with flow. In teaching, flow is easiest to obtain and most enjoyable when you share it with others, which is why we consider it an element in the interpersonal domain. The concept of flow has been around for years, but preK–12 educators do not widely discuss it (Csikszentmihalyi, 2008). Most experienced teachers have had at least one lesson that seems to go perfectly as planned, with time seeming to fly. While most teachers focus on the elements of a lesson plan that create these conditions, other factors contribute to this phenomenon that are within the control of the teachers and school leader.

To illustrate, read Tyler's fictional story.

> Tyler, a seasoned fifth-grade teacher, loved teaching fifth graders and preparing them for middle school. Due to population shifts and teacher attrition, the school required Tyler to move to the first-grade team. He had never taught first grade but embraced the opportunity. Instead of moving to a different school, he decided the change in his current school would be good—and he was up for the challenge. He already knew teachers he would be working with on the second-grade team. They were

all younger, so he was excited about being the seasoned veteran who could mentor them. He really didn't have the opportunity to do that while he was on the fifth-grade team because everyone had been teaching about as long as he had. Tyler visualized being in the groove as a mentor, with new synergies and successes making time fly in the new school year.

But Tyler didn't anticipate the difficulty in switching from reading to learn to learning to read. He did have fifth-grade students who struggled with reading, but these students struggled mostly with text complexity, vocabulary, and background knowledge. He quickly realized the skill set for teaching reading was much different from what he remembered from his undergraduate days.

During their collaboration time, his team members discussed activities and skills they learned during a reading workshop and subsequent professional learning. Tyler was teaching fifth graders during those learning opportunities, so he did not participate and didn't pay much attention to the primary years' meetings. While the other teachers talked, Tyler sat and listened, but he was having difficulty following what they were saying. It seemed like they were in a real groove of mutual understanding—almost finishing one another's sentences with impressive subtlety in interaction. Tyler kept his mouth shut—he was the veteran teacher, after all! It was painful for him, something he would not admit, possibly not even to himself at first.

Several weeks passed. Things weren't getting better. Tyler was at a loss when it came to helping students who struggled after initial instruction. He dreaded the district-mandated reading instruction part of the day. Every day, Tyler watched the clock and counted the minutes, which made the days seem to take so long to get through. Some students had no issues at all with reading; however, those who struggled were getting frustrated and so was Tyler. It was agonizing. Minutes seemed like hours, and unlike his colleagues, Tyler was not effortlessly lost and loving the moments. He was keenly aware of the punitive purgatory of his daily

> grind, where every tick of the clock made him ever more aware of the weight of his circumstance.

Figure 3.1 provides an anticipatory set for the element of flow. The reproducible "Next Steps: Chapter 3 Recap Activity" (page 69) gives you the opportunity to fill in your own ideas.

The Interpersonal Element of Flow in Mattering
Enjoyment of an activity to the extent that one loses track of time
One Way to Conceive:
Imagine a week in school when you could not even conceive value in anyone saying, "Thank goodness it's Friday (TGIF)!"
One Way to Believe:
Search effortlessly for anything you can do to eliminate designations of weekdays that wish away parts of the school week for the weekend. Look instead at what you're doing in the moment and find ways to celebrate during those days.
One Way to Achieve:
Implement a reminder strategy so you don't forget to move from one activity you love to another, and those at your next destination can greet the best of you, as you move from one immersive activity to another.

FIGURE 3.1: The interpersonal element of flow in mattering.

In this chapter, we get started with flow by getting lost in some background on flow and what it's about. We then identify the essentials necessary to achieve flow (and what this might look like in a classroom), including knowing what to do, how to do it, how well you are doing, and what to consider as being done. We continue with efficacy in perceiving significant challenges and skills as well as embracing and minimizing distractions on topics both academic and practical. Following are implications for teachers and school leaders. We conclude the chapter with the reproducibles "Next Steps: Chapter 3 Recap Activity" (page 69) and "Your Personal Professional Development: Thought Experiment—Flow" (page 70).

Getting Started With Flow

Psychologist Mihaly Csikszentmihalyi (2008) describes the concept of *flow* as a state of total immersion in what you're doing. Flow is when concentration on the task at hand is effortless. When you're in a state of flow, it is easy to lose track of time and self (Csikszentmihalyi, 2008). Robinson (2009) uses the term *the element* to describe flow. When someone is in the element:

> They are doing the thing they love, and while doing it, they feel like their most authentic selves. They find that time passes differently and that they are more alive, more centered, and more vibrant than at any other time. (Robinson, 2009, p. 21)

Performing activities you love fills you with energy, even when you're physically exhausted (Robinson, 2009). Finding flow is important to your well-being. According to Barker (2017), in *Barking Up the Wrong Tree*, to find flow, you must identify and use your signature strengths. These strengths are the keys to your happiness. The more hours per day you spend doing what you are good at, the less stressed you feel, and the more you laugh, smile, and feel others are treating you with respect (Barker, 2017).

People do not necessarily need to engage in something they love to achieve flow; they can turn a routine task into something they enjoy doing. Csikszentmihalyi (2008) says the key to happiness is the ability to transform even tedious, uninteresting tasks into something enjoyable. We investigate that notion further when we examine another element of mattering, assimilation, in chapter 5 (page 91). Pink (2009) notes that achieving flow through signature strengths or even mundane tasks leads to the most satisfying experiences in people's lives. When people are in the state of flow, they live in the moment so much that time and place seem to disappear. People engage so deeply in what they are doing, they lose themselves in the task.

Teachers tend to have a difficult time finding flow in their daily work. It can happen, but it's rare. (Teachers who have experienced flow know exactly what we are talking about.) It is losing all sense of time when teaching a lesson or completing an activity with students. The bell rings, and everyone in the room is surprised at the time. You don't want class to end. And once you experience flow, you always hope to return to that feeling. It is truly a magical moment in the classroom *and* between teachers and students. According to enjoyment and flow researcher Owen Schaffer (2013), the requirements for achieving flow include the following.

- Knowing what to do and how to do it
- Knowing how well you are doing
- Knowing what's necessary to accomplish to consider the task done
- Perceiving significant challenges and skills
- Embracing and minimizing distractions

Often it is extremely difficult for teachers to get in the state of flow. In fact, in some cases, teaching is counterintuitive to being able to achieve flow. The following sections examine these requirements in more detail.

Knowing What to Do

To a nonteacher, *knowing what to do* may seem rather obvious—teach. Oh, if it were only that simple! The teaching profession has become more and more complex, requiring teachers take on more responsibility in loco parentis. Teaching is not just about content or learning; it is about addressing emotional, behavioral, and social issues and, in some cases, physical needs . . . all the while trying to teach. Teachers struggle to figure out which needs to take care of first and which needs can go on the back burner. It's complicated.

Standardized test performance measure school success, but test scores are seldom the most pressing issue. This puts many school leaders in a quandary. Do leaders sacrifice the perceived success of students to take care of nonacademic needs first, or do they continue pressing forward, putting the performance mandate above all else? Schools that struggle to perform successfully on state academic achievement tests risk losing students, community support, and subsequently funding. Without adequate funding, it is extremely difficult (if not impossible) to meet the nonacademic needs of students. The *what to do* becomes difficult to determine, but at the same time, it's still a foundational building block of flow.

We suggest teachers develop some key principles for knowing what to do in a professional world—a world that makes this difficult to discern because of a surfeit of edicts and conflicting priorities. First, do things equitably by leveling the playing field for learning. Ensure all students have the tools and materials to start from where they are academically and move to a better place—start to finish each day. Don't make it more complicated; a frenzy of competing interests could confuse things. Next, handle issues that are both urgent and important first, issues that are only urgent second, and de-prioritize issues that are neither. Utilize an organizational tool such as the Eisenhower matrix to assist in this endeavor (Nevins, 2023). Save those issues that are important but not urgent for when you have time to address them well, and be OK with this type of prioritization. Stop playing a carnival whacking game on everything that comes your way. Finally, always take the high road when it comes to maintaining dignity, and understand students will spend an inordinate amount of time and energy trying not to be embarrassed in front of their friends. These will keep your *what* headed true north and positively influence the chances for flow in your day.

Knowing How to Do It

Again, to someone outside the education profession, it would seem rather absurd that a teacher would not know how to teach. However, some pre-service teaching preparation only scratches the surface of what a teacher has to do on a regular basis. New research uncovers better teaching methodologies and practices leaders expect teachers to review, learn, and implement. As educators become more aware of neuroscience and cognitive development, views on how to teach have changed. Knowing how to teach reading, for example, takes additional training and support for teachers to know how to do it correctly.

Keeping up with new developments in education and how to implement new methodologies is a full-time job. Separating the wheat from the chaff of research and various education-related articles takes a tremendous amount of time—a resource most teachers do not have because they are busy teaching! Leaders also expect teachers to implement new methodologies with little practice. How often have teachers sat through an hour or two of a professional learning session on the best particular way to teach and then have the leader expect them to go into the classroom the next day and execute the method flawlessly? Learning how to teach and updating teaching skills is an ongoing process that takes time, effort, and energy. Often teachers who struggle to change effectively default to familiar practices, as knowing how to do what's new and most effective takes time and energy they do not have. Ironically, time would fly, and energy would be recharged if this component of flow were more the rule than the professional exception.

To enhance the possibility of knowing how to do what others ask you to do, we suggest a few tips. First, keep current in your reading. Browse books before buying and be selective in what you digest. When you find thought leaders you trust, stick with them, and follow them until you start hearing them repeatedly say the same things. Second, ask your teaching colleagues, principal, assistant principals, counselors, instructional coaches, and paraprofessionals what they are reading. Borrow one of their books, enjoy it, and ensure you give it back. If worth it, then pick up your own copy. This will enhance the chance that those who have influence will positively receive, notice, and reinforce your actions. You will enjoy the confidence to apply best practices to fit your needs—doing things your own way—and thus achieve moments of flow. Finally, take risks and embrace your agency. Teacher agency is an often-underused opportunity; done well, it really does make time fly.

Knowing How Well You Are Doing

Teachers can look at the variety of ways their schools measure the effectiveness of teaching and learning to see how complicated it is to know how well they are doing. Ironically, the most effective schools often have difficult-to-measure nuances that make it almost impossible to determine, with any sense of reliability and validity, which schools are doing a better job than others. Unfortunately, for many districts and leaders, the metric itself becomes the goal. Although the overall goal is to ensure high levels of learning for all, the metrics leaders use to measure the goal can confound. In contemporary schools, instead of focusing on ensuring high levels of learning, leaders focus on trying to increase the achievement of each metric. This can lead to shortcutting and implementing creative practices to meet a metric without fundamentally changing the underlying practices that promote learning. When the metric becomes the goal, the focus on student learning is lost. When the focus on student learning is lost, the focus on teaching excellence becomes deflected, at best.

At the teacher level, knowing how one is performing is just as daunting a task. Factors outside the teacher's locus of control can impact the academic success of students in the classroom. Just look at the myriad of teacher effectiveness rubrics available. There are multiple ways of attempting to measure effective teaching. However, teaching is tremendously complex and is impossible to measure on a rubric. The upshot is when teachers do not know how well they are doing, a requisite component of flow is absent. Like anything else, missing just one component might not always be disastrous, but just like bricks in a wall, the more missing, the less structurally sound the whole.

When the metric becomes the goal, the focus on student learning is lost.

Remember the chapters on community and authenticity? Increasing one element of mattering helps in other areas as well. We suggest you consider the Irish proverb, "The best looking glass is the eyes of a friend," and find a work friend who will be honest with you. Then, get permission for classroom coverage and offer each other clinical observations. Be in charge of the look-fors. Invent your own clinical supervision model; re-embrace those years when you had frequent, helpful, honest feedback on methods you were trying for the first time under the watchful eye of a colleague. Utilize peer-to-peer observation protocols. Some districts allow teachers to integrate these observations into the formal evaluation system, but they can be just as powerful (or perhaps even more so) when it is not part of formal evaluation. With countless management-of-the-month gurus offering up new and refabricated checklists to those who officially evaluate, keep in mind the true instructional leaders in the building are the master teachers, and those who are superstars are probably most giving of their time on your behalf (or would be honored to if you asked). Best of all, you'll have a gauge of how you're doing, and this will enhance the potential for flow.

Knowing What's Necessary to Accomplish to Consider the Task Done

Teaching is an infinite game. Sinek (2020) describes an *infinite game* as one in which there is no agreed-on objective, fixed rules, or end, and no one is declared the winner. There will always be more students, students with different challenges, and changes to lesson plans. There will always be disagreements on the most important elements of teaching and learning. When examining the requirements to attain flow, this one seems the most difficult to attain because in education, there is no *done*. Thus, when confronted with a reality that runs counter to the mindset teachers must have for the optimal outcome, they must either search for better answers or determine how to ask better questions. In the case of teachers, the question is one of perspective. Ask yourself, "What way of thinking should I adopt?"

Educators must have an infinite mindset. They need to understand their job in education is never totally complete. There are milestones, indicators, and goals to achieve, but there is always more to do. This is the way your thinking needs to continually improve and grow.

Sometimes, teachers need to create indicators with an end. For example, set the goal of having zero emails in your inbox. It is something you can see, but it may not mean you have taken care of everything on your to-do list, however, clearing your emails is a goal at the start of the day. Another goal could be updating all grades by a certain date. Certainly, that goes over well for someone down the hall who is checking, and that's extrinsic; yet even intrinsically, there always is a sense of accomplishment at the end of a semester or grading period. When you can click the *submit* button to put in final grades, it feels good. Unfortunately, except for the end of the school year, chances are by the time teachers click *submit* on those final grades, there's already a stack of papers they need to grade for the next term.

Sinek (2020) makes the distinction between those who have a *why* and those who have a *just cause*, which is more about difference making and being part of something larger than yourself. To maximize flow, we suggest moving more toward the latter than the teaching profession has in a long time. Moving your perspective toward your just cause has a forward focus in terms of where you want your world to be and your place in it. If you do this, you can enhance the possibility of flow in your daily life because you will have a clearer distinction between those situations where *done-ness* is appropriate and those things that are, by design, a never-ending state of *undone-ness* (like education, improvement, or student learning). You might be thinking this is too simplistic given the social and political forces focused on education as a finite game (with winners and losers). How can educators possibly view education any other way? The metrics educators use to measure student achievement (such as state test scores) are lagging indicators of success. If you view education as an infinite game and continue to focus on student achievement, those lagging indicators will take care of themselves.

Perceiving Significant Challenges

Teaching is rife with challenges. Some challenges even seem insurmountable. If individual teachers try to address these issues individually, they most certainly are impossible to tackle. Any educator can rattle off a litany of significant challenges to the school, teachers, student needs, public pressure, and so on. The problem isn't perceiving these significant challenges; perceiving significant challenges adds to flow, but this can perplex educators. The issue is perceiving that significant challenges *exist* coupled with the necessity of feeling the efficacy to successfully address these same problems. That's what invites flow into the mix—the healthy combination of both. When you face a mountain of challenges and get the feeling there is no way to overcome them, you can feel overwhelmed and disheartened. There's certainly not too much chance for flow in this instance. Yet, this is sometimes your reality. All too often, leaders expect teachers to address issues with students they were never trained for and never expected to deal with. Without a way of moving through these challenges toward success, teachers will certainly struggle to find flow. But when teachers can connect these challenges with the significant skills we note in the next section, hope abounds and so does flow.

Perceiving Significant Skills

As we mention in the previous section, along with perceiving teachers have certain challenges, leaders must be aware of significant skills to address these challenges. It is extremely easy for leaders to identify significant challenges in the workplace, from addressing numerous student concerns to dealing with difficult adults. But just pointing out the problems doesn't solve anything. All too often, teachers feel underprepared and lack the skills necessary to address the many facets of *all* their students' complicated lives. As schools become a more critical institution in the lives of students socially, emotionally, academically, and behaviorally, it is ever more important to have the skill set to address all these challenges. In many ways, teachers must be specialists and generalists in multiple disciplines to feel successful, and of course, be successful.

The larger the gap between teacher challenges and their skill level, the more difficult it is to attain flow. If a task is too difficult and challenging, and the teacher's skill level is low, then the activity is frustrating and can seem hopeless. If the task is too easy and the teacher's skill level is high, then the task can become boring. There is a *sweet spot* for having the right amount of challenge with the right amount of skill. The key is to determine what areas are highly challenging, so leaders can provide training and support for teachers to increase their skill level, and enter that *Goldilocks zone*.

Embracing and Minimizing Distractions

Any classroom teacher will find this particular element of flow humorous. Some days it seems like the classroom is nothing but distractions. Sometimes, these distractions are no one's fault,

such as mandated emergency drills and state assessments. Then, there are those distractions from outside the classroom, such as surveys students must complete, the administration pulling students from classrooms, and receiving a notice from the guidance office for a student to report. At other times, distractions are from inside the classroom—a student has a meltdown, two students start yelling at each other, and countless others. It can feel, at times, like teaching is the afterthought with everything else going on.

Of critical importance in teaching is establishing a way of doing classroom business in which the teacher and class embrace the typical distractions of childhood and youth in a way that is . . . well, unruffled. Accomplish this by employing a high-altitude understanding of three science strategies: (1) brain science, (2) learning science, and (3) improvement science. Note that often, each of these strategies is noticeably absent not only from pre-service preparation programs but also from quality professional learning and in-service training. Establishing competence in those three strategies puts you well ahead of the pack in reactively embracing teachable moments in the discipline, establishing a focus on factors that prevent student misbehavior, as author Ryan Donlan (2022) notes in *All Other Duties as Assigned: The Assistant Principal's Critical Role in Supporting Schools Inside and Out*. These science strategies include maintaining student interest in both the teaching and the teacher; engaging students so their energy is spent on productive activities; and ensuring students are successful in full view of others (Donlan, 2022).

Additionally, consider your disposition. You have two choices in being free from distractions in your classes to *till the soil for the flow potential*, so to speak. You can either be part of the solution or you can be the biggest contributor to the problem. Teachers must know the collective attitude of the room is probably about the same as their own. If you're stressed, the students will be stressed. Teachers must also know they have two choices with addressing the unexpected while in flow—to react or choose not to react to the distraction. Finally, know everything that happens in your classroom, including freedom from distractions, happens through relationships first. It pays to keep these relationships in mind, as you put your disposition in full view, every day.

MAKING *FLOW* MATTER

In this chapter, we share a clinically straightforward way for you to attend to all the factors that comprise flow—or, said differently, the factors that can maximize the chance of flow happening, if you learn about and attend to them. Admittedly that's a lot to do! There's research to review, books to read, skills to refine, and many other things to consider. Here's your first step: by concentrating on one thing at the outset, you'll find you can dedicate right-sized portions of the rest of your energy to learning about knowing what to do, how to do it, how well you're doing, what to do to be done, and all the rest. Quite simply, get yourself a hero.

Yep—a hero in flow. Find people you admire who you have heard tend to self-actualize while getting lost in what they do. Find clips of interviews with them on the internet. Read reports of how these people spend their days, and what they prioritize, what

> they eat and don't eat, and how they exercise. Find out their perspective. Get inside their heads if they allow. What do they do to motivate themselves when the going gets tough? What do they do next when they fail at something? How do they maintain perspective and self-honesty? In short, find heroes worthy enough of your interest, excitement, and time by doing your homework. Strive to be a bit more like them if that works for you. We're not suggesting you create a shrine in your home office of all these potential heroes' doings and life events. Just learn from someone you admire, and in doing so, that person may provide a potential on-ramp into some grooves in life you also have, and that may invite some flow in you too.

Implications for Teachers

To find flow, teachers need to be in an environment where they can enjoy doing activities with others. The simplest way to do this is to work with those whom you enjoy being around. In chapter 1 (page 19), we identify the difference between collegial and congenial workplace friendships. When working together, flow requires a congenial relationship (Csikszentmihalyi, 2008). If teachers do not like who they are working with, it is even more difficult—sometimes impossible—to achieve flow.

Teachers must identify areas where there is a challenge due to a skill gap and pursue professional learning opportunities to help remedy the situation. If teachers find they have difficulty completing aspects of the job because they lack certain skills, they should actively pursue ways to decrease the gap. This foundationally requires teachers to identify the difficulty, name it, share it with those who have the resources to help them, ask for help, and most of all, embrace the difficulty as natural. Once they've done so a few times, teachers' confidence, trust, and agency will build, promoting what management thinker Jim Collins (2001) calls a *flywheel effect*—gradually gathering momentum toward a point of breakthrough—of their personal and professional development efficacy.

We concede that identifying and addressing these skill gaps can invite teachers' feelings of vulnerability. Depending on the culture of the school and the relationships in the school, the emotions involved with vulnerability can be extremely difficult. If teachers feel psychologically unsafe in a school environment, one of two things will happen: (1) they will ignore the skills deficit and bluff their way through, in which case, there will be immense teacher frustration, or (2) they will try to address the skill gap alone. In the latter case, teachers each addressing the skill gap can be exhausting and challenging without the support of building leadership in place.

When thinking about the daily struggles, it may seem like finding flow while teaching is impossible. More than any other aspect of mattering, flow takes patience and time. Learning a new crochet stitch, for example, does not come naturally, but over time, it becomes second nature. The following to-dos provide some pointers.

- Know and accept the fact that you need and deserve flow in your school workplace. Seeking a desired state of flow is a given, not an outlier or something unprecedented. Consider regular flow as the best-positioned natural order of things, one you require. Then go after flow, using what you now know and can do for you.

- Pursue every opportunity you can to close the gap between the skills you have and the challenges you face. Select no more than two or three skills to develop over this next year. We would suggest one skill be relational and another, task specific. Then, set out at a reasonable pace to get better at both, providing yourself some space to do so and with permission for any implementation dips that may occur.

- Commit to memory Schaffer's (2013) requirements of flow that we note earlier in the chapter (see page 58). You might even assign some wall space to these requirements in your classroom and model for students how you are curious about what you and your students can do as learners to get more into the groove in a positive way. In short, make visible this learning commitment and don't go about it solo.

- In the post-pandemic world, student misbehavior is increasingly a factor that prevents flow in the classroom. Behavior disruptions are more often and intense than ever before (Institute of Education Sciences, 2022). If you find yourself in this situation, spend time learning and using trauma-informed practices. Identify colleagues who are skilled at leveraging teachable moments from disciplinary challenges borne of students' manifested circumstances. Strive to find others who seemingly handle these behavioral challenges unconsciously (you'll find there's much behind their success, of course). Learn from them. Watch them closely. Ask them what they do outside class to garner in-class success with traumatized or disenfranchised students. Learn what they read and are currently studying.

- Finally, find people you enjoy working with, and do so as much as possible. This will get you closer to the goal line of flow because people working together accomplish most tasks. We're hard pressed to imagine how you can achieve flow if you are around folks you do not appreciate.

Implications for School Leaders

Flow is most likely when there is a balance between the skills one has and the challenge at hand (Csikszentmihalyi, 2008). Educational leaders identifying needed skills and then providing effective professional learning to improve the skill to match the challenge will help teachers' sense of flow. Assisting with creating a personalized professional learning plan can help a teacher close the gap between skills and challenges. Personalized training, coaching, and practicing must support this plan. Leaders who cast away one-size-fits-all professional learning for a more personalized approach can create a very impactful (albeit more difficult to manage) experience—a challenge well worth embracing.

For teachers to identify skill gaps, they must feel psychologically safe. School leaders can ensure teachers can take risks without fear of repercussions. Teachers need the ability to expose vulnerabilities and lack of skills instead of trying to hide them. The more psychological safety a leader invites into the school environment, the more open teachers will be regarding areas needing improvement. When teachers feel psychologically unsafe, they will not want to discuss skill gaps for fear of others mocking or punishing them. Leaders cannot assume teachers feel psychologically safe. Leaders should model vulnerability and explicitly address teachers or staff members who violate a psychologically safe environment.

Leaders can also use the school schedule to help achieve flow by building into the schedule distraction-free zones where no disruptions will occur. This can help reduce variables impinging on flow daily. With preplanning, leaders can cluster together some unavoidable distractions. For example, scheduling announcements to follow a fire drill and finishing up a district-required survey clusters three distractions together to allow for longer stretches of uninterrupted learning time.

> Leaders cannot assume teachers feel psychologically safe. Leaders should model vulnerability and explicitly address teachers or staff members who violate a psychologically safe environment.

Because teaching is an infinite game, it becomes even more critical for leaders to clarify their expectations for being successful as a teacher in your building or district. Providing regular, valuable, timely, and relevant feedback allows teachers to have an idea of how they are doing and if they are meeting set objectives. Allowing teachers feedback from other teachers can be even better. Teacher feedback must be authentic. Authentic feedback can mitigate the impact of the Dunning-Kruger effect. The *Dunning-Kruger effect* is a tendency of highly skilled people to underestimate their abilities when compared to their colleagues (Kruger & Dunning, 1999). Often, the strongest teachers in a school are more critical of their skills and teaching abilities than those who struggle.

Another critical component of flow is people must have a feeling of control over the task. Again, educational leaders can create a climate that empowers teachers to have a certain amount of control over various tasks. We discuss this concept in more detail in chapter 8 (page 143).

Leaders must recognize when teachers are struggling with flow. Regular visits to classrooms will help you keep a pulse on how teachers are feeling. Keep a mindful eye on barriers that may be blocking flow. The following to-dos may help.

- Be intentional in planning individually relevant professional learning so you address any skills or challenge differentials among teachers and staff. Doing so may very well contribute to a school climate of trust and excitement for growth because of the calculated way you are going about providing fertile ground on which flow can germinate. Teachers will feel the professional learning they receive is helpful and relevant.

- Just as we encourage teachers, leaders should commit to memory Schaffer's (2013) requirements of flow. And like teachers, consider giving teachers wall space in the school. Model for your teachers and staff how you are curious about what everyone can do as adult learners to get more in the groove of what they do professionally

in a positive way. We encourage you to make this learning commitment visible schoolwide.

- While we realize and understand the advantages of allowing district- and building-level data to inform teacher and staff training and professional learning, be intentional about individualizing professional learning based on the interests, aptitudes, and abilities of your teachers. That way, each teacher can pursue passions that may invite flow into the workspace.

- In the post-pandemic era, recognize and acknowledge the shift in student behavior. Teachers and staff may need to update classroom management techniques and reteach students school rules and policies. Being supportive and focusing on solutions help both teachers and students. Step up in your role and model for teachers how to address and restoratively support traumatized students. Ensure you know how to do what you are asking teachers to do, and then do it in full view of them.

Conclusion

To close this chapter, we provide some closure on Tyler's story.

> Tyler finally had enough. He knew he could not continue doing this for the rest of the year. The principal reached out to Tyler and stated he was concerned with his continuing frustration. Tyler decided he was going to open up to one of his teammates. He was extremely nervous. He had so much more teaching experience than this colleague did. What would she think about his needing help with something like teaching reading?
>
> After school, Tyler went into her room and just let it all out. He felt he was over his head in first grade. He didn't understand the complexity of teaching reading. As opposed to what he had learned in his student teaching years prior, it was now so much different. He was frustrated; the students were frustrated. He was embarrassed that he wasn't doing a better job. He was vulnerable.
>
> "Oh, Tyler!" she said in a calm and caring voice. "I am so glad you came to me with this. Teaching reading is complicated. We're all still learning. We learn every day." She continued, "I'm so glad I can help you with this. We are a team. Someday soon enough, we'll need your help for sure."

> They sat together and made a plan that included peer observation and coaching—a teacher-driven model of collaborative clinical observation. They went to the principal for his approval so they could get class coverage for a couple of days. The principal was able to quickly grant the request because the district had a system in place to allow for peer-to-peer observations.
>
> By the end of the year, Tyler felt more confident and capable at teaching reading. His skills had improved to close the gap with the challenge he faced, and he had a much better sense of what he was doing and how to do it. He still had a way to go, but he was well on his path. He actually started looking forward to the reading block during the day and working with the struggling readers. While it certainly wasn't every day, Tyler found that he was able to slip into a state of flow at times as he helped his students improve. "We are learning this together," he would say, and the students would just smile back.

Considering everything that occurs in the daily life of a teacher, it might be a reach for some to conceive flow occurring at all. While it may be difficult at times to achieve (as Tyler finds), attaining flow is possible. Flow experiences beget more flow experiences. En route, however, it's important to have the capacity to identify the requirements of flow and create the conditions to achieve it. This is not to say that every day will seem like it zooms by effortlessly, but flow brings enjoyment to tasks. There are likely quite a few teachers reading this book who have never experienced flow in their profession. Those who have experienced it undoubtedly remember those moments because they are so special.

Achieving flow is a wonderful thing. Educational leaders and teachers must be intentional about creating the environment in which flow can occur. This will mean changing some previous practices and embracing others anew. Some structural variables can be as easy to manipulate, such as changing the way announcements take place over the public address system to prevent interrupting a classroom in flow. Other structural variables can take more time to alter, but it is possible—such as creating individualized professional learning plans to meet the needs of individual teachers. Most of these variables land somewhere in between.

In the next chapter, we'll move to the first element in the intrapersonal domain: purpose.

Next Steps: Chapter 3 Recap Activity

Fill in the following diagram from the chapter's beginning, this time with unique information pertinent to you and this foundational element in mattering.

The Interpersonal Element of Flow in Mattering
Enjoyment of an activity to the extent that one loses track of time
Your Way to Conceive:
Your Way to Believe:
Your Way to Achieve:

Ensuring Teachers Matter © 2024 Solution Tree Press • SolutionTree.com
Visit **go.SolutionTree.com/teacherefficacy** to download this free reproducible.

Your Personal Professional Development: Thought Experiment—Flow

The following thought experiment gives you an opportunity to imagine a different reality. Take time to visualize the scenario. You may want to revisit these questions several times to get a complete picture. It takes practice. Find your quiet space and consider the possibilities.

Imagine tomorrow, you achieve flow with your students:
What would it look like?
What would it sound like?
What is the biggest obstacle preventing you from achieving flow for that lesson?
What additional skills do you need to achieve flow?

Have you ever experienced flow?
If so, how did it make you feel? If not, what do you think you can do to help move in that direction?

How do you think students would feel in your class if they could achieve flow?

Make an action plan to experience flow. What is one skill or challenge gap you want to address?

How can you address the skill or challenge gap?

Who can help you address it?

If you have time and interest, keep a pad of paper, smartphone, or the like close so you can jot down information and list of anything you see in anyone's workplace that can psychologically impinge on flow for one week. Keep in mind, anything that wishes away the present for the future (figuratively or literally) counts here. It could be comments the cashier at the local gas station made to what educators utter, value, and celebrate while in school. You might be surprised to find many past and present colloquialisms for what educators say in passing and identify parts of the workweek or time actually working against the flow that is necessary for teacher mattering (hint: TGIF).

Once you've got your list, take control of only things you can control. Don't become a zealot or grandstander for the elimination of everything you find; however, do be more mindful of these things, and take some steps to address what you can. You might create some norms in your own classroom for what you say or do, so you celebrate people's immersion into the present moment more.

You could even share with students your involvement with this thought experiment and what you discover. How about encouraging students to do the same and then having a discussion as a class? Students can help create new norms in your domain and theirs that promote the possibility of flow. Ask them what they need to achieve flow themselves. Don't make flow a secret. Don't bemoan when flow is not there either. Just celebrate when you look up or at one another and hear the bell ringing, and realize flow *was* there. Best to you with this!

Questions to ponder:

How important to you is flow in your workplace?

What resonates most with you about flow?

Do you see flow in your building? If so, where?

What is one small thing you can do to strengthen flow in yourself?

What can you do to expand flow for others?

Ensuring Teachers Matter © 2024 Solution Tree Press • SolutionTree.com
Visit **go.SolutionTree.com/teacherefficacy** to download this free reproducible.

CHAPTER 4

Staying the Course, En Route to My Why: *Purpose*

Purpose is the first of two elements we classify as belonging to the intrapersonal domain of mattering, meaning they come from within the individual. The other is assimilation, which is the subject of chapter 5 (page 91). Purpose is the most apparent of the two as an intrapersonal characteristic. Fulfilling one's mission and passion is a unique and individual pursuit. Teachers each must identify their own life purpose and determine if that purpose aligns with their school and district's mission, vision, and values.

To help illustrate how critical *purpose* is to a teacher's sense of mattering, we begin with the following fictional vignette.

> Soon after college, Jennifer found a teaching job several hours away from her hometown. She enjoyed the work and her colleagues tremendously and couldn't imagine doing anything different. Due to life circumstances and needing to take care of elderly parents, Jennifer decided to take a teaching position in a district closer to where she grew up. She was looking forward to the change and excited about the new venture in a different locale. Her new school was high performing and had been on the list of best schools in the state for the past several years.

Jennifer's new school had the following mission statement: The mission of Midway School is to ensure the success of all students. It was rather generic, but similar to her previous school's mission. As the new year approached, Jennifer became more and more excited about the new setting and meeting new colleagues. The accolades the school had received in recent years made Jennifer somewhat concerned she wouldn't meet her new coworkers' expectations. After all, the school she came from did everything it could to ensure all students succeeded but still seemed to fall short, at least in the eyes of the state and on state assessments.

After the first few days of school, Jennifer became concerned about the things she heard from colleagues. Lower-performing students were placed in remedial classes with little hope of obtaining grade-level standard expectations. She heard colleagues saying unsettling things like, "You know who Tim's parents are; you can't really expect much from him," and "Allison has difficulty learning, so you really can't have the same expectations from her that you do other students."

New to the school, Jennifer was careful not to say too much about what others were saying. After all, it was the beginning of the school year, so perhaps she was just still adjusting to her new environment. The school was using the PLC process, just as her old school had, and Jennifer was looking forward to the meetings with her collaborative teammates. At the first meeting, Jennifer spent time with three other grade-level teammates as they planned the next unit. In Jennifer's job interview prior, the principal had spoken about the PLC process and how well teachers worked together.

But Jennifer found the collaborative team meeting time underwhelming, to say the least. The team members were very friendly and seemed to get along with one another. However, most of the forty-five minutes were spent discussing how much students were behind from the previous year—not about what to do to catch them up. Her teammates just complained. This was in stark contrast to her experience using her previous district's PLC process.

That night, Jennifer went home and cried. What had she done? She left a wonderful school district she loved and colleagues she cared about. On the outside, the new district seemed to be similar—the mission was almost identical, and the state's school grade showed the new school was even more successful. But this didn't seem to be the case. A few weeks passed, and Jennifer decided it was time to talk to the principal about how she was feeling.

"Of course, we believe all students can learn," the principal said confidently. Jennifer felt immediately relieved. But then he continued, "But the parents and students have to take responsibility for their learning. It is our job to teach, and it is their job to learn." Her heart sank. This mindset was not in line with what she was used to in a PLC. She prodded a bit more. "And when they don't learn?" she asked.

"Look, we are an A school," the principal responded. "Our teachers work hard, and there are just some kids that won't be as successful as others. These kids have tough backgrounds, and there isn't much we can do about that," he chided.

It was time to get to class, so the conversation abruptly ended.

As Jennifer reflected on her conversations with colleagues and the principal, she wrestled with uneasiness and discomfort. It wasn't just what she heard that upset her; it was the fact that something critical was absent from the entire school community—a conviction to fix something glaringly wrong. What was wrong was the lack of resolve to attend to what was right in front of everyone. The school so desperately needed a feeling of obligation to focus its efforts and provide strength—an overall sense of purpose about what members of the staff must do and who must accomplish it.

Figure 4.1 (page 76) provides an anticipatory set for the element of purpose. The reproducible "Next Steps: Chapter 4 Recap Activity" (page 87) gives you the opportunity to fill in your own ideas.

The Intrapersonal Element of Purpose in Mattering
Feeling of fulfilling one's mission and passion
One Way to Conceive: Imagine filling in your weekly calendar first asking "Why?" for each "What?" "How?" and "With Whom?" you include.
One Way to Believe: Take a bit of extra time explaining to others the reasons behind your actions or decisions, even if these conversations are difficult or do not satisfy those with whom you're talking.
One Way to Achieve: When you haven't purposefully prioritized something you simply cannot attend to, understand it is not as central to what you are all about. You can rest easier knowing you haven't relied on elevating others to attend to it.

FIGURE 4.1: The intrapersonal element of purpose in mattering.

In this chapter, we start with purpose by staying the course en route to your *why*. We explain the importance of aligning personal with professional purpose. All too often, the district's stated mission, vision, and values (de jure) are different from the lived version (de facto) within the collective or within those individually responsible for carrying them out. Additionally, a teacher's sense of personal or professional purpose can change over time, depending on life experiences. The school and district's lived mission, vision, and values can also shift with changes in leadership or community sentiment. It is important for teachers to reflect continually on their sense of purpose, and for educational leaders to ensure they are living the stated mission, vision, and values of their school or district. Soon to follow are implications for teachers and school leaders. We conclude with the reproducibles "Next Steps: Chapter 4 Recap Activity" (page 87) and "Your Personal Professional Development: Thought Experiment—Purpose" (page 88).

Getting Started With Purpose

People need a sense of purpose in their work to be satisfied with their jobs, and the teaching occupation is no exception. According to social psychology researchers Vlad Costin and Vivian L. Vignoles (2020), having and working toward a goal in life gives people a sense of purpose. In *Grit*, author Angela Duckworth (2016) defines *purpose* as the desire to contribute to the well-being of others, while in *Drive*, Pink (2009) states having a strong sense of purpose will lead people to try to extend and expand their abilities. Additionally, "participation in meaningful occupations appears to be an important component of well-being" (Haim-Litevsky et al., 2023, p. 3).

Similarly, Sinek (2009) describes *purpose* as one's cause or beliefs. Sinek (2009) popularly refers to this as the *why*. Finding purpose allows people to perform at their highest levels. It "is the most authentic expression of your innermost nature, or your true self. It represents our inner truth that seeks expression through a myriad of activities as life is happening to us" (Dhiman, 2007, p. 30). Purpose in life is a defining element in a person's well-being (Ryff & Singer, 2000). A sense of purpose is essential if people are to become the best version of themselves. People strive for perfection and are driven to fulfill their potential, whatever that may be (Joseph, 2019).

Needing a sense of purpose is certainly not new. Aristotle discussed the concept of *eudaemonia*—a life of happiness and well-being (as cited in Joseph, 2019). *Eudaemonic well-being* is the condition of having a sense of life purpose and growth (Flett, 2018). It is indeed a complicated and winding road, as people's purpose changes as their life circumstances change (Mitsuhashi, 2018).

One way to help identify your purpose is to examine the similarities and differences between passion and purpose. From there, you can consider how your purpose connects to your work.

Passion and Purpose

Your *passion* and *purpose* are closely connected, and sometimes people use the terms interchangeably. *Passion* is about emotion. As author and speaker Terri Trespicio (2015) notes, "Passion is not a plan, it is a feeling—and feelings change." *Purpose*, rather, is *why* people do what they do—how they contribute to society. According to Duckworth (2016), passion is not just something a person cares about; rather, it's something that person cares about consistently over time. It is something people direct their attention to. *Passion* is a feeling or activity people think about constantly; their actions continually drive them toward their passion (Duckworth, 2016).

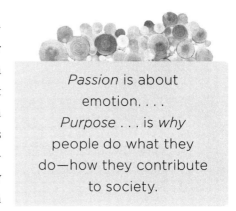

Passion is about emotion. . . . *Purpose* . . . is *why* people do what they do—how they contribute to society.

Finding one's passion and purpose is typically not a straightforward process. Author and entrepreneur Liz Forkin Bohannon (2019) encourages people to stop trying to find their passion as part of the passion and purpose equation; people discover their passion and purpose over time and through life experiences. Purpose is not something you *find*; instead, it is something you *build*. You build purpose through *pluck*, which means spirited and determined courage (Bohannon, 2019).

Psychiatrist and Holocaust survivor Viktor Frankl (1992) developed an approach that stems from existential psychotherapy called *logotherapy*. *Logotherapy* rests on the premise that a "will to meaning" motivates human beings; people thrive when they have a sense of purpose and meaning (as cited in Victor Frankl Institute of Logotherapy, n.d.). All humans have the drive to create purpose and meaning in their lives (Smith, 2012). Frankl (2006) contends people have the freedom to derive meaning from what they experience and how they react to those experiences.

Purpose in Work

Do you define what you do in school each day as your *job, career,* or *vocation*? You might be asking yourself, "What's the difference?" Your *job* is about earning a paycheck. Your job is a means to an end. People need money to do the things they want to do, so they have a job. In a *career*, people seek opportunities for advancement and promotion. They hold a long-term view with goals for growth. Your career is a marathon of achievement over time, not a sprint. A *vocation* is something even larger—*a calling*—or something that draws you to it. It is a feeling that you are doing what you were meant to do. A vocation is your professional purpose. At this point, you might be thinking that at times, you have felt teaching can be any or all of these.

You are right. There are days when you are counting the days to your vacation—putting in your time on the job for a paycheck so you can do more enjoyable activities; that's treating education as a *job*. There are times when you think about sustainable advancement and long-term goals in the education profession; that's treating education as a *career*. Then, there are days when you feel you are in the right spot, that you are absolutely where you need to be—where your calling led you; that's treating education as a *vocation*. The key is how much time you spend on each of these three definitions. If you view teaching as a job or career, you have less meaning and purpose.

You can find meaning in your work by perceiving the value of that work (Smith, 2012). When people find meaning in their work, their productivity and ability to solve work-related problems increases (Pink, 2009; Sinek, 2009). Purpose gives people the ability to overcome obstacles and challenges (Duckworth, 2016). Finding purpose in work allows people to define *meaning* and maintain a sense of engagement (Flett, 2018). A WorkHuman Research Institute (2017) survey finds employees search for meaning in their work, and frequent, value-based recognition is one of the best ways employers can meet this need. However, employees in many companies do not clearly understand *why* they do what they do daily. When employees do not understand the purpose of their work, they do not engage in highly productive activities or find deep satisfaction in their jobs (Sinek, 2009).

Ikigai is a Japanese concept that encompasses one's purpose in life, or the point at which one's mission, passion, profession, and vocation converge (García & Miralles, 2017). In other words, *ikigai* is what people obtain when they focus on doing what they are skilled at, what they love, what the world needs, and what they are paid to do. Freelance journalist and writer Yukari Mitsuhashi (2018) describes *ikigai* as happy living and finding joy daily. Ikigai is whatever gets you up and going every day. A paycheck, job security, or a pension is insufficient to keep employees at the same company for their entire working lives; humans embrace a sense that life involves more than making money (Jaramillo, 2019). According to Mitsuhashi (2018), a person may have more than one ikigai at any given time, and that person's ikigai may change over time. Like Duckworth (2016), Mitsuhashi (2018) views *ikigai* as a way for people to move forward toward something they value in life. Teaching is one such avenue, if you allow it to be.

Embracing a vocation such as teaching over a job or career may sound simple, but it is deceptively hard. It takes deep reflection and self-awareness. In the book *Let Your Life Speak*, educator Parker Palmer (2000) states:

> Vocation does not mean a goal that I pursue. It means a calling that I hear. Before I can tell my life what I want to do with it, I must listen to my life telling me who I am. I must listen for the truths and values at the heart of my own identity, not the standards by which I must live—but the standards by which I cannot help but live if I am living my own life. (pp. 4–5)

Embracing your vocation is indeed a difficult and lofty task; it not only requires deep self-awareness but also the ability to suspend cultural expectations of how you respond and react.

Even then, it is easy to lose sight of your calling. As Kanold (2021) states in *SOUL!* "May we remember why we chose this vocation, even on our worst days" (p. 66).

MAKING *PURPOSE* MATTER

We suggest a few self-conversation starters to help you begin exploring your purpose. A similar professional learning activity in *All Other Duties as Assigned: The Assistant Principal's Critical Role in Supporting Schools Inside and Out* inspires these starters (Donlan, 2022). First, think about the following questions. For step one, write each question on the front of an index card and your answer on the back.

- » Why did you wish to become a teacher?
- » Who was your favorite teacher when you were in school and why?
- » What do you see when you look into your mind's eye and imagine your best self?
- » What do you like to do in your spare time?
- » What do you wish people say about you when you cannot hear them?
- » Who is your hero and why?
- » When do you feel most like your authentic self?
- » When you were happiest in life? What made you so happy?
- » What does *professional autonomy* mean to you?
- » What about your school life energizes you the most?

Step two: Write the following statements on your index cards and prioritize them.

- » Getting to my *why* allows me to be strong when the going gets tough.
- » Getting to my *why* brings meaning to both success and failure.
- » Getting to my *why* allows me to make things happen.
- » Getting to my *why* is fun.
- » Getting to my *why* is discomforting.
- » Getting to my *why* is a useful tool to meet my objectives.
- » Getting to my *why* allows me to build inclusivity at work.
- » Getting to my *why* is where I am most authentic around others.
- » Getting to my *why* is of little importance to me.
- » Getting to my *why* occasionally gives me a much-needed booster shot.

Put your top three priorities from this list next to one or two starters that caused your most profound thinking and self-learning from the first list.

Step three: Consider the following statements and write your answers on index cards.

- » Identify the two or three of the most challenging goals you wish to succeed at in the future, and why you wish for this success.

» Identify the two or three hardest achievements you accomplished over your lifetime, and what influence overcoming these difficulties had on your perspective and feelings.

Step four: Determine which of Kahler's (2008) psychological needs are most prevalent in you. Kahler's (2008) discoveries regarding personality note eight psychological needs people have; these needs will be met positively or, in their absence, people will experience personal or professional repercussions. How each person's personality develops throughout life determines the priority of needs. Write each of the following needs on index cards and select the two that resonate most deeply with you: What provides you the energy to get up and do what you do each day, despite obstacles?

» Recognition of productive work

» Recognition of meaningful work

» Time structure

» Recognition for your convictions

» Recognition of personhood

» Sensory awareness (smells, textures, and so on)

» Contact with others

» Incidence (meaning risk or a rush)

» Solitude

Using the information you collected in steps one through four, develop a short self-statement. Use the following format.

The reason why I find passion and purpose as a teacher is this role fulfills my own psychological needs (from step four) of _____. Difficulties I experienced in the past (from step three), such as _____, are doable because of why I do what I do (from step two), including _____ and _____. I maintain a sense of perspective by keeping (from step one) the following things I can contribute in mind: _____, _____, and _____. This helps me better understand the intersection of my passion and purpose.

Implications for Teachers

It is imperative for teachers to identify their purpose. They do this by ensuring their purpose aligns with the mission of the organization. If your purpose does not align with the school's mission, there will always be a disconnect. Not all teachers want and need the same things, and not all organizations emphasize the same values and beliefs. People must pick a context and environment that works for them (Barker, 2017). *Measure twice, cut once* when selecting a career destination. A teacher can be a huge success in one school but an average teacher in another. This is because when a teacher's abilities and talents align with the school's mission and values, great outcomes are natural by-products. In his book *When: The Scientific Secrets of Timing,* Pink (2018) discusses the

importance of *team synchronization*, which we touch on in chapter 1 (page 19). Teachers need to sync with a boss, a group, and their heart. This can only happen if you are in the right pond (Barker, 2017). If a teacher is out of sync with the boss and group, it might be time to find a different pond (Barker, 2017).

There is a distinction between life purpose and professional purpose. For teachers, when the two converge (or at least run closely parallel), teaching is a vocation. Teaching can also move from a vocation to a career to a job, but you don't want things moving in that direction. Teaching should be a vocation. It is too difficult, too complicated, and too hard to simply be *just a job*. All teachers know someone in their school who's just teaching for a paycheck and upcoming holidays. To these teachers, it's just a job. And although they may say this feeling doesn't impact their teaching, it quite certainly does. They know it, you see it, and, most assuredly, the students feel it. Some teachers quit and leave, but the teacher who quits and stays is worse.

Treating teaching as a vocation is not an excuse to exploit teachers and cajole them into poor working conditions. In fact, the opposite is true: those who believe teaching is their vocation should be exemplars. These teachers are the reason why the field of education needs better pay and working conditions. If people's professional purpose is to teach, society should lift them up!

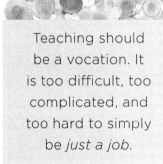

Teaching should be a vocation. It is too difficult, too complicated, and too hard to simply be *just a job*.

How many teachers continually and powerfully reflect on their sense of purpose? Given the emotionally exhausting conditions teachers navigate every day, their north star or purpose can become clouded. Take time to pause and review—to see through the clouds. What is your *ikigai*? It is completely natural for there to be days, weeks, or months when teaching feels like a job? The important thing is to not stay in that realm too long. If you do, dissatisfaction, stress, and burnout will most assuredly follow.

Before and during pre-service undergraduate work, students ideally will identify teaching as a way to fulfill their unique sense of purpose. What they might not experience enough is a frank conversation about how not everyone is meant to be a teacher. Even the most successful teachers have particular areas in education where they are better suited. For example, when deciding to teach at the elementary or secondary level, consider that these schools have radically different student environments and appeal to different people in different ways. Not all can "retrofit for the grooves" they pursue. This should be your first professional implication—soul searching early on to ensure your personal purpose aligns with your personal suitedness.

As people live and grow, it is very possible for their purpose to change and grow in many different ways due to their life circumstances. Sometimes, people simply lose sight of their purpose and need to refocus. Other times, their purpose may have shifted so greatly that teaching does not fulfill a deep-seated need they must fulfill to truly be happy and satisfied with life. People rarely say or write this sentiment because it may seem controversial. As people live and interact in society and the world around them, it is very possible for their purpose to develop into something new they cannot fulfill. If this is the case, teachers need to take stock and decide whether they can reinvigorate or redirect their purpose.

People often take passion for granted. Because of this, it is important to spend some time regularly reflecting on your purpose as a teacher. The following to-dos can help.

- Be active in developing, articulating, and reinforcing your own purpose statement within yourself. Keep it brief and meaningful. Just like muscle memory, do the necessary repetitions so your purpose becomes an inescapable part of who you are and what you think about daily. Be diligent to the point that you can make quick decisions with a filter of purpose in mind. Remind yourself of your purpose in subtle ways—notes on your vehicle dashboard, mnemonic devices, notes on a mirror at home, an exercise regimen mantra—whatever works. Tweak as needed. Make this a living conversation with yourself. Give your purpose a voice inside your head; see it in your mind's eye.

- Identify your own personal mission statement and leverage your passion to align it with that of your school. If necessary, create a Venn diagram and strive to identify what might be in the middle to find your energy.

- Dedicate a portion of your classroom wall space to your *why*. Create a collage of photos, images, and artifacts that represent the intersection of your passion and purpose. Doing this will not only provide visual affirmation for what resides in your mind and heart each day while teaching but also a great opportunity to articulate this to students. This might even be a good activity for students to develop purpose in their studies.

- Borrowing the title from Harvard professor Richard F. Elmore's (2011) book, *I Used to Think . . . and Now I Think . . .*, create a T-chart and list five to ten meaningful issues that occupied your values as a pre-service teacher and a similar number of issues that occupy your values today. Then, examine your two lists to see how congruent they really are. For any of the recent items you may derive from negative professional experiences that remove your initial idealism regarding the profession or your place in it, strive to identify how you can maintain your current wisdom and sophistication yet move closer to the idealism you once enjoyed. This may even create ongoing minds-eye relief, regardless of whether or not you reach idealistic utopia.

- Spend time with students who aspire to be teachers. Work to affirm their purpose and passion with mentoring and support so that as a teacher, you are talking others into joining the profession for the right reasons. Verbalization can become more of your lived reality than if you did not attend to it. And, if you invite students into your classroom to see your intersection of passion and purpose in operation, you'll become more mindful of including your passion and purpose in your lesson plans. We see little, if any, downside.

Implications for School Leaders

Many books and much research addresses a person's sense of purpose. Some of the better-known titles include *The Element: How Finding Your Passion Changes Everything* (Robinson, 2009), *The Last Lecture* (Pausch, 2008), *The Power of Habit: Why We Do What We Do in Life and Business* (Duhigg, 2014), *The Happiness of Pursuit: Finding the Quest That Will Bring Purpose to Your Life* (Guillebeau, 2014), and *The Purpose-Driven Life: What on Earth Am I Here For?* (Warren, 2012). Fulfilling your mission and passion in life is important to overall life satisfaction. Educational leaders help teachers carry out their sense of purpose by keeping the long-term success of students an ever-present focus in decision making. This may seem obvious, but too often, district and school leaders make decisions without clearly articulating to teachers *how* these decisions will ultimately help students. Often leaders assume but do not articulate the benefits to students, but they should.

Some who pursue teaching careers realize after they start their career choice is not right for them. They discover they have other purposes for fulfillment. Purpose offers clarity. Professional purpose offers clarity related to what is important in work. Not everyone has the same professional purpose. That's OK. School leaders can find ways to assist these teachers in finding other career paths or encourage them to re-examine or rekindle their individual passion and purpose. Teachers who do not have a passion for teaching can still be effective, yet they will most certainly be less fulfilled or even miserable over time, which will have a negative impact on others, including students.

The job of the organization's leader is to communicate the purpose of the work to employees. If leaders are not telling the story, others will, and that story might not connect effectively with the purpose of the work. Leaders who communicate what they believe draw in teachers: "Their ability to make us feel like we belong, to make us feel special, safe and not alone is part of what gives them the ability to inspire us" (Sinek, 2009, p. 55).

The average person spends eighty to ninety thousand hours at work over a lifetime (Pryce-Jones, 2010). With so much time spent at work, employees and their leaders must engage purposefully in their work. Consider these troubling statistics: in the United States, 51 percent of managers are not engaged, and 14 percent are actively disengaged (Murray, 2017). When employees start believing in their leaders and feel they share their leaders' sense of purpose (that is, the employees' values align with those of their employers because leaders adeptly and adequately communicated those values), trust begins to form. When there is trust, leaders emerge at all levels. Educational leaders who build trust oversee teachers whose professional purpose motivates them. Great leaders offer people a sense of purpose not tied to external incentives (Sinek, 2009).

Teachers most engage in their work when the school or district's mission (or purpose) makes them believe their job is important and gives them opportunities to learn and grow. This means leaders must communicate the purpose of the organization clearly and consistently for employees to be effective (Murray, 2017). Leaders must continuously examine and access the organization's mission and vision. The mission must authentically resonate in the hearts and minds of employees (Jaramillo, 2019). Leaders can accomplish this through the stories they tell, as well as *how* and *what* they recognize. Leaders who prioritize outcomes (such as test scores) over purpose de-emphasize the qualities that make an organization great (McLeod, 2016). By making the focus of the organization separate from its purpose, leaders erode the purposeful meaning employees seek.

Teachers need time for reflection and rejuvenation to maintain focus on their purpose. This can take many forms, including further education, job swapping, or fellowships. Gain leadership support and intentionally provide time for teachers to reflect and rejuvenate during the regular school day. For your purpose to flourish, policies must encourage such experiences, with or without adequate funding. Educational leaders at the school and district levels must purposely advocate funding teacher-rejuvenation projects, when practical.

For example, in Indiana, the Lilly Endowment (n.d.) selects one hundred teachers per year to receive funds to pursue personal growth projects through its Teacher Creativity Fellowship Program. The program funds travel (both domestic and international), artistic endeavors, genealogical research, and writing. Each of these projects is deeply personal to the individual with an indirect impact on the classroom. The projects are a way for the participants to rejuvenate professionally in pursuit of something personal. As the title of the program suggests, successful project proposals include creative activities not used for traditional teacher training or additional college coursework. While it would be difficult for a district to fund a program of this scale, there could be opportunities for a district to fund smaller projects for a handful of teachers.

Educational leaders might explore cost savings for teachers who avail themselves of higher-education opportunities. Leaders can encourage pursuing quality, relevant graduate studies as a way to rejuvenate and re-center a teacher's sense of purpose. Since the late 2010s, while direct financial gains have waned in many states for teachers pursuing graduate degrees and staying on as classroom teachers, studying beyond a bachelor's degree can help solidify a sense of purpose (Darling-Hammond & Podolsky, 2019). Through cost-sharing programs, districts can create financial plans to assist teachers with tuition costs. This is often a win-win situation, as districts can grow leaders from within while ensuring teachers stay up-to-date on current pedagogy.

With some planning, school districts in areas without a local university offering postgraduate education courses can work with a university to bring a regional program to the district or offer virtual opportunities. As an example from our experience, Warsaw Community Schools in northern Indiana partnered with Indiana State University (ISU) to bring the master of education and educational specialist programs to the district. Successful applicants took local, in-person classes in the school corporation's administration building in the evenings throughout the semester and had a residency on the ISU campus in the summer. District leaders were able to harness funding from various grants to assist with tuition.

Teacher job swapping is another avenue education administrators can curate for teachers to define and refine their purpose. Having the ability to view teaching from different perspectives in different settings can sometimes provide clarity for teachers, especially teachers who've taught in the same district their entire careers. Having the ability to embed and teach in a different district for a semester (or a year) can provide teachers with a unique opportunity career teachers rarely receive. For example, teachers would receive the ability to teach in a demographically different district or area of a state to gain valuable insight into other teaching practices.

It is critical to keep teachers' sense of purpose in mind when discussing activities and actions. Here are some to-dos to try.

- Earmark at least the first ten to fifteen minutes of any classroom observation follow-up meeting to explore the *why* behind the teachers' instructional and behavioral choices. Curate conversations at the intersection of the teacher's passion and purpose. Dedicating this time will not only allow for teacher agency in reflection but also encourage teachers to reflect with their supervisor more purposefully.

- Initiate what can be, at times, difficult—yet healthy—conversations about topics you need to discuss with those you're having impasses with professionally, particularly those who have a different life or professional purpose than you. Seek ways to find agreement on these topics together. One strategy here is to acknowledge you are feeling a bit of dissonance and would like to learn more about the person or situation. Share with the person that as supervisor, while your expectations might remain high, if the path to meeting those expectations is unreasonable, you would like help in discovering another way to reach mutual goals more effectively. Doing so will engender mutual confidence you can work through differences together.

- Ensure you inquire into what rejuvenates your teachers each term or academic year. Ask teachers what they did to recommit to the challenges and rewards of being teachers, and you'll help them tap into their purpose. Successful commitment to your teachers' purpose for being in education and thus in mattering, necessitates many visits to this well to quench their purpose mindfulness.

- Take notes regarding the purpose of your teachers and staff and set a monthly goal to structure some time and attention to commit resources to this endeavor schoolwide. In other words, what you support with time, money, and other resources reflects what you value, so show teachers and staff you value where they find purpose by committing to helping them find it. And consider this a sound investment.

Conclusion

Now, we'll revisit Jennifer to see how the gap between the school's purpose and her own played out.

> Jennifer was torn. She enjoyed being around her new colleagues and they were extremely friendly and gracious. But in many ways, she felt her new school hoodwinked her. So much on the outside seems to be so similar to

> her old district. What she discovered was the new school's lived mission was much different from its stated mission. She could have tried to change the culture over the next several years, but she was close to retirement and, with her ailing parents to think of, it wasn't a burden she was ready to take on. At the end of the year, Jennifer was drained. The dissonance between what she felt in her heart was important—all students can learn, and it is our job as teachers to ensure that happens—and what was actually going on in the school was too much. As Jennifer walked out on the last day of the school year, thoughts of retirement or recommitment elsewhere were difficult to ignore.

Jennifer's circumstances bring sorrow. Where educators can turn sadness into resolve is with knowledge that leaders have a responsibility to attend to the elements of mattering, and while teachers should be aware of and open to using opportunities to increase their sense of mattering, leaders cannot expect them to move mountains by themselves. Leaders must step up to provide both opportunities for and sustainability in mattering. And they must do so purposefully.

Before we end this chapter, consider that people are often too hurried in their lives to stop and think about their purpose. They go about their days without reflecting on *why* purpose is important or how one's purpose can change over the years. Teachers must clearly understand their professional purpose, and their purpose must closely connect to the education of students. Anything less makes teaching a job or, at best, a career, not a vocation.

As an occupation, teaching is too difficult to have a disconnect between one's professional purpose and the day-to-day activities of teaching. It can be emotionally exhausting on the best days for the most dedicated teachers who have a clear purpose that connects to teaching. It is nearly impossible for someone who feels teaching is just another job. Even the most dedicated teachers who view teaching as a vocation will sometimes slip into the *teaching is just a job* mindset. When that happens, it's important to recognize and address it, so that a person does not dwell in that realm too long. Never underestimate the power of reflecting and rejuvenating as ways to reconnect with teaching as a vocation.

In the next chapter, we'll move on to the intrapersonal element of assimilation.

Next Steps: Chapter 4 Recap Activity

Fill in the following diagram from the chapter's beginning, this time with unique information pertinent to you and this foundational element in mattering.

The Intrapersonal Element of Purpose in Mattering
Feeling of fulfilling one's mission and passion

Your Way to Conceive:	
Your Way to Believe:	**Purpose**
Your Way to Achieve:	

Ensuring Teachers Matter © 2024 Solution Tree Press • SolutionTree.com
Visit **go.SolutionTree.com/teacherefficacy** to download this free reproducible.

Your Personal Professional Development: Thought Experiment—Purpose

The following thought experiment gives you an opportunity to imagine a different reality. Take time to visualize the scenario. You may want to revisit these questions several times to get a complete picture. It takes practice. Find your quiet space and consider the possibilities.

Imagine your purpose perfectly matches the occupation of teaching. What would it look and feel like?
Where are the gaps in how you teach now?
What needs to change?
Imagine your purpose perfectly matches the organization's purpose. What would it look and feel like?
Where are the gaps in how you work now?

Ensuring Teachers Matter © 2024 Solution Tree Press • SolutionTree.com
Visit **go.SolutionTree.com/teacherefficacy** to download this free reproducible.

What needs to change?

Consider your school's mission. How is the school's lived mission different from its stated mission?

How is the school's lived mission different from your own mission (or purpose)?

How do you view teaching? Is it mostly a job, career, or vocation?

When you feel like teaching is just a job, what do you do to move to the vocation mindset?

Questions to ponder:
How important is *purpose* to you in the workplace?
What resonates most with you about purpose?
Do you see purpose in your building? If so, where?
What is one small thing you can do to strengthen purpose in yourself?
What can you do to expand purpose for others?

CHAPTER 5

Seeing the Downside as a Necessary Upside: *Assimilation*

Assimilation is the second of the two elements of mattering in the intrapersonal domain, and it's a bit more difficult to succinctly define. We conceive of the concept as self-regulation, particularly a mix of regulation through identification and integrated regulation. These two terms derive from self-determination theory (Ryan & Deci, 2000). They state that regulation through identification is "a conscious valuing of a behavioral goal or regulation, such that the action is accepted or owned as personally important" (Ryan & Deci, 2000, p. 72). University of Rochester professors Richard M. Ryan and Edward L. Deci (2000) are also of the view that integrated regulation "occurs when identified regulations are fully assimilated to the self, which means they have been evaluated and brought into congruence with one's other values and needs" (p. 73). Ryan and Deci (2000) recognize identification and regulation as extrinsic motivation. However, because one has to internalize the activity, we incorporated the concept of assimilation into the intrapersonal category.

Assimilation, therefore, is *self-regulation*—or doing things you consider necessary, but unpleasant. You assess these parts of your job as congruent with what's important to you. Not all tasks teachers engage in are pleasant. However, many teacher tasks are extremely important for the functioning of the school and the safety of students and staff. Teachers must find connections between their sense of purpose and these unpleasant tasks. Educational leaders must ensure these required tasks are necessary and clearly connect to the mission, vision, and values of the school.

To help illustrate how assimilation plays into a teacher's sense of mattering, we'll begin with the following story, a fictional classroom account fashioned from a real-life dog story.

> Students sat with rapt attention as teacher Seamus McMillan perched on a stool at the outset of class on a Monday in March and pitched the need to embrace annual standardized test preparation. His point was not simply one of method and motivation; it was one of embracing even what sucked about it, although he was careful to more tactfully craft that sentiment for students. Just how to embrace this annual test preparation escaped many of his colleagues' wheelhouse, yet Seamus tried an approach with both poignant and pungent visuals to bring students into the moment and energize their efforts.
>
> First, Seamus noted the difference between what he was asking and not asking students to do. "I'm not asking you to be taught to the test," Seamus said. "I'm instead asking you to be open to test-taking training, as there's real strategy in doing well with this sort of training." So, with the task ahead delineated, Seamus began framing a perspective with which to charge the incline motivationally.
>
> "You all know that I've had a very energetic dog, Zachary, a Weimaraner, for the past few years, right?" he asked. Students nodded in affirmation; after all, Seamus was known for sporting pics of his "dog-child" on his phone. Students were used to seeing the pictures nearly every day. "Well, what happens each winter is that Zachary gets let out in our small, fenced-in yard at least two or three times each day and, for a few months, the snow doesn't allow me to get out there with a scoop or shovel. You can imagine the condition of the yard in early March, when the snow begins to melt," he said. "So, it takes quite a bit to motivate me to get out back and do the deed, giving the yard a thorough scooping before the springtime warm-up, when I can be out more regularly and stay on top of things."

"How do you psyche yourself up to shovel all that stuff?" one student asked.

"It's a matter of perspective, really," said Seamus. "You see, I embrace what's good about it, and ensure I'm in a great mind space when doing so. In short, I link the task to what's important to me, and do this task at an intentional time, on a specific day, every year."

"When's that?" the students asked.

"Well, it's the weekend nearest St. Patrick's Day. You see, each year on the Saturday closest to the holiday, our community hosts one of the largest St. Paddy's Day parades in the state, as you all know."

"Yeah, Mr. McMillan . . . we see you march in the parade each year!" one called out.

"You're always wearing that weird green sash and using a cane," said another.

"That's an authentic Irish walking stick, from Dublin, Ireland," Seamus responded.

He added, "The point is, our St. Patrick's Day parade is one of the most special times each year, arguably, a harbinger of good times to come. So, what happens is each year, after I march in the parade, I arrive at home in a great space, mentally and physically. The clean, crisp, fresh March air and the three-mile walk fill me with energy, and the general vibe of the audience all along the parade route—and my friends in my local Irish group—bring out the best and most hopeful parts of me."

"What does that have to do with shoveling dog poop?" someone asked.

"Everything, really," said Seamus. "And it's not really what I'm shoveling; it's how I'm going about the project, and the sense of accomplishment I have when I'm finished."

"You see, this is how I do it. I take my spring-loaded scoop and a big bag, and I go to the middle of the yard and stand. Then, I pick up a few scoops

and put them in the bag, as I rotate in a small circle. I keep going in circles and moving with larger arcs outward from the center, all the while filling my head with 'harbingers of good times to come'—in other words, thoughts of things I wish to do over for the coming year."

"This is really my own version of a New Year's resolution," Seamus noted, "except one that I make for myself. I consider doing this very important. You might say it's one of the most important things I value—taking the time and space annually to elevate my thoughts, clear my head, and—you know what's crazy about it—all of the sudden I'm nearly done! I look up and almost all the yard is clear. And I've had the best time getting in touch with what's important to me while recharging to live the next leg of my best life, even while doing what would seem like a job that is not at all fun to do."

"So," a student said, "you choose something awful that you don't really have a choice to do, but you make sure you're doing something at the same time that makes it all worthwhile?"

"Something like that," Seamus responded. "While it's a job that nobody would really want, it does serve the greater good. And while doing it, I align it with the things I value about myself and about the choices I make, and, in the end, it all comes together in a way I can live with. In fact, I feel pretty darned good when I get it done, and I even don't dread it the day before. I find peace with it because . . . it fits. Reminds me of the quote by Matt Haig (2021), in The Comfort Book, 'It is easier to learn to be soaked and happy than to learn how to stop the rain' (p. 128)."

Figure 5.1 provides an anticipatory set for the element of assimilation. The reproducible "Next Steps: Chapter 5 Recap Activity" (page 106) gives you the opportunity to fill in your own ideas.

The Intrapersonal Element of Assimilation in Mattering
Integration of necessary, unpleasant tasks with one's own values to achieve a goal
One Way to Conceive:
Imagine how you can best handle tasks you really don't look forward to at work, both in terms of the benefits to others and yourself, by taking care of them personally.
One Way to Believe:
Seek opportunities to choreograph how you might "take one for the team" at work, and discuss positively why your supervisor might assign those things to you and relieve you of other duties taking up your time.
One Way to Achieve:
Take action to build a winning team around you to embrace unpleasant tasks at work. Think of what you all might address together to ensure others succeed as well as what you can do with a trusted, efficient, and effective group of individuals.

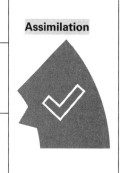

FIGURE 5.1: The intrapersonal element of assimilation in mattering.

In this chapter, we get started with assimilation by seeing the downside as a necessary upside. We explain the importance of assimilation, along with the roles of positivity, teacher stress, and freedom of choice in assimilation. Following are implications for teachers and school leaders. We conclude the chapter with the reproducibles "Next Steps: Chapter 5 Recap Activity" (page 106) and "Your Personal Professional Development: Thought Experiment—Assimilation" (page 107).

Getting Started With Assimilation

Assimilation is linking your purpose to something you don't like to think about or do. It's like connecting what you must do with an internal reason to "take one for the team" and feel good about it because *you* are best suited for the personal challenge. Further, assimilating adds to the overall value of your environment.

Assimilation recognizes what you value and moves you to connect with whatever you must engage in, even if unpleasant. In their article "The Motivation at Work Scale: Validation Evidence in Two Languages," Marylène Gagné and colleagues (2010) state as people identify tasks with their purpose, even undesirable or mundane activities become acceptable because they connect to motivation. We discuss in chapter 4 (page 73) the importance of aligning your purpose with your work as an educator, and in chapter 3 (page 55), how skills and action can contribute to flow. Assimilation is about the mindset that allows those things to happen. Teachers should understand *why* they must do certain things, especially those things they do not enjoy doing. A typical school day is filled with mundane tasks teachers must complete. As teachers identify work activities, they develop *integration*, which is "identifying with the value of an activity to the point that it becomes part of a person's habitual function and part of the person's sense of self" (Gagné et al., 2010, p. 629).

Thus, teaching becomes an essential part of who teachers each are as a person. In a sense, as you genuinely assimilate, you become more authentic (see chapter 2, page 39). Your actions and mindset change who you are over time. This is more than intrinsic motivation. Goals and values drive integration, whereas emotions you experience while engaging in an activity drive intrinsic motivation.

Teachers may not enjoy particular tasks, such as performing semiannual book room return duty, but if they can identify the task as an integral part of education or understand how it helps achieve educational goals, the task becomes more manageable.

Akin to this, Sinek (2009) discusses the *Golden Circle*, which he describes as the center circle of a set of three concentric circles. The outermost circle is *what* companies or employees do. Employees in the organization understand what the work is and what they must do to accomplish the job's tasks. The second circle is *how* companies or employees do the work. This is slightly more nuanced than the *what* circle, but it is still relatively apparent to those who engage in the work. The innermost circle is the *why* (or purpose) of the work. Sinek (2009) terms this innermost circle the *Golden Circle*; it is the part of the three circles many companies or employees do not consider or understand. Companies fail to reach their potential and employees are disengaged or unfulfilled because they don't focus on the Golden Circle.

When people achieve assimilation, they have found their why in the Golden Circle. The more disconnected one's why and the tasks one needs to perform, the more stress. Granted, people can overuse the phrase *know your why*. This is especially true for those who take Sinek's (2009) words *know your why* out of context and simply use the phrase as a simple statement of *why* something is necessary to do. Those who know the meaning behind the message understand the *why* Sinek (2009) discusses *is* the mission, *is* the purpose. Unfortunately, people have a tendency to simplify and lose the nuance of the true message of *know your why*.

When leaders start conversations with the phrase "This is *why* we are . . ." and continue with whatever the task may be, they can get the false sense they have answered the *why* question. It is extremely important to know the why of a particular task, but that is just part of it. After you answer the *why* question, a disconnect often continues between the why of the task and how it truly relates to the overall mission and vision. Instead of just answering the why, follow up with *why, and*. (That is, "This is *why* we are doing it, *and* this is how it connects with our overall purpose.")

When the why is unclear, efforts to make the work environment positive can backfire and stress can rear its head.

Positivity and Assimilation

When teachers have difficulty reconciling actions with their purpose, stress and negativity will follow. Stress and negativity are natural functions of human emotion and teachers must validate and acknowledge them to reconcile them in a healthy way. Some mistake optimism for *toxic positivity*, which can prevent this necessary validation. Not all optimism and positivity are toxic, but not having any optimism and positivity certainly is. It is important to understand the difference between what is toxic and what is not. In the article "It's Okay to Be Okay Too: Why Calling Out Teachers' 'Toxic Positivity' May Backfire," University of Winnipeg researchers and coauthors Laura Sokal, Lesley Eblie Trudel, and Jeff Babb (2020) differentiate the two:

> Toxic positivity seeks to reject, deny, or displace any acknowledgement of the stress, negativity, and possible debilitating features of trauma, and instead looks

only through rose-coloured glasses. In contrast, a positive outlook acknowledges both the negative, challenging aspects as well as the more optimistic frames and pathways. (p. 3)

The absence of any optimism and a focus solely on the negative leads to continually dwelling on doom and gloom. As exhaustion sets in, becoming more negative is natural. It takes less energy to have negative emotions than positive emotions. Being positive and optimistic takes energy. When there is no energy, negativity can become overwhelming. Before you know it, there is a black hole of toxicity that sucks the energy out of anything positive or optimistic in an organization.

To leverage your personal capacity for assimilation, it is important for you to take a step back and examine if what others are saying is just viewing things through an optimistic lens or actually toxic. We want to reiterate—*optimism* means acknowledging and accepting the realities but viewing the future and change as something that can create something positive. *Toxic positivity* ignores the current reality.

For some, embracing positivity is a coping mechanism for stress (Sokal et al., 2020). Performing an undesirable task positively and optimistically can help people attain meaning with the task and assimilate the task into their purpose. You cannot assimilate a task when your only thoughts about that task are negative. In a school climate where all positivity is seen as toxic, it is extremely difficult—if even possible—for teachers to gain a sense of assimilating tasks.

Stress and Assimilation

There's no doubt: teaching is a stressful profession. Look at any survey about various professions and you will see teaching ranks as one of the highest in stress levels (McCarthy et al. 2022; Watson et al., 2010). Consider that as of 2017, about 61 percent of teachers said their work is always or often stressful, while that number was only 30 percent just two years prior (Stice, n.d.). Stress for teachers can present as anger or depression (Agyapong, Obuobi-Donkor, Burback, & Wei, 2022). According to Kyriacou (2011), when the three following conditions are present, teacher stress occurs.

Not all optimism and positivity are toxic, but not having any optimism and positivity certainly is. It is important to understand the difference between what is toxic and what is not.

1. When teachers must deal with demands
2. When teachers do not feel they can deal with those demands effectively
3. When there will be a negative outcome if teachers do not handle the demands satisfactorily

The issues students bring with them to school add to the stressful environment for teachers. One such example is *adverse childhood experiences (ACEs)*, which include experiences such as violence or abuse that lead to lasting trauma and toxic stress. ACEs impact students' brain development and physical, emotional, social, mental, and behavioral health and well-being (Bethell, Davis, Gombojav, Stumbo, & Powers, 2017). These adverse experiences are not usually isolated events but a series of events that accumulate over time (Bethell et al., 2017). Teachers typically lack the training and resources to adequately address the effects of ACEs, which is not only detrimental to students but also places further strain on teachers. ACEs seemingly worsened during the prolonged shutdown of schools during the COVID-19 pandemic and even since, in the aftermath (Anderson et al., 2022).

To deal with ACEs, schools have increased their focus on student behavioral health, yet have teachers received adequate preparation and support? We do not believe so. Schools are expected to provide emotional, social, and behavioral health supports and address the needs of students. Schools must adopt practices that support a wide range of student needs, including additional mental health support (Bailey & Hess, 2020). To do this, schools should consider increasing their number of counselors, social workers, school psychologists, and nurses (Bailey & Hess, 2020); however, limited resources can make this impossible, not simply impracticable. Bethell and colleagues (2017) estimate approximately 20 percent of U.S. children have experienced two or more ACEs. The pandemic only exacerbated an already alarming issue. The CDC reports three of four high school students experienced at least one ACE during the pandemic (as cited in Anderson et al., 2022). The same report indicates 37.1 percent of U.S. high school students reported poor mental health during the pandemic and 19.9 percent considered suicide. Most alarmingly, almost 9 percent attempted suicide in 2020 (Anderson et al., 2022).

The realities of the teaching occupation—dealing with difficult students and complex societal issues, coupled with inadequate resources and funding—are likely to continue. People in educational organizations have attempted to create policies and procedures to mitigate this reality through stress-reduction and stress-management techniques. Given the current state of education, organizations and individuals with the best stress mitigation will only curb the amount of stress. In other words, it's likely impossible to mitigate stress to an extent that it does not impact individuals in the organization. Assimilation impacts stress. As you assimilate, you feel less stress. Doing tasks you perceive as unnecessary and unpleasant is stress inducing, especially when coupled with all the things you deem more important but can't do at that time.

So, if stress-reduction and stress-management techniques only get you so far, what is there to do? Take, for example, the U.S. Navy BUD/S (Basic Underwater Demolition/SEAL) training. Most people would agree (given the reputation of Navy SEALs) the training regimen is likely to be stressful. Researchers Eric N. Smith, Michael D. Young, and Alia J. Crum (2020) examined individuals going through the BUD/S (phase 1 training) with a focus on the *stress-is-enhancing* mindset. Individuals with a stress-is-enhancing mindset view stress as a way to learn and grow. Smith and colleagues (2020) posit individuals with a greater stress-is-enhancing mindset performed better in physical activities, lasted longer in the program, and received more positive ratings from peers and instructors (Smith et al., 2020).

This is not to say teachers are under the same type of stress that occurs during BUD/S training! The study only focused on phase 1 of the training, which lasts eight weeks (with minimal sleep) of the twenty-five-week BUD/S training. Teachers, on the other hand, are with students thirty-six weeks each year. While stress on teachers is assuredly not as intense, it certainly has more longevity. Schools expect teachers to endure year after year.

Conversely, individuals with a *stress-is-debilitating* mindset view *stress* as a factor in decreasing performance and productivity. The daily realities of teaching make it impossible to completely reduce stress in most situations. There is a difference between *toxic stress* and *tolerable stress*. Everyone has a different level of tolerance when it comes to managing stress. And that is OK. What is tolerable stress for one may be toxic for another. What makes the issue even more complex is some teachers have been dealing with unhealthy amounts of stress for so long they no longer realize it's abnormal. Coauthors Alia J. Crum, Peter Salovey, and Shawn Achor (2013) note that in an effort to reduce stress and emphasize the negative impact of stress, educational leaders have inadvertently encouraged a stress-is-debilitating mindset. Constantly trying to avoid stress and stressful situations can actually lead to increased stress. Crum and colleagues (2013) further point out, "Even hardiness and resilience approaches to stress, while acknowledging the enhancing outcomes, still ultimately affirm the mindset that the debilitating effects of stress must be managed or avoided" (p. 718).

How does this stress-is-enhancing mindset translate to the educational environment? In 2020, researchers Joungyoun Kim, Yeoul Shin, Eli Tsukayama, and Daeun Park conducted a longitudinal study of 310 preschool teachers. In their *Journal of School Psychology* article, they state, "Teachers who can see the positive side of stress felt less job stress and were less likely to leave their jobs within a year than were their coworkers who saw stress as strictly harmful" (p. 19). Chinese University of Hong Kong researchers Sau-Lai Lee, Hiu-Sze Chan, Yuk-Yue Tong, and Chi-Yue Chiu (2023) find teachers with a growth mindset have higher life satisfaction.

The effects of stress, no doubt, have negative implications for teachers. Your mindset regarding stress, whether it is a stress-is-enhancing or stress-is-debilitating mindset, will have an impact on your response to stress. This is not to say that someone with a stress-is-enhancing mindset who is under an extreme amount of stress will not suffer from negative effects, but this mindset can stave off some extreme effects. Think about it in terms of getting a flu shot. The flu shot may not prevent you from getting the flu, but it can prevent you from getting a severe case of the flu.

> There is a difference between *toxic stress* and *tolerable stress*. Everyone has a different level of tolerance when it comes to managing stress. And that is OK.

Finding the sweet spot of stress is difficult (although having a stress-is-enhancing mindset can help), and finding it won't eliminate the need to keep stress at a manageable level. There is a Goldilocks zone for stress. Too little stress leads to boredom, fatigue, frustration, and dissatisfaction. Too much stress leads to exhaustion, illness, and low self-esteem. In fact, there are two types of stress. *Distress* is the type of stress typically what people refer to in education. *Eustress* is moderate or normal stress that leads to a feeling of accomplishment and fulfillment (Šćepanović, Constantinides, Quercia, & Kim, 2023). These key ingredients can promote and foster assimilation in reasonable and right-sized doses.

In chapter 4 (page 73), we discuss the work of Frankl (1992) and how his work relates to purpose; that work also connects to assimilation in people's freedom to draw meaning from their experiences and reactions to those experiences. *Freedom of will* is the idea people have control over how they react to obstacles. Frankl (1992), a Holocaust survivor, states that when everything else is taken away, "What alone remains is 'the last of human freedoms'—the ability to 'choose one's attitude in a given set of circumstances'" (p. 9).

To be clear, if the amount of stress on an individual is too great and becomes toxic, no amount of assimilation will help. Educators must believe they have the ability to act rather than react to situations. By acting on the stress, they gain the feeling of control. When people are constantly reacting, they feel out of control. By choosing your attitude about stress, you can change your narrative and perception of the task at hand. Again, this doesn't mean the stress will be eliminated, but it can increase your tolerance for stress and allow stress to enhance rather than debilitate. As you assimilate to necessary tasks, your stress level becomes more manageable. The ability to connect what you are doing with why you are doing it is powerful.

MAKING *ASSIMILATION* MATTER

Making assimilation matter is really a choice between two options. You can handle it (1) individually, by buckling down or (2) as a team, by barn raising. The first is rather obvious and often well expressed with phrases like "Suck it up, buttercup." (Another one, "Embrace the suck," we have used in presentations.) It's about lowering your head, putting on the figurative helmet, and—any of the other variety of metaphors that mean *at the end of the day*—dealing with it. Then, on top of that, resign yourself to the fact that there really is an upside to your downside.

The other way to handle things is communal. With a big project, the whole neighborhood or town comes out to help, such as happens with a barn raising. Putting the team in action allows members to share some of the discomfort; team camaraderie can even offset that discomfort, as the outcome is greater than the sum of the parts of the contribution.

Buckling down or barn raising are key ingredients to making assimilation matter. Other foundational ingredients (such as trust, respect, and in modest degrees, feelings of healthy altruism) must be on board to prepare for making assimilation matter. Obviously, the quality of a school's leadership and management can help or hinder assimilation potential.

Implications for Teachers

Everyone has things they don't like to do. It doesn't matter what field you are in or job you have. This is true in people's professional and personal lives. People don't particularly like cleaning bathrooms; but they can't really ignore it as that would be gross—not to mention unsanitary. So, they can either grumble their way through the entire time and be miserable, or they can think about

how awesome it is to have a nice clean bathroom once it's done—or in the case of the teacher Seamus from this chapter's story—a clean yard after his pet Zachary's very productive winter. The end goal is worth the experience of doing the task.

Teachers can understand assimilation and determine how it impacts their attitude about certain activities they may not particularly like to do. Once teachers integrate undesirable activities and understand the tasks are necessary to meet their ultimate goal, the task becomes less unpleasant and, in some instances, creates a paradigm shift in thinking about how certain tasks relate to the overall goals.

To get there, ask yourself: "What is my end goal? How is this going to help me get to where I want to go?" If you still can't come up with the answers, talk to your school administrator. Building leaders have a larger view and may give you insight into *why* the school does something a particular way. If the administrator doesn't have a good answer, then it's time to re-evaluate why and if the school can change the activity to make it more purposeful. Discontinuing ineffective or outdated activities is just as important as implementing new ones.

If you don't feel psychologically safe to challenge the status quo or ask those types of clarifying questions, then perhaps you're not in the right place—or your leader quite possibly is not. We discuss this possibility in chapter 3 (page 55) on authenticity. School administrators and district leaders must be open to teachers asking tough questions and seeking clarification. They shouldn't see these questions as a challenge to their leadership, but rather a way for teachers to gain meaning and purpose for the activity.

Teaching will never be a stress-free profession. It is important for teachers to adopt a stress-is-enhancing mindset over a stress-is-debilitating mindset. Know the difference between toxic stress and tolerable stress. Be self-aware enough to understand when stress is tolerable and when it becomes toxic. Don't overschedule your free time. We've heard people say, "I need a vacation from my vacation." They cram so many activities into a trip, they are exhausted when they return. Vacations should be refreshing, rejuvenating, and re-energizing. Don't overschedule yourself so much you don't have enough time to recharge your batteries!

Be aware of self-imposed stress. Are you constantly trying to keep up with the teacher next door who changes her impeccable bulletin boards every other week? Other teachers might spend hours putting together cute decorations and scouring image-sharing social media sites for the latest ideas. Perhaps crafts aren't your thing, but if you feel like you have to change your bulletin board or keep up with that other teacher, stop. Just stop. Your bulletin boards don't have to be perfect. Your classroom decor does not need to be prime-time worthy for all onlookers. Now, if creating showstopping bulletin boards is your jam, great. Have at it! Perhaps doing crafts is your way of de-stressing. People are all different and bring different skills, interests, and talents to the profession; embrace these differences—don't let them become sources of stress.

Teachers have lots to do beyond actual teaching, and stress is impossible to avoid. Here are some ideas to take tasks from unpleasant into bearable.

- Get in the habit of offering yourself a chuckle or laugh when you're doing something you don't enjoy. The neurochemical energy will help carry you through and beyond; evidence suggests even laughter that's *not* genuine can make a difference in your mood (Greene, Morgan, Traywick, & Mingo, 2017). Don't take yourself too seriously; give with grace to the team (but not selflessly). Maintain friendly boundaries and don't let others take advantage of you. Allow yourself to smile—you're in the driver's seat!

- Strive to understand how certain tasks your administrator asks you to do have impacts beyond your classroom and may influence the progress of the entire school's overall goals. While this is challenging, be effortful in shifting your own paradigm regarding the importance of schoolwide goals or your need to be actively involved, even if it's unpleasant. This shift starts within you and can influence those around you.

- Take certain steps when discussing unpleasant tasks with colleagues. First, focus on the solution; have an idea how to improve the situation. Principals do not intentionally do everything in the most inefficient, ineffective way possible. Some unpleasant tasks are truly unavoidable, but others might not be or at least might be improved. Say you're willing to *embrace the suck* while others find a solution, committing to colleagues you will be solution focused and not mired in negativity, saying, "Until we find a better way, we're going to do the best with what we have."

- Make yourself available to others to help with unpleasant tasks for which they're directly responsible. Instead of considering these tasks a distraction, reframe them as part of your sphere of responsibility. Consider and model the proverb, "Many hands make light work." We hope good karma comes your way so that you draw a helpful crowd to help you with your next unpleasant task.

- When you hear that an unpleasant task you did was specifically helpful to someone, write down exactly what, how, and why. Keep these notes, so in future instances, you can serve as the beacon of reason in a staff meeting for why embracing unpleasant tasks can reap dividends. Specifics help, and memories fade without documentation. Be your school's institutional memory for the benefits of assimilation, and be sure to note when your school administration lends a hand. Often, administrators need someone with teaching credibility to send a few deserved props their way (and especially when they're planning to ask for help again over pizza . . . there's typically no free lunch).

Implications for School Leaders

Administrators can focus on assimilation by helping teachers understand why they need to perform certain tasks and the benefits of doing the tasks for the school's overall goals. Before teachers can internalize a task as an important part of their job, they must understand the reasons behind

the task itself. This goes beyond just stating the ultimate outcome; leaders must clarify *how* completing the task helps teachers. Remember the *why, and*: *Why* is the task important, *and* how does it help achieve the school's overall goals?

For example, a principal can explain to a teacher who does not like recess duty why it is important for student supervision. However, this does not go far enough to engender assimilation. The administrator should also discuss how the teacher can interact with students in a different way during recess, which can lead to building relationships with and among the students. This will have an impact on how students behave in the classroom and the teacher's overall relationship with each student. Fewer student behavior problems translate to more time and energy spent on the more enjoyable aspects of teaching and learning. The farther the connection from task to goals, the harder it is to assimilate. If the connection is far removed, administrators may need to make the tasks a vital activity.

Educational leaders must be willing to admit and accept negative situations. It is important to identify and discuss the hardships teachers face in education. There's a delicate balancing act between identifying and discussing these issues and using them as excuses. Leaders simply can't ignore that everything isn't perfect. When leaders try to ignore negative circumstances, it can lead to a feeling of toxic positivity. Leaders must also admit there are things beyond their control, making their job harder. That's not an excuse; it's reality.

Leaders must understand teachers can't just blatantly ignore circumstances impacting a student's educational experience. At the same time, continuing to focus on the things leaders can control in the school setting is of the utmost importance. All too often, leaders are afraid teachers will use them as excuses to avoid doing different tasks, so they avoid talking about the situation altogether. This leads teachers to believe administrators are out of touch with reality and don't understand the challenges teachers face every day in the classroom.

Leaders must be willing to allow teachers the opportunity to ask tough questions. Challenging the status quo may seem to challenge leaders. However, teachers may be simply trying to gain insight into why they must complete a particular task and how completing that task is going to positively impact students. Leaders have a more global overview of the entire district or school, so it is highly likely teachers might not at first understand how their activities fit into the bigger picture. Leaders should welcome teachers seeking clarification. It's much better for them to ask and get an answer than to go around the teachers' lounge complaining!

This also serves as a good check on what and how leaders are asking others to perform tasks; if leaders cannot articulate why something is done a particular way and how it impacts student success, then perhaps it's time to reevaluate the task itself. Leaders can discontinue performing tasks that don't make sense anymore or are outdated. Just as leaders expect teachers to change their practices as new information is available, leaders should be willing to do the same.

Leaders have the burden of mandates, regulations, and requirements that make some unpleasant tasks unavoidable. Others are self-inflicted. The number one rule is: do not ask a teacher to do anything you aren't willing to do yourself. Roll up your sleeves and get in the trenches. Here are some ideas.

- Ensure you are transparent with faculty and staff about the probable unpleasantness of some of the tasks you ask them to do. Discuss the tasks fully and connect how completing them will help both the individual directly and indirectly—benefiting the entire institution. If you are unable to make individual connections, be truthful and consider amending how you currently approach tasks.

- Don't feel the need to accommodate or refute the perspectives of teachers who emote over necessary unpleasantries during staff meetings. It's not worth the energy. Acknowledge them, use the word *and* more often than *but*, and ask for their help. For some particularly onerous tasks, provide teachers the opportunity to follow up with you and offer assistance instead of forcing all issues in front of a crowd and expecting a willing slate of candidates. Sometimes, there's pressure to stay away from what could appear to be sucking up.

- Keep a quiet and modest repository of resources or opportunities on hand for teachers who successfully and consistently assimilate. Ironically, these are probably the same teachers who resist external incentives for their work, but that doesn't mean they don't deserve the generosity and kindness you dole out (quietly and without fanfare). Possibly, you could give these teachers a gift card when they're heading to a conference or a thoughtful release to attend some meaningful professional learning. Use wise discretion with these opportunities for those who assimilate more selflessly than others. And don't advertise you do it.

Conclusion

We'll now revisit Seamus to see how he has continued to apply this element of mattering to his personal and professional life.

> A few years hence and long after Seamus's dog Zachary passed, one of Seamus's own children now in kindergarten, Erin, was nearing the end of activity time in what looked like a busy, cluttered, and colorful, student-friendly maker space section of the classroom. Hearing their teacher share that it was clean-up time, Erin's friend Seth offered a sigh of disappointment, tossing a toy toward a basket and looking with exasperation at the perceived unsavory tasks ahead. "Don't worry, Seth," Erin said, "I know what we can do. Let's start in the middle, crawl in circles, and not look up 'til the basket is full and the carpet has space to roll around." As their pace quickened, both giggled while the

teacher looked down with a smile. Erin clearly picked up this assimilation mindset from Dad.

Later in the day at the other end of the school, Principal McMillan (yes, Seamus!) was participating in a grade-level collaborative team meeting. Interest was high, as were appetites, as Seamus often liked to accompany afternoon meetings with snacks. This time, Seamus would deliver pizza to the group himself as members continued their work. With data in hand and a small group of students the topic of conversation, one teacher shared with the group, "While it might seem unpleasant to do some extra collaborative planning this evening in order to offer some reteaching in one another's classrooms, what I'm excited about is to learn a few more best strategies to reinforce the content my students are not understanding, rather than to dip into my plan B in how I might try the same thing differently." Another noted, "I'm excited to meet our new pizza delivery driver, some guy named Seamus." Smiles were evident, as Mr. McMillan realized the vicarious value of living assimilation, in full view of others. Mr. McMillan shared with the team that they'll be first on his route, right before he delivers a pizza to his wife and children. The teachers appreciated that Mr. McMillan never asked them to do something he wouldn't find the positive in and take an active role to support himself.

In the next chapter, we share an element that invites educators to matter from the outside in (in most cases). That's the extrinsic foundational element of mattering: compensation.

Next Steps: Chapter 5 Recap Activity

Fill in the following diagram from the chapter's beginning, this time with unique information pertinent to you and this foundational element in mattering.

The Intrapersonal Element of Assimilation in Mattering	
Integration of necessary, unpleasant tasks with one's own values to achieve a goal	
Your Way to Conceive:	
Your Way to Believe:	Assimilation
Your Way to Achieve:	

Ensuring Teachers Matter © 2024 Solution Tree Press • SolutionTree.com
Visit **go.SolutionTree.com/teacherefficacy** to download this free reproducible.

Your Personal Professional Development: Thought Experiment—Assimilation

The following thought experiment gives you an opportunity to imagine a different reality. Take time to visualize the scenario. You may want to revisit these questions several times to get a complete picture. It takes practice. Find your quiet space and consider the possibilities.

Think about what brings you joy and happiness. What are your hobbies? When you are not working, what do you work on?
How can you incorporate what brings you joy and happiness into your classroom?
What is one activity that creates self-imposed stress in your professional life?
What action steps can you take to reduce that stress?
At work, what is an activity you must do that you hate doing?
What is the purpose of this activity? How does it help students and the school's mission?
What are some strategies to change the way you do the activity to make it more enjoyable?

Ensuring Teachers Matter © 2024 Solution Tree Press • SolutionTree.com
Visit **go.SolutionTree.com/teacherefficacy** to download this free reproducible.

Questions to ponder:

How important is assimilation to you in your workplace?

What resonates most with you about assimilation?

Do you see assimilation in your building? If so, where?

What is one small thing you can do to strengthen assimilation in yourself?

What can you do to expand assimilation for others?

CHAPTER 6

Getting Real With How Educators Stack Up: *Compensation*

Compensation is the first of three elements of mattering that fall into the external domain, which includes factors that outside forces control, and over which an individual has little direct control. The other two elements in the external domain are stability (see chapter 7, page 127) and job crafting (see chapter 8, page 143). Compensation is clearly an external force; the amount of compensation a teacher receives is based on school district contracts. The amount of money a district has to fund teacher salaries is based on federal, state, and local funding sources.

To begin to illustrate how compensations fits into the elements of mattering, we'll begin with a story grounded in real life from long ago, with a few fictional details.

> First-year teacher Zane Loran was traveling with twenty-year veteran teacher Tim VanLorie to a statewide reading conference. It was the only conference they could attend that year because of limited professional learning funds, so they had to choose wisely. Both teachers taught English language arts at the high school level, with students spanning the gamut from those who struggled to read to those taking advanced courses in writing and literature.
>
> Reviewing the conference booklet available from their statewide reading association, the two chatted one day in the teacher's lounge on

| 109

session attendance and making the most of the conference experience. Zane thought it best that they divide and conquer, ensuring to expose themselves to the widest array of sessions available and then coming back and taking responsibility to teach what they learned to colleagues in the department. Tim found this new energy delightful, and commended Zane on his ambitious plan to make the most of what the conference would provide in terms of experience and professional learning.

Tim then took the time to offer some additional perspective on how they could make the most of their impending road trip. "Zane," he said, "I want you ready to go Sunday afternoon by 1:00 p.m. Wear a suit, the best you've got. I'll pick you up, we'll drive three hours to the hotel and convention center. The bell team will take our bags to the room while we enjoy a few drinks in the hotel lobby. After, we'll dine in an adjacent steak house, before getting to know some others at the sponsored preconference. Make sure you wear your suit."

Zane responded, "I'm happy to do that, Tim, but won't most others be wearing khakis and comfort wear? Why the suits?"

Tim shared, "There is one thing we must keep in mind, always. We're teachers. We're important, and what we do is critical. When we arrive somewhere, we must project that we're on par with any principal or superintendent in the place, and that they're similarly on par with us."

Tim continued, "What we do matters, and how we do it is in direct proportion to how we see ourselves and what we're worth as professionals. It's what we deserve, and we have a responsibility to provide this first, and expect others to provide for us similarly. How we roll reflects how we wish others to value us, and that part is entirely up to us. When we are working with students in the classroom, we dress differently—we're getting on the floor, moving around, and wearing more comfortable clothes with students. However, this a must because when we are working with and around other adults, how we dress—whether we like it or not—sends a message."

Tim then said to Zane, "It's a shame that our profession is not valued monetarily in a way comparable to similarly credentialed college

> graduates. Yet, if we're going to continue to drumbeat that conversation—insisting teacher compensation changes for the better because we make all other professions possible and, by the way, allow all parents to work for their own paychecks—we have to ensure we leverage as many positive perceptions as we can. Let's not let this compensation conversation subside anytime soon."

Figure 6.1 provides an anticipatory set for the element of compensation. The reproducible "Next Steps: Chapter 6 Recap Activity" (page 124) gives you the opportunity to fill in your own ideas.

The External Element of Compensation in Mattering	
What one receives (which is fair and equitable based on experience and education) for what one does	
One Way to Conceive: Imagine stepping out of your vehicle each day as you arrive at school and return home, feeling of high worth in terms of knowing your game, selling your craft, and being respected and connected in what you do—most of all, thinking yourself of high value.	**Compensation** 
One Way to Believe: Ensure self-fullness each day, either believing or acting you exist at a level of remuneration above conventional, societal, or media depictions of the profession. Know yourself as one of high worth, and be effortful in this visualization.	
One Way to Achieve: Commit to selling the profession to those coming after you—to students in your classes or your own children at home whom you love. In doing so, you actively promote compensation increases for the profession in a way that go beyond those monetary, to all things extrinsic and intrinsic you can provide as benefits. And continue expecting, requesting, and at times, when appropriate, insisting on higher pay.	

FIGURE 6.1: The external element of compensation in mattering.

In this chapter, we get started with compensation by getting real with how educators stack up. We discuss this complex concept in a way that often transcends a paycheck; we define *compensation* here as simply what one receives for what one does. An increase in monetary compensation alone will not remove the stresses and emotional fatigue many teachers feel; however, an increase in pay is something that matters in terms of one's foundational needs and leaders do need to address it. We present public perceptions of teaching and meaning as compensation. We try our best to offer reasoned perspectives and even a broadened definition on a topic admittedly challenging to control from the inside of the profession. After getting started with what compensation is in the context of mattering, we'll move on to implications for teachers and school leaders. We conclude with the reproducibles "Next Steps: Chapter 6 Recap Activity" (page 124) and "Your Personal Professional Development: Thought Experiment—Compensation" (page 125).

Getting Started With Compensation

Compensation is most often thought of in terms of the size of one's paycheck. Historically, teaching in U.S. public schools has rarely been a high-paying profession (Goldstein, 2015). Education historian Dana Goldstein (2015) states this is due to the feminization of the teaching profession, beginning in the early 1800s. Back then, people did not view teaching as a career. It was a philanthropic vocation or missionary work rather than a professional occupation. Women were the building blocks of an inexpensive labor force in the 1800s and still compose approximately 76 percent of teachers in the United States (Goldstein, 2015). The idea that virtuous ideals or philanthropy *calls* teachers to the profession continues to keep teaching salaries low. Being called to a profession is important; however, that should not mean low salaries. If a doctor is called to practice medicine, should that doctor be paid less? What would you think if your doctor said, "Yeah, I think my calling was accounting, but replacing knees paid more so that's what I decided to do." You can be called to a profession and be paid well. They're not mutually exclusive.

Historic precedents of low teacher salaries have become a growing concern among teachers, school leaders, and elected officials. Coauthors, researchers, and worker advocates Sylvia Allegretto and Lawrence Mishel (2018) show over a twenty-one-year period (1996 to 2017), the weekly wage of U.S. public school teachers *decreased* by an average of $27 (adjusted for inflation). While this might not seem like a tremendous amount of money, during the same period, the weekly wages of other occupations *increased* by an average of $137. Allegretto and Mishel (2018) call this discrepancy the *teacher wage penalty*—a difference between what a teacher earns and what others with the same education background make in the private sector. The teacher wage penalty grew from 5.5 percent in 1979 to 23.5 percent in 2021 (Allegretto, 2022).

U.S. school districts are expected to do more with less money year after year (Allegretto, 2022). Strained budgets have a big impact on the salaries of teachers. Darling-Hammond and colleagues (2016) note many states cut their education budget during the late 2000s due to the Great Recession. In 2015, according to the Center on Budget and Policy Priorities, twenty-nine states were still spending fewer dollars per student than before the recession when adjusted for inflation (Leachman, 2017).

Allegretto and Mishel (2018) suggest although states cut taxes to relieve the tax burden on citizens during the recession, the tax cuts remained long after the recession ended. For example, although the tax cuts may have affected Indiana's ability to generate revenue, the state tax revenue rebounded since the recession; as of 2019, the state had produced $2.3 billion in government cash reserves (as cited in Davies, 2019). In some states like Indiana, local school districts rely on referenda to make up for the state's funding shortfall. Organizing these referenda uses valuable time, money, and energy the state could more effectively use in school systems in other ways. Districts perceive a referendum as the only way to compensate for decreased funding without cutting staff, closing after-school programs, eliminating art and music classes, and ending intervention programs (Herron, 2019).

Teachers do have a benefits advantage. In 2021, teachers had a 9.3 percent advantage in benefits over other professionals. But as Allegretto (2022) points out, the net penalty is still 14.2 percent. It is also worth mentioning that the Great Recession (2007 to 2009) necessitated cutting education budgets, which in turn impacted teacher salaries. Yet, despite the economic recovery since that time, school budgets and teacher salaries have not risen to pre-recession levels, reflecting state officials' policy decisions (Allegretto, 2022).

According to the twelfth annual *Education Next* (*EdNext*) survey of public opinion, the percentage of people who believe teacher salaries should increase rose by 13 percent from 2017 to 2018; in some states, as many of 63 percent of respondents agreed with an increase (as cited in Cheng, Henderson, Peterson, & West, 2019). However, the overall percentage is still only 49 percent. In response to Allegretto and Mishel's (2018) report, National Education Association president Lily Eskelsen García addresses the findings: ""It is time to show respect to those professionals who dedicate their lives to students and building the future of our communities. Professional work deserves professional pay" (as cited in Busser, 2019).

Low teacher pay is a particularly thorny problem, one suffering a public perception of the teaching profession exacerbates. Simply raising salaries, even if possible, will not necessarily provide redress for all compensatory challenges, so here we'll discuss ways *meaning* can contribute to compensation as a modest part of what teachers can control. We offer the following and hope robust conversation will keep this issue at the forefront until educators can attain a resolution.

Public Perceptions of Teaching

Teachers' public perceptions and even their self-perceptions of the profession have been a struggle. The oft-misused saying, "Those who can't do, teach," is not only inaccurate but also harmful to the status of the teaching profession. People who "can't do" one occupation will find little refuge in teaching. Teaching is complicated, as teachers need to deliver their knowledge as performances in all directions, depending on daily context and learner readiness. So teachers must be ready to shift directions at a moment's notice. Also, being successful in a different career path and knowledgeable about a subject is one thing. Adding the layer of teaching is like the popular comparison of Fred Astaire to Ginger Rogers; as the *Frank and Ernest* comic strip famously pointed out in 1982, Rogers did the same dance moves as Astaire but "backwards and in high heels," adding an increased level of difficulty (as cited in Pronko, 2019).

Educators and specifically K–12 classroom teachers are the linchpins of a successful education system. However, classroom teachers are also often the scapegoats for failures in society. Since the publication of *A Nation at Risk*, the general public has perceived the education system as failing the United States, communities, and students (as cited in National Commission on Excellence in Education, 1983). Politicians and policymakers deride the K–12 education system and, directly or indirectly, the people working in it (Kirst, 2010). This has led to a loss of autonomy and control over how educators operate in their schools, a process known as *deprofessionalization*. As a result of decades of politicians using the education system as an example of mediocrity to generate campaign support, teachers are more deprofessionalized than ever before in American history (Bruno, 2018).

For example, special-interest groups have succeeded in deprofessionalizing the teaching profession (American Federation of Teachers, 2017). Teachers lack a voice when it comes to deciding discipline policy, performance standards, and resource expenditures, which all have an impact in their classrooms.

In 2022, 91.2 percent of the U.S. population twenty-five and older completed high school or college (U.S. Census Bureau, 2023). Most adult U.S. citizens have at least thirteen years' experience as a student. Too often, people mistake their own experience for understanding the intricacies and nuances of teaching. It's almost as odd as thinking educators can all serve as plumbers because they used the restroom this morning. Everyone's a backseat commentator, and despite decades of education reforms, teachers continue to bear the brunt of the criticism. Federal legislation such as No Child Left Behind (2002) and Race to the Top (as cited in GovTrack.us, 2023) reiterate criticism of the American education system but prove to be of little help in making headway. State initiatives focus on improving the education system but provide little direct support to classroom teachers, instead focusing on policy rather than practice (Petrilli, 2022). Changes to state testing, new graduation requirements, and career-focused initiatives are just a few areas where policy changes occur with a "school districts just need to figure it out" approach for funding. This leaves even less money for teacher salaries. Teachers are under an enormous amount of pressure; however, actually empathizing with them and providing the resources to make a difference often seems almost an afterthought.

In the face of public opinion, teachers struggle to feel valued. The Organisation for Economic Co-operation and Development (2014) released the results of the *Teaching and Learning International Survey (TALIS)*, which indicates approximately 30 percent of teachers believe society values teaching as a profession. A 2018 study comparing Finnish and U.S. school systems finds a stark contrast in the way wider society views teachers (Hemphill, 2018). The survey asks respondents if they agree or disagree with the statement, *I think the teaching profession is valued in society*. Only 33 percent of U.S. teachers agreed or strongly agreed, while almost 60 percent of Finnish teachers agreed or strongly agreed (Hemphill, 2018). That's a stark contrast!

In another survey, Phi Delta Kappa finds 52 percent of U.S. teachers said their community values them "a great deal or good amount," while 31 percent of the teachers felt their community ascribes them "just some" value (PDK Poll, 2019, p. 6). Teachers who feel their community values them less are more likely to support striking for higher pay and less likely to give an *A* grade to their school (PDK Poll, 2019). In the United States, teachers need politicians who respect and value their expertise (Scholastic, 2012). When public perception of the teaching profession is more favorable, teachers will likewise have a more favorable view of their profession.

Coauthors and researchers Andy Hargreaves and Michael O'Connor (2017) discuss the need for financial support to have successful school systems. In their article "Cultures of Professional Collaboration: Their Origins and Opponents," Hargreaves and O'Connor (2017) state professional collaboration that characterizes high-performing systems requires a strong and well-compensated teaching faculty with highly developed expertise, as well as time and resources for teachers to meet with colleagues during and beyond the regular school day. Successful schools depend on systems that taxpayers support. Society needs to value the systems' contribution to communities and general public good. High-performing systems that contribute to the local community carry a price tag—hard-earned tax dollars. This a price some interest groups and political systems are reluctant to pay (Hargreaves & O'Conner, 2017). This puts districts in the position of limited and sometimes scarce resources for necessary personnel success.

Meaning as Compensation

Compensation in mattering admittedly includes the size of a teacher's paycheck, yet it can mean other things too. An adequate salary and benefits package is only part of a complicated answer to the teacher-compensation problem, so it's important to acknowledge that money is necessary to meet the most basic needs of employees (Corna, 2021). This is critical for understanding the complexity of teacher pay. Pay must be high enough to allow for a comfortable life and comparable to those in other professions with the same experience and education level. Seventy-four percent of teachers do not believe their salary is fair for the work they do (Will, 2022). *They are correct.*

However, having a singular focus on pay can ultimately be detrimental. The idea of a $100,000 per year teacher salary for all may exacerbate an already complex problem (Denver Classroom Teachers Association, n.d.). Pink (2009) and Sinek (2009) illustrate that external validation or rewards have demotivating effects in the long term, which can do more harm than good. A more substantial salary may increase satisfaction in the short term, but the monetary reward is unlikely to bring about lasting effects (Pink, 2009). Often, leaders will use rewards to motivate individuals, but those rewards may undermine a person's intrinsic motivation, thereby creating the opposite effect (Reeve, 2018).

Increasing pay can become a *hedonic treadmill*—the phenomenon that describes how happiness is susceptible to change over the short term based on events but then returns to a set point (Tanzer, 2019). It is akin to chasing rainbows. Teachers dissatisfied with their career often think an increase in pay will lead to more satisfaction. While it may be temporarily satisfying, a pay increase does not bring lasting satisfaction—and thus, monetary compensation alone is not the answer. Leaders must consider other ways to think about compensation.

Some suggest higher pay is not always worth sacrificing the work-life balance. Writer Bassam Kaado (2023) says employees are more likely to take a pay cut if it means a better work-life balance. In fact, 20 percent of respondents to the *2022 Pulse of the American Worker Survey* state they would be willing to take a 10 percent pay cut if it meant better hours (Kaado, 2023). However, according to a Gallup study, money is a bigger concern for disengaged employees or those who feel undervalued—who don't feel like they matter (Corna, 2021). Another 2022 study finds meaningful work and colleagues rank above compensation as the top factors driving educators to stay in teaching, but for those who had already left, compensation was the top factor (Bryant, Ram, Scott, & Williams, 2023).

We conclude there are limits to how much a pay increase will actually increase teacher job satisfaction. The paycheck is certainly part of compensation, but it's just that—a part. A primary factor in job satisfaction is how much people feel their leaders appreciate the work they do (Chapman

& White, 2019). However, the compensation versus other factors is a complex issue beyond the scope of this book.

In the post-pandemic era, most people prioritize stability (which we address in chapter 7, page 127) over more money. While a higher salary may encourage job seekers, it doesn't guarantee retention, motivation, or engagement (Kaado, 2023). "Money is not a sustainable motivator. People want money; they also want meaning" (McLeod, 2016, p. xii). Thus, meaning is compensation as well.

Where things get a bit fuzzy in contemporary parlance is educators often do an analysis solely in terms of motivational influences—what is *extrinsically* motivating versus *intrinsically* motivating. But motivation cannot take the place of validation. As we establish, teachers must feel a sense of belonging in their building or district, a sense of purpose in teaching, and validation—from external sources—of the work they are doing. Pay raises are only a short-term solution if not coupled with other improvements in the teaching environment. Earning more money alone will not necessarily improve the culture or reduce stress in a dysfunctional environment.

Teaching requires problem solving, creativity, and complex planning. These activities build teacher efficacy and a realization of personal and professional empowerment—or *validation*. This is the opposite of an external compliment or even a performance reward. Validation through extrinsic rewards is counterproductive for much of what teaching demands because rewards help people be more productive when there is a clear path to finishing a task. Teaching is anything but clear. With complex tasks (those without a clear end point or are difficult to measure quantitatively), external rewards have a negative impact (Pink, 2009).

> Validation through extrinsic rewards is counterproductive for much of what teaching demands.

This is not to say your acknowledgment of appreciation will all be for naught. You just need to appropriately and selectively deliver your appreciation. Leaders can avoid inappropriate use of appreciation by ensuring it is authentic and not given to manipulate or for selfish motives (Chapman & White, 2019). Authentic appreciation from leaders and coworkers can lead to a more supportive work environment. This is what we consider integral to be part and parcel of compensation—*a focus on employees' value.* The U.S. Department of Labor finds 64 percent of Americans who leave their jobs state they did so because their leaders did not appreciate them (Robbins, 2007). When employees do not feel leaders appreciate them in the workplace, negativity increases. Lackluster performance, tardiness, and a lack of connection with work start to emerge when employees do not feel valued (Chapman & White, 2019).

MAKING *COMPENSATION* MATTER

Teachers can make compensation matter by establishing guardrails around their time and talents. They need to develop the confidence to know when their professional time ends and their personal time begins. Whether teachers choose to live their work lives through *confluence* (working various hours of the day, within reason) or *compartmentalization* (leaving work at work and disconnecting to their teacher life while at home), they must be fair in allocation of professional investment.

Just as teachers want a guaranteed and viable curriculum for students, leaders want a viable workload for teachers. Determine what teachers can do in an eight-hour workday and utilize systems to maximize their time. Additionally, if you struggle with too many things to do and not enough time, check out *Fewer Things, Better* by Angela Watson (2019). Watson also has some great online resources (see https://truthforteachers.com), including a course called *40 Hour Workweek for Teachers, Administrators, and Instructional Coaches*.

Teachers can also make compensation matter with sound and wise investments. Invest a portion of what you earn when feasible, and do so consistently. You'll see wealth accumulate over time; using a frugal strategy to navigate your future is more a marathon than a sprint. While many school districts have done away with local pensions, many states continue to offer retirement programs for teachers, as well as self-contribution methods to save additional income. While this certainly does not help beginning teachers in the short term, it is a benefit that will literally pay off in the future. Some teachers are living paycheck to paycheck and think that investing for retirement is impossible. Take time to get help and advice on financial management and budgeting.

Finally, educators should make compensation matter by knowledgeably and reasonably talking about it. To change the public perception of teachers, they must continue to voice a clear and steady message at the grassroots level. Protesting for higher teacher pay at the state capitol might feel gratifying, but calls to action like these shouldn't replace sustained, consistent discussions with national, state, and local communities. Reasonable testimony in appropriation hearings for targeted, thoughtful, and intentional bills is the wiser move, especially for those who provide local autonomy for teacher pay incentives, allowing boards of education to compensate teachers in a way local families support.

When talking to lawmakers, educators should target specific issues, including student loan forgiveness, creating a special tax cut for teachers, and establishing a special home loan interest rate for teachers. Not only will these incentives possibly entice some people to go into the teaching profession but also help already established teachers make up the salary shortfall.

Per-pupil spending directly and positively associates with improved student outcomes (Barrett, 2018). Inadequate funding leads to high dissatisfaction among teachers. Phi Delta Kappa's annual poll finds 54 percent of teachers say the public schools in their community have too little money, and they have "seriously considered leaving" the profession (PDK Poll, 2019, p. 7). In the same poll, the most common reasons for teachers leaving the profession are inadequate pay and benefits. This 2019 poll marked the eighteenth consecutive year a lack of funding has been cited as the biggest problem facing public education; 60 percent of parents and 75 percent of teachers indicate their community school is not adequately funded (PDK Poll, 2019).

> Working in local communities with parents and local business leaders is also a must. Leaders should continue the conversation regarding the importance of highly effective teachers to ensure students receive a quality education, and what a quality education can do for individuals and their community. When education fulfills families, parents love their children's teachers and want teachers to take care of their children as their own.

Implications for Teachers

The discussion about appropriate teacher compensation is at the forefront of many state and local education discussions. Unfortunately, the discussion often involves only conversations about paychecks. This is shortsighted because district administrators have little or no direct control over the amount of funding the states receives. Teachers are well aware of the teacher pay gap and understand the gap increases each year. So, what can be done? Well, leaders can be persistent in noting this is unacceptable, for sure. Leaders must continue to advocate for fair and equitable pay with state and local officials to create solutions that work. The pay gap really started to increase in the early 1990s (Allegretto & Mishel, 2016). It took thirty years to get teachers in the predicament they are in right now, and leaders will not solve the compensation solution overnight.

So, what else can teachers do? They can work with administrators to invite business leaders and elected officials to classrooms for a day—not just a quick visit, but for the entire school day. Teachers can also create a teacher–business partner exchange with local chamber of commerce members: teachers spend a day learning about a chamber member's role in business and then chamber members spend a day learning about teaching. Remember, most business professionals' experience with school happened when they were students. Often their perception is skewed of what happens in contemporary schools.

Teachers can own a higher status as teaching professionals by visualizing every day that their professional contributions are on par with their school leadership team members. Teachers can metaphorically position themselves as surgeons in their institution, requesting that chiefs of staff ensure their operating rooms are well staffed, well resourced, and ready for their expertise. Teachers can walk with an air of confidence, encouraging students into the profession. Let students know this is the best time to be in education and mean it. Higher status comes more from the inside out. You cannot impress on others in society that a teacher's reputation should be more like a Finnish teacher's until you start believing it yourself. This is not delusional; it is simply a choice of how you envision yourself and the contributions you make. Teachers make all other professions possible, for goodness' sake, so start (or continue) acting like it! For social and economic changes to occur, people first must reimagine the role of teachers. When experts introduce a change, it is less likely to occur (Jennings, Lanaj, Koopman, & McNamara, 2022; Shughart, Thomas, & Thomas, 2020).

Finally, teachers can take control of their space. They can ensure schools impeccably outfit spaces where teachers gather—lounges, breakrooms, and otherwise—and reflect the accoutrements they deserve. Teachers can expect the school will honor their creature comforts and don't need to be

shy in advising administrators of these expectations. The *why* is simple—because they're teachers! After all, meeting environmental preferences *is* compensation and certainly within the control of those providing resources and making budgetary allocations each year.

This sort of outfitting is typically well within a building's mission statement, and school leaders should better articulate this. The best leaders know achieving their mission and vision involves the best educators, whose needs are preeminent. It's all about compensation. Teachers must think about things with a clear head, an honest heart, and a lens widened appropriately to see themselves for who they are and what they deserve. Teachers have agency to increase what their schools, the teaching profession, and society provide.

When it comes to action steps in moving the needle on mattering through teacher compensation, teachers should think big and strategize legislative and policymaking solutions, yet at the same time, take immediate, incremental steps to own what they can about the problem and move solutions forward. Teachers could try the following.

- Know (in your head and heart) you deserve higher pay for what you do as a teacher. Many who receive higher wages cannot do what you do; in fact, probably most of them cannot. Believe and accept that. Don't get angry about it. Just find peace, and consider this compensation issue a *long game*.

- Advocate with positivity and persistence for fair and just compensation and, along the way, ensure you suggest and model cost-saving options that can result in shifting funds to salaries and benefits packages.

- Make an appointment with a financial planner and take stock in your current wealth, financial security, and where you wish to be when you retire. This will serve as a reality check as to what you need to do, or begin doing, to get where you wish to go and where you deserve to be.

- List the internal rewards you have received in your teaching career and those you continue to receive from your students, families, and especially friends and colleagues at work. Quite possibly, the latter prevents you from celebrating the profession publicly. Consider developing a written memoir from your list and, if you can find the time and interest, begin writing just one page about each reward. Developing a tangible artifact can serve as an intrinsic indication that you are incredibly worthwhile.

- Advocate for other indirect teacher compensation, such as federal or state low-interest home loans for teachers or increasing the teacher tax credit. Teachers can also advocate at a local level for perks in compensation, such as school or district enrollment in hotel chain discounts, rental cars for personal use cost savings, travel discounts, online or local shopping discount programs, and similar services those in higher education and the business industry often provide for their employees.

Implications for School Leaders

Available funding for school districts can hamstring district leaders, but not completely. Grant funds can provide a temporary reprieve, though these are admittedly in short supply, preventing long-term solutions. Federal title funds fluctuate from year to year and never fully fund programs they are designed to help. Districts rely on the political whims of elected state officials to appropriate most school funding. Local school referenda are time-consuming and expensive for the district, but only sporadically succeed because they increase local tax rates. Still, leaders should never shy from leveraging the modest control they have over resources.

Administrators should first have a clear understanding of *compensation*, which not only includes salary but also benefits, status, validation, and authentic acknowledgment. Key is knowing when and how to move each lever. Leaders can influence available monies and identify potential efficiencies that can lead to more funds for teacher salaries. Investing in energy-saving technologies and participating in purchasing groups are two ways many district leaders utilize to cut costs. Leaders should also take a hard look at the administrative positions to ensure the central office or school office staff are the right size. With new technology and efficient systems, fewer staff can do more clerical work. Leaders should use the district's mission, vision, and beliefs as a lens to look through for how to spend money. Sometimes, leaders must learn to say "no" to requests not in line with these values.

Additionally, compensation includes benefits such as providing free or low-cost health clinics and mental health services for teachers. A robust wellness program is an additional benefit that also reduces health insurance costs. If leaders audit what they offer, they can envision their own families as their employees. What do leaders want for employees holistically? If employees were going through a tough time, what might leaders wish were available? Leaders can strive for these kinds of compensation for everyone. Leaders can have a fair and just compensation perspective.

Leaders should also make every effort to ensure teachers have status in the school, including messaging about the value of teachers each time they connect with community influencers or the community in general. The best leaders serve as talent agents for their teachers and staff, recognizing them appropriately for achievements, risk taking, successes, going the extra mile for students, or their dedication. The best leaders leverage district resources to get the word out about teacher accomplishments; they elevate teachers in the minds of others every time they go to a service or civic organization meeting, visit the hair stylist, or sit in the waiting room while their car is getting an oil change. The best leaders serve as teachers' champions and spokespersons.

District leaders can begin to change the community narrative by inviting community leaders and stakeholders to participate in community engagement meetings. Hold these meetings as part of strategic planning or building projects. Citizens participating in a series of meetings relating to school finance, educational programming, demographic studies, and facilities audits can invoke a sense of community responsibility and educate the public on the complex issues the district faces.

Provide teachers opportunities to personally validate themselves. Leaders can allow for risk taking, provide stretch opportunities, encourage failure (at times), and protect the school's willingness to

fail forward with grace and honor. In their understanding of psychologist Lev S. Vygotsky's (1978) *zone of proximal development*, leaders recognize how discomforting this space can be. Leaders should talk to staff members about how developing their best selves happens when they are at their own edge of discomfort. Tell staff some of the best compensation you receive is when your team gets out of the way and lets you charge forward in the unknown. Leaders can also model this in practice. Teachers need to see leaders growing in their leadership and honoring themselves.

Leaders must authentically acknowledge themselves and others. They are not trite cheerleaders for everyone or all that's done; doing this frustrates those hustling the most and scoring the best. Best to offer praise selectively and in a way that works for each individual. Some prefer you to praise them privately, some publicly. It's best for leaders to provide some praise for all, but do it with targeted intentionality and proportionally to the breadth and depth of their legitimate contribution.

Encourage failure (at times), and protect the school's willingness to fail forward with grace and honor.

As public servants entrusted not only with students and families but also teachers, school administrators have an obligation to make progress on the lack of adequate teacher compensation. Leaders can do the following.

- Seek to identify cost savings and efficiencies that allow lateral fund transfers to salaries and compensation packages for teachers and staff. Invest in other benefits, such as perks programs, on-site health care options, behavioral and mental health services, and employee wellness programs.

- Strive to compensate with latitude, liberty, and job security when you cannot provide more money. This starts with trust in your leadership. Let your people know you'll help them achieve what they dream if it will benefit them—even if it means leaving the building or district. Be authentic and helpful to staff when you find these benefits.

- Prioritize *equity* over *equality*, where you can and when appropriate. Your teachers and staff each have individualized circumstances needing your time, attention, and grace. Be as transparent as you can with your bargaining unit about this perspective if you work in a unionized school, or with your faculty or staff shared governance representatives, if not. Some of the best compensation you can offer outside salary includes respecting the individual, familial, and personal circumstances of your people—all the complexities of what their loved ones bring to them on any given time of day.

- Design tuition reimbursement programs for teachers on an incremental basis, factoring in longevity and requiring sustainable commitment to the school, as this may encourage teachers to stay in the profession and grow professionally. Doing so for hard-to-credential areas is advantageous for both teachers and schools, with a resultant positive impacts on students.

Conclusion

Now, we'll return to veteran teacher (Tim) and new teacher (Zane).

> In the teacher's lounge, Tim and Zane were readying for some eventful conferencing—they will both represent the status of the teaching profession well. Zane, pondering Tim's excellent advice with anticipation of a memorable conference ahead, said before leaving the lounge, "Tim, I hate to ask, but do you know a good resale shop where I can buy a class-act suit? The only one I have barely made it through the job interview last summer."
>
> Tim said, "Better than that, my friend. I have one I'll give to you—high-quality, fine-stitched wool, and one I wore well when I was a bit slimmer around the middle. I think it'll be just right for you after a quick trip to my tailor."
>
> Zane was grateful, and felt good for Tim's investment in him. Zane was hopeful that over time and through his commitment in teaching, he could accumulate high-quality suits to pass along, as well as a tailor he knew by name and an air of confidence that would make a lasting impression. Having the support of a trusted colleague, while unable to supplant the meager paycheck he made, helped Zane establish enough self-worth to represent his profession to the best degree possible, find peace in status, and help him make an indelible impression at the upcoming conference, which was both a personal and professional delight to experience.

No doubt compensation is one of the most complicated elements in mattering. Partly, this is because people need to tease out a more encompassing working definition and get sophisticated about what *compensation* entails. Plus, for many readers, *compensation* means money . . . period, and we get that. We're not trying to avoid that definition by widening the conversation. That said, compensation is the one element school districts have the least control over. There is a limited amount of funding available and the only way to increase the funding is to increase taxes or decrease spending on other programs. Politicians don't win elections by running on a platform of increasing taxes. This is even true with the best intentions, such as raising teacher pay. Because there is so much social and political baggage with increased funding for schools (which would mean increased salaries for teachers), teacher compensation has declined since the 1990s (Allegretto & Mishel, 2016). The teacher pay penalty continues to increase and there has been little headway in stopping this trend.

Leaders could utilize certain tools much more effectively, such as tax cuts for teachers, easier and faster student loan forgiveness, and special subsidized home loans for educators. Additionally, having special tuition-reimbursement programs for teachers who have a continued commitment to the school or district could also assist with overall teacher compensation and leverage incentives for them to stay, grow, and earn. Probably most effective will be teacher and administrator efforts to bolster elements of compensation they *do* have control over, and work to reframe how they perceive themselves, so others can do so vicariously. Perhaps, over time, an acceptable amount of monetization will follow.

In the next chapter, we'll discuss the element of stability.

Next Steps: Chapter 6 Recap Activity

Fill in the following diagram from the chapter's beginning, this time with unique information pertinent to you and this foundational element in mattering.

The External Element of Compensation in Mattering	
What one receives (which is fair and equitable based on experience and education) for what one does	
Your Way to Conceive:	
Your Way to Believe:	Compensation
Your Way to Achieve:	

Ensuring Teachers Matter © 2024 Solution Tree Press • SolutionTree.com
Visit **go.SolutionTree.com/teacherefficacy** to download this free reproducible.

Your Personal Professional Development: Thought Experiment—Compensation

The following thought experiment gives you an opportunity to imagine a different reality. Take time to visualize the scenario. You may want to revisit these questions several times to get a complete picture. It takes practice. Find your quiet space and consider the possibilities.

Practice a conversation with an elected official or taxpayer who could provide meaningful dialogue on increasing teacher pay—not just a one-sided "telling" conversation but a two-way conversation. What questions could you pose to get the other person thinking? It is so easy to get defensive! Yes, you could rattle off a bunch of facts, but the conversation needs to be about changing the person's heart as much as their head.

Questions to ponder:
How important is compensation to you in your workplace?
What resonates most with you about compensation?
Do you see adequate compensation in your building? If so, where?
What is one small thing you can do to enhance compensation in yourself?
What can you do to expand compensation for others?

Ensuring Teachers Matter © 2024 Solution Tree Press • SolutionTree.com
Visit **go.SolutionTree.com/teacherefficacy** to download this free reproducible.

CHAPTER 7

Taking Care to Take Care: *Stability*

Job stability, the second external element of mattering, not only refers to keeping a job but also to the steadiness of employer expectations and job responsibilities. It is the feeling that one's job is secure and not likely to disappear or change radically. Stability is another element with an obvious fit for the external domain, as it ties to funding, population shifts, and school leadership decisions, which can include alterations to teaching assignments and other changes, up to and including job loss. Some changes and planning for changes in any school are in the natural order of things, but the ways in which they occur, and the planning that goes into these changes, can influence teachers into feeling their jobs are unstable.

To illustrate this element, we'll begin with a fictional story.

> When Sandra's telephone rang, she noticed it was her brother Cam calling from out West. It was early 2020, and waves of concern were growing since the COVID-19 pandemic's onset; states were starting to take emergency measures in response. It appeared the two restaurants Cam owned were being shuttered temporarily through state executive order. His employee team was strategizing what it could do to offer take-out orders

with a skeleton crew to salvage some of the work opportunities Cam was providing.

The situation was heartbreaking. With sixty employees total between the two businesses, Cam only had a limited amount of emergency funds to maintain jobs for all. With the impending loss of revenue looming, state emergency appropriation, while a discussion point, was not yet a reality. Cam's crew was important to him, and it seemed there was little he could do. He examined options for a personal business loan to stave off family hardships.

Worse, as he told Sandra, Cam's community was home to many food-processing plants and supply-chain emergency providers of goods and services, and it seemed many who worked in those industries were getting sick. Those businesses were ground zero for infection rates, with employees who largely had limited access to health care and employee benefits if they missed work because of illness. It was a trying situation that lent little to personal or business stability. The outlook seemed bleak, with few answers in sight.

Offering as much support as she could in love and care, Sandra ended the telephone call with a heavy heart but also with a sense of deep gratitude. Sandra was a teacher, and while wise and arguably desperate measures were in emergency planning to keep students and staff safe in local schools—amid emergency one-to-one technology purchases and virtual technology struggles to continue with coursework—there was not one discussion locally about teachers losing their jobs or students losing the ability to continue their education.

Figure 7.1 provides an anticipatory set for the element of stability. The reproducible "Next Steps: Chapter 7 Recap Activity" (page 139) gives you the opportunity to fill in your own ideas.

The External Element of Stability in Mattering
Knowledge that the job is secure and not likely to disappear or change radically

One Way to Conceive: Imagine *you* being the first person your students, colleagues, parents, and principal would think of if they had to identify someone they could not operate or attend a school without.	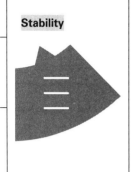
One Way to Believe: Begin effortful self-development, assignment acceptance, and reliable establishment as the go-to person for elements others find invaluable and you are passionate about for school and students.	
One Way to Achieve: Enjoy a daily deep, relaxing feeling that no matter what might happen in your school tomorrow, you will be the hottest commodity around if you need to seek opportunities to teach elsewhere. In other words, own your value and potency to a degree that gives you find great comfort and reassurance.	

FIGURE 7.1: The external element of stability in mattering.

In this chapter, we get started with stability by taking care to take care. We acknowledge while teaching may be a relatively stable profession, it is not without problems that can cause teachers to fear for their jobs. To feel they matter, teachers must feel stable. Fair, equitable, and transparent evaluation systems must be in place. Involuntarily changing teaching assignments multiple times, moving to new buildings often, and changing grade levels year after year can adversely impact job stability. One might argue that stability has been the bedrock of what has drawn talented professionals to the teaching profession for decades. Here, we'll share contemporary thoughts and opinions. Soon to follow are implications for teachers and educational leaders. We conclude with the reproducibles "Next Steps: Chapter 7 Recap Activity" (page 139) and "Your Personal Professional Development: Thought Experiment—Stability" (page 140).

Getting Started With Stability

Stability has the potential to be the most misunderstood of all the elements of mattering. Stability includes job security; economic challenges highlight this most obvious area of job stability. Businesses that focus on nonessential services such as entertainment, recreation, and leisure are often hit the hardest during economic downturns. In times of recession, for example, many businesses feel the impact to some extent, and layoffs occur. Unemployment rates skyrocket. However, when we examine teachers' jobs during these difficult economic times, few teachers (if any) are laid off. School districts will cut programs, field trips, supplies, and materials. Thankfully, it is difficult for a school district to perform a wholesale layoff of teachers due to a short-term downturn of the economy or a recession. For example, in Elkhart County, Indiana, in March 2009, the unemployment rate hit 20.6 percent, and in April 2020 (due to COVID-19), 30.7 percent (U.S. Bureau of Labor Statistics, n.d.). However, we observed teachers were not laid off anywhere close to those rates both times.

This is not to say teacher layoffs do not occur—indeed, they do. Layoffs usually have more to do with a drop in student enrollment, a reduction in funding from other sources, or long-term budget adjustments. Funding issues may not seem like the case for a teacher who is actually laid off when compared to other industries. The teaching profession is relatively stable. While budget cuts due to economic recessions happen, they will more likely translate into no pay increases or a reduction in extra programming.

It is unfortunate when a *reduction in force (RIF)* takes place. Administrators are wise to mitigate the number of RIF actions each year through long-term planning and natural attrition. However, sometimes, a RIF is necessary. In some cases, due to a radical shift in state budgeting or local taxation, RIFs can occur quite unexpectedly, but this is not typical. Most districts have a policy explicitly stating and following a strict timeline of notification of the possibility of a RIF *before* it occurs.

The hours a contract requires a teacher to work and the pay the teacher receives are other important areas of stability. Typically, districts contract a start and end time each day, along with a maximum number of hours worked per day. A common narrative from educators is *Teachers could make more money working at a fast-food restaurant or as a cashier at a local superstore.* However, this is a false equivalency. Pay is at a premium for those workers because they must work weekends and evenings. Scheduling can also be erratic and sometimes make it difficult to swap shifts with others. Again, while it's true many teachers work evenings and weekends (for example, lesson planning and grading), they are not monitored as closely and, if there is a personal milestone event, they typically don't have to worry about missing it entirely because of their work schedule.

WORKING A SECOND JOB

About ten to fifteen years into her teaching career, Shelly decided to get a part-time job working at a local superstore. She did this for a couple of reasons. First, she wanted to experience a job many of her students and parents experience. Shelly had worked in a factory for three summers while attending college but wanted to experience something different. She also wanted to make a little extra income to help with some unexpected personal expenses.

Shelly worked after school, evenings, and weekends, plus holidays (such as the day before Thanksgiving, Thanksgiving, and Black Friday). It also meant working Christmas Eve and New Year's Eve. An unexpected result was that Shelly re-examined her homework policies. For the first time, she was experiencing what many of her students were. Go to school all day, head straight to an after-school job, then go home and prepare for the next day (homework). Wow—what an eye-opener!

Sick days at the superstore were different as well. One evening while she was working, Shelly got sick and went home. She was scheduled to work the next morning (a Saturday) and couldn't go in due to illness. Shelly called in sick and received a "point" because she missed her shift. Once employees receive so many points within a certain time period, they would be ineligible for a raise, or worse, they could be fired. This was the first time Shelly had called in sick, but it didn't matter. As a teacher, she received seven

> sick days to use during the 184-day contract. She could call in just a few hours (or less) before school began, with no deductions or "points" whatsoever.
>
> While working at the superstore, her employer limited the number of hours Shelly could work—even in the summertime. This was not because she couldn't fit it in her schedule, but rather because she couldn't work enough hours to be a full-time employee. Becoming a full-time employee would have meant more benefits, such as health insurance. While the hourly rate might have looked OK, it did not include any type of insurance. This lack of insurance wasn't an issue because Shelly had insurance through her school district; however, had she not been a teacher, she could not have afforded to just have her job at superstore alone.
>
> Shelly enjoyed her time working with her coworkers at the superstore. In fact, she still sees some of them when shopping. She learned so much from her colleagues during her time there. Prior to her experience, Shelly would often lament, "I wish I could just work at _____." Once she had the opportunity to do so, she realized all jobs have advantages and disadvantages.

But even with this relative stability, many educators would say there is a need for major changes in the education system, noting the state of crisis in the teaching profession. No doubt some things need to change—and change radically—soon. The workload, stress, and public pressure make the job of being a teacher unsustainable. We see this compounding each year, as more leave the profession and fewer enter (Morrison, 2022). Few teachers would list the likelihood of losing their jobs as a major worry. So why is job stability one of the elements of mattering?

When we talk about *job stability* and having a job that does not change radically, we are targeting specific issues. For teachers to increase their sense of mattering, certain aspects of the job must feel stable, including the likelihood of forced transfers and performance evaluations.

Stability and Forced Transfers

When a district forces a teacher to transfer from one grade to another, one subject to another, or one building to another, it can produce a feeling of instability for the teacher. Sometimes, shifts in assignments or a RIF can happen due to budget cuts, enrollment shifts, or lowering enrollment. Other times, this is a tactic district administrators or building principals use to force change in a certain building for a certain group of teachers. While this tactic may successfully take care of the issue at hand, you can also create much angst and undue stress. Some leaders believe regular forced transfers can also help keep a teacher "fresh" and more open to change. Again, while this promise may seem valid on the surface, it can most assuredly do more harm than good.

Teachers typically enjoy a certain student age group or subject area more than others. Moving a teacher from a second-grade classroom to a fifth-grade classroom without the teacher's consent can create an atmosphere of powerlessness over that teacher's own career path. Sometimes, these forced transfers are necessary, such as in the case of balancing class sizes. A principal may just need another fifth-grade teacher, and the school has too many second-grade teachers. The alternative would be a RIF, including the teacher who didn't want to transfer. A principal may also believe the teacher struggles with that age group (second-grade students) and fifth grade may be a better fit for the teacher's personality and strengths—although, of course, it's better if the teacher makes this move voluntarily. The principal will have difficult conversations with the teacher, even if the principal deliberately and carefully crafts the conversations. The principal should be open and honest with the teacher about why the change must occur. Sometimes, it's just a necessity; the school is overstaffed in one area and understaffed in another. Fortunately, in most cases, leaders can anticipate and discuss rapid fluctuations in the student population well in advance of any moves. Unfortunately, at certain times (which should be extremely limited) leaders need to make adjustments, even after the school year starts. This may be true when looking at incoming kindergarten classes and determining the number of students "on the bubble" of needing a new teacher or removing a teacher from teaching kindergarten.

Forced transfers are not just limited to elementary school teachers. Some principals believe secondary teachers should change subject areas. For example, social studies teachers might teach U.S. history one year and U.S. government the next. Again, while sometimes changes should occur (like due to student enrollment in particular subjects or grades), leaders should not make wholesale changes just for the sake of changing.

> It takes time—not just weeks or months but *years* to hone the craft of teaching. The more stability teachers have in their surroundings, the better.

When teachers must transfer to different grades or teach different subject areas, they lose the grade-level or subject-area expertise they built over the subsequent year. It takes multiple years of teaching the same thing for teachers to anticipate possible areas where students may struggle and how best to help them in those areas. Sometimes, it's just trial and error. Each student is different and has unique needs. As teachers fill their toolbox with new strategies, those new strategies will help teachers meet unique student needs more effectively and with less effort.

It takes time—not just weeks or months but *years* to hone the craft of teaching. The more stability teachers have in their surroundings, the better. Think of stability through the lens of a professional athlete. Are athletes better when they're with the same team for multiple years over their career or moving to a different team every year?

Stability in Performance Evaluations

Schools and districts expend so much time, effort, and money on teacher-evaluation systems. However, evaluation reforms of the early 2000s have not had the impact many reformers once hoped. Research shows teacher-evaluation reforms do not improve student outcomes (Bleiberg, Brunner, Harbatkin, Kraft, & Springer, 2021). Teaching is such a complex endeavor it's impossible to quantify everything a teacher thinks, says, and does on a regular basis. Plus, the makeup of each class of students is unique.

Not only is there evidence evaluation systems have null effects on student achievement but also may add additional stressors. Researchers Matthew A. Kraft, Eric J. Brunner, Shaun M. Dougherty, and David J. Schwegman (2020) show evaluation reforms actually *decrease* teacher job satisfaction. At the same time, evaluation forms also impact administrators. A large demand on the principal's time is spent conducting teacher evaluations, which leads to more paperwork. The additional time leaders spend working on evaluations takes away time from their focus on other issues that often show a positive impact on students (Neumerski et al., 2018).

One of the criticisms is evaluation reform still falsely identifies an overwhelming number of effective and highly effective teachers. When leaders began enacting these evaluation reforms, many thought a large number of teachers would be revealed to be ineffective or in need of improvement. However, that has not come to fruition. In our experience, this makes sense in most districts: ineffective teachers often leave the profession prior to the end-of-the-year summative evaluation. Also, it's fair to say a school district is not going to replace every ineffective teacher with another ineffective teacher. Therefore, it makes sense that most districts would find very few, if any, ineffective teachers. Conversely, some administrators rate ineffective teachers higher because of the consequences of a low rating (such as probation or performance pay), or for example, the principal simply likes the teacher. Critics say if a district employs mostly effective and highly effective teachers, student achievement in that school should also be high, but studies show teacher evaluation has little impact on actual student achievement. Again, teaching is complex. It is definitely more complex than what a rubric can represent.

We are not suggesting you eliminate teacher evaluations. But time spent on evaluations must be proportionate to the influence they have on student improvement. The purpose of teacher evaluations must be teacher improvement. Principals are more productive when they have the ability to fast-track certain teachers. Compare this to a fast pass you can get at an amusement park. Effective teachers do not need the level of scrutiny and feedback on all indicators of a particular rubric leaders use in teacher evaluations. A principal could spend that time discussing various career goals and improvements a teacher would like to make. This would be more of a conversation between the principal and teacher. Teachers can select one or two areas they really want to improve on and those become their focus for the year. Meanwhile, this will free up time in the administrator's schedule to meet and observe new or struggling teachers more often.

MAKING *STABILITY* MATTER

Teachers and principals make stability matter by getting involved politically and playing the long game with elected officials. Elected officials can create policies, including those that focus on school funding and evaluation systems, ensuring teachers have a sense of job stability. With adequately funded schools, teachers might be less concerned about losing their jobs, and using student achievement to evaluate teachers is not only ineffective but also counterproductive. State and local officials must prioritize education as a way to improve communities.

Investments in education translate to fewer expenditures in the future on, for example, prisons and other social services (Baron, Hyman, & Vasquez, 2022). The better educated students are, the better educated citizens they become. Studies continually show the better educated students are, the less likely they are to rely on social services in the future (Mitra, 2011), and the more likely they will be to have civic and social engagement (Campbell, 2006).

Educators must smartly and tactfully approach conversations with elected officials, speaking in a language they understand, if the educators wish to help sustain and bolster stability in the profession. We have learned from lobbyists and staff members close to elected officials that an individual voice really does matter *if* it is prudently leveraged and exercised, which is sometimes not the case.

Consider sending an individual a handwritten letter. Do this during a legislative downtime, when elected officials are not under the pressures of a legislative session. First, thank the representatives for what they do for education, especially given the wide swath of other items needing their attention in other key industries, such as health care, social services, and public safety. Know legislator committee assignments and show you understand what those committees do. If the legislator receiving your letter is on an education subcommittee or committee, all the better! Tell a story about how legislative support made a difference in the life of a student. Be specific in your example, and weave the theme of teachers' need for stability into your narrative. For example, you might relate how a law your representative voted for enabled you to spread nine months' pay over a twelve-month period, meaning you can volunteer for a summer camp for students with physical and mental exceptionalities. The new law also provides stability in terms of your own children's needs while home on summer break. Thus, the policymaker's action allows you to give part of yourself to others because you can tend to your own basic needs.

To leverage the generosity political leadership provides, when writing to lawmakers, ask them to consider an idea you have about how teachers can make an even bigger impact. Again, plant this seed when the pressure of a session is not on representatives' shoulders. Say your idea may help economic security of teachers, performance and evaluation systems, or the grading and ranking of schools, which often put pressure on teachers who choose to serve in communities of high need. In other words, advocate smartly through the side door while presenting your best self and leveraging theirs. Finally, offer to lend a hand by assisting with wording of legislation or helping them understand complex issues if they are willing to sponsor legislation. (Rarely, if ever, do legislators not want a selection of good ideas they can offer as a new session opens and they forge consensus opportunities.) Writing to lawmakers this way (with specific and attainable requests) adds *arrows to their quivers* (that is, resources or strategies to help them meet ongoing challenges), while protesting at the state capitol alone may only serve to *shoot those arrows back* (that is, use those resources and strategies against those who could be willing to help).

Implications for Teachers

Job stability emerges when teachers believe they will not be arbitrarily fired or are under constant threat of a RIF. But as we've explored so far in this chapter, it also comes from teachers' ability to stay at the same school and teach at the same grade level, if they so desire. Obviously, this is not always feasible, as student population shifts require shifts in school personnel. Teachers should be proactive by working with educational leaders to mitigate unwanted shifts in teaching assignments.

It is also important for teachers to continue to advocate for fair evaluation systems. Evaluation systems should be *equitable, not equal*. That means some teachers will have different evaluation requirements. Experienced, successful teachers may be fast-tracked in their evaluation through quick or fewer evaluations. This allows the administrator more time to help struggling teachers improve and grow.

Shifting to a growth mindset for teacher evaluations may be difficult for both teachers and administrators. Some districts operate from a deficit view of teacher evaluations, so evaluators spend time trying to find areas where teachers come up short. In this type of culture, having an improvement or growth-minded evaluation system is extremely difficult. It is important to continue to work with district leaders to make this shift happen.

Some immediate actions teachers can take to leverage the foundational element of stability of mattering include the following.

- Be mindful of the stability of the teaching profession. It's better than most. This gives you a foundational point for leveraging your voice to do many other things. You're fairly certain you'll be collecting a paycheck and have relatively stable employment for the immediate future. The COVID-19 pandemic publicized and solidified this stability.

- Advocate with persistence, positivity, and pleasantness for equitable and fair evaluation systems that empower teachers to hold one another accountable. This creates organic stability, along with teacher empowerment more in line with the faculty governance models in college or university settings. Consider this model for teaching professionals at the preK–12 level.

- When teacher and staff openings occur, give of your time and energy to be involved with the hiring processes so you will have both empowerment and ownership in changes to come in your professional life. When it is not feasible to be directly involved in hiring, perhaps a good first step is to suggest interview questions or offer to vet potential candidates.

- Pay attention to and value your network, both in- and outside your building. We address developing relationships with legislators (see page 133), and completing the reproducible "Your Personal Professional Development: Thought Experiment—Stability" (page 140) will help you do just that. However, do not forget that stability in teaching comes from one's internal network as well. It's your work friends and colleagues who will lift you when you're down. Teachers who focus on making continual investments in the people they work with will find those people there for them when it's critical.

- Be active in letting your school leadership team know what you need to increase perceptions of a stable workplace. There are things these team members cannot control, of course, but believe us when we say they worry about stability. They worry about you leaving for other school districts. Don't leave them guessing. Be a teacher leader and share with your leadership team members ideas about what they can control.

Implications for School Leaders

By proactively planning for population shifts, district leaders can mitigate the necessity of an involuntary RIF. For example, reducing staff through attrition by retirement rather than forced layoffs helps teachers feel they have a stable job. It is important to carefully examine population shifts and potential staffing changes well in advance of making any decisions. While some unexpected events make a RIF necessary with little notice, avoid this whenever possible.

Ensuring equitable and fair evaluation systems also helps teachers feel a sense of job stability because they will not be too concerned with arbitrary firing or an unexpected loss of their job. Teachers should know exactly how they are doing and have a plan for future improvement. Administrators should never take the attitude that teacher evaluations are there as a "gotcha" or way to catch teachers doing something wrong. Evaluations must be done through the lens of teacher improvement and growth. Some teachers are ineffective. Just as teachers work with students to improve in areas of struggle, it is important for leaders to work to improve teachers. Not all teachers will come into your district with all the tools necessary to be successful. It is important to help them learn and grow. Still, not every teacher you hire is destined to be effective. It is your responsibility to students to have effective teachers in every classroom. So unfortunately, there will be times when it's necessary to let someone go. Students need school leaders to do this, and, just as important, students deserve teachers committed to learning and growing.

> Teachers should know exactly how they are doing and have a plan for future improvement.

School administrators are the first lines of offense in ensuring teacher job stability and for anything else attempting to infringe on that feeling of stability. They can do the following to ensure teachers' job stability.

- Proactively plan to avoid reductions in force due to economic challenges or the possibility of them, and work creatively to handle these challenges through attrition and comprehensive communication.

- Implement fair, clear, and transparent supervision and evaluation systems for teachers. Allow their input into necessary improvements you can implement

to enhance feelings of stability and parity. Don't surprise teachers with new requirements or unclear components in evaluation and supervision that make them uncomfortable. If you're planning to make changes, let your teachers know twelve to eighteen months prior, if possible, and involve them in exploring options and making decisions.

- Provide teachers each a visual depiction of Maslow's (1943) hierarchy of needs, and ask if they are willing to define *self-actualization* as teachers. Also, ask teachers to populate the areas farther down in the hierarchy as look-fors in the school setting that could provide love and belonging, safety and security, and so on. Ask them to complete the hierarchy using actionable leadership behaviors, so you're not left guessing what they wish to see from you to foster more of the foundational needs that lead toward high-level need fulfillment.

- Become the most serious student you can of governmental legislation and state policy and their implications for schools. Stay ahead of financial, emotional, or other actions that could impinge on stability in your teaching staff. Establish respect as a consumer of thoughtful political reasoning on all sides of the statehouse aisle, and offer your elected officials at least two to three ideas for each concern you cite. Become a trusted go-to for your teachers and staff.

Conclusion

Here we return to Sandra's story and consider how stability affected her sense of mattering.

> Sandra deeply pondered Cam's plight. And while she was thankful that a job-loss circumstance was not on teachers at nearly the same rate, her profession had been upended with many of the same fears and realities as others—risks of infection and transmission of COVID-19, technological barriers to home-based instruction, and continuation of school-provided critical services to families logistically burdened (such as food provisions, community-based counseling and intervention, and aftercare programs for working families). Sandra particularly worried about the severe learning losses predicted by those who knew the importance of what teachers and schools do every day on site. However, there was a brief respite amid these concerns in that those providing students with care and learning would be safe and secure in their employment while continuing their all-important work. In short, and despite the many other challenges

> the pandemic threw at teachers, Sandra had stability during the most difficult and unprecedented of times.

When taking into consideration all the occupations available, teaching is relatively stable. Especially in times of economic downturn, teachers can feel a little more confident in job security. Compared to some jobs, teaching ensures a relatively stable schedule. These are two positive aspects of a career in teaching. Not all occupations afford the same.

The biggest change in the job stability element of mattering is the focus and direction of teacher-evaluation systems. Since the United States started to reform evaluation systems, it has taken more time and energy to conduct them, and there is little proof that the amount of time spent on evaluations has a dramatic impact on student achievement. It is time to reconsider some of these evaluation reforms. It does not make sense to continue doing evaluations in ineffective and counterproductive ways. That's not to say there shouldn't be evaluations. Some changes, such as those that address equity and fast-tracking, make evaluations effective; however, there must be an emphasis on improvements and growth for the teachers.

In the next chapter, we'll move on to the last external element of mattering: job crafting.

Next Steps: Chapter 7 Recap Activity

Fill in the following diagram from the chapter's beginning, this time with unique information pertinent to you and this foundational element in mattering.

The External Element of Stability in Mattering
Knowledge that the job is secure and not likely to disappear or change radically

Your Way to Conceive:

Your Way to Believe:

Stability

Your Way to Achieve:

Your Personal Professional Development: Thought Experiment—Stability

The following thought experiment gives you an opportunity to imagine a different reality. Take time to visualize the scenario. You may want to revisit these questions several times to get a complete picture. It takes practice. Find your quiet space and consider the possibilities.

Imagine reaching out to a legislator who represents your community or school. Do some homework. What recent legislation has your state senator or representative sponsored or cosponsored that has been helpful to you as a teacher?
How might you thank your legislators for what they are doing for education, given what you know about the sponsored legislation, committee assignments, and constituent events, on their plate?
Jot a few notes here regarding a story you can share about your ability to make a difference in the life of a student because of the support of your legislators. Be specific in your example, and weave a theme of the teachers' need for stability into your narrative.
Develop a thoughtful and finessed way of asking your legislator to consider an idea you have about how teachers can make an even bigger impact. This, of course, means you actually have such an idea. If not, take some time to think about it. (That's why we call this *a thought experiment* and ask you to revisit these questions if needed.) Be encouraged to set this aside, allow your ideas to percolate, and come back to it when appropriate.
Finally, do some homework about what might be coming your way during the next legislative session. Often, principals are good sources of this information (through their statewide principal's association), so meet with your principal before attending. Then, write a few sentences foreshadowing what legislators might be working with, share your thoughts with them, and offer to lend a hand or helpful testimony if they are willing to sponsor legislation important to you.

Questions to ponder:

How important is stability to you in your workplace?
What resonates most with you about stability?
Do you see job stability in your building? If so, where?
What is one small thing you can do to strengthen job stability in yourself?
What can you do to expand job stability for others?

CHAPTER 8

Letting Things Be Loose or Tight: *Job Crafting*

Stability ties to funding, population shifts, and school leadership decisions. The concept of job crafting is a bit more nebulous than some other elements in this book. *Job crafting* is the capability to make subtle changes to the work environment to meet individual needs. While this element has intrapersonal characteristics, we determine it falls among external factors. Supervisors, administrators, or policymakers create conditions that allow job crafting to occur. Of course, teachers need to recognize when their leaders empower them to make changes, but we recognize that the ability to do so comes from others.

One way to think about job crafting is as a balance between teacher autonomy and district consistency. Teachers need the ability to craft tasks that best suit their needs whenever possible. In short, teachers must receive the latitude to act with agency, with respectful deference to their creativity, ingenuity, and ability to keep their eye on the ball, while playing the game of school—to a certain degree—their own way.

To illustrate the element of job crafting, we'll begin with a fictional story.

> Chandra, a fourth-year teacher, stared into a mirror that hung across from her at the back of a sushi bar while she awaited her order from the chef. She was grabbing a quick dinner after traveling more than two hours for a weekend graduate class. It was late Friday afternoon, approaching

dinnertime. Her first class began at 6:00 p.m. and would go late into the evening. There would be more to follow in an all-day Saturday session, with a trip home after.

While sipping on her hot tea, Chandra thought of the last few years. Great teaching reviews. Awesome students. Family support. Good relations with those on both her grade-level and content-area teams. What Chandra could not ignore, however, was a slight emptiness in the pit of her stomach—a soft yearning that something about how she was teaching was incongruent with her identity but which she was unable to recognize. It was unsettling in both its presence and its ability to escape clear identification.

Chandra's image in the mirror stared back at her. It was a rather blank stare when others might expect her to have a look of assurance, confidence, and contentment. It was strange that she lacked something to be complete. Her sushi arrived.

Pondering the chapter she was reviewing for course discussion, Chandra thought of the twenty-five question prompts her professor provided and asked the graduate students to answer. She pulled the prompts from her purse for another look. One was, Why did you pursue a career in education? Another was, Who was your favorite teacher or adult figure in school, and why? The last one really intrigued Chandra: What would you be doing if you could have a career do-over?" (Donlan, 2022, p. 20). The professor had asked her to sort the prompts into similar themes.

That weekend, the professor asked the graduate students to prioritize some additional statements he would provide. The students would be performing some more sorting and prioritizing activities, and even delve a bit into who they are as people and how they best represent their individuality. Creatively, the professor would ask them to weave all of their information into a statement constructed to help these graduate student educators discern something unique about themselves they really needed to take time to discover—their professional signature.

> Chandra thought the exercise might be a bit hokey, but she respected her professor, so she was willing to be a good sport and give it a shot. What she did not realize, and what was forthcoming, was a fairly emotional weekend—a closer inspection of herself and how she needed to leverage her unique gifts in teaching, in her own way. Amid all the successful aspects of her teaching career, for some time Chandra had not investigated if any parts of her were conforming to an industry standard, especially when there might be a better way.
>
> Before returning home on Saturday evening, Chandra was invited to take time for herself, and investigate if her current interests, aptitudes, and abilities align with how she did her job in the finite hours she had each school day. But this time, she investigated with a deeper sense of how she might do things differently within the established parameters of her school and district.

Figure 8.1 provides an anticipatory set for the element of job crafting. The reproducible "Next Steps: Chapter 8 Recap Activity" (page 158) gives you the opportunity to fill in your own ideas.

The External Element of Job Crafting in Mattering
Capability to make subtle changes to the work environment to meet individual needs

	Job Crafting
One Way to Conceive: Imagine if you could share your best ideas about doing things your own way in your classroom (within reason), and receive great ideas from others around the world on the same.	
One Way to Believe: Discover and leverage online groups that share ideas, as these groups can be powerful. Involve yourself with an online community to support, encourage, and brainstorm with others.	
One Way to Achieve: Confidently employ your most effective persona to deliver the *how* for the *what* supervisors or policymakers ask of you—and enjoy success in it! Oh, and be humble as well (but don't overdo it) as you find creative and powerful ways to live your passion and make a difference within the boundaries leaders establish for teachers.	

FIGURE 8.1: The external element of job crafting in mattering.

In this chapter, we get started with job crafting by letting things be *loose* (provide flexibility) or *tight* (not up for discussion). The key is knowing when, where, and in which areas job crafting is most effective. We focus on what job crafting can look like and the when and where of teacher job crafting. We compare and contrast job crafting with autonomy. We also note implications for teachers and school leaders, and conclude with the reproducibles "Next Steps: Chapter 8 Recap Activity" (page 158) and "Your Personal Professional Development: Thought Experiment—Job Crafting" (page 159).

Getting Started With Job Crafting

We often hear about teachers wanting more autonomy. The word *autonomy* (n.d.) comes from the Greek origin of *autos* (self) and *nomos* (law). It is similar in meaning to *independence*. While independence is a laudable commodity, the needs of students vary in both breadth and depth. It is impossible for an individual to serve all the needs of all students in the most effective ways possible; it takes a team. Long gone are the days of *Just let me shut the door and teach*. There are behavior issues, cognitive concerns, and students struggling in multiple subjects. Teachers must rely on the expertise and guidance of others, such as mental health therapists, counselors, learning disabilities specialists, and those who specialize in trauma-informed practices. The most certain way to burn out in the teaching profession is to want independence and actually get it. It's easy to conflate independence and autonomy; teachers want *some* say in how they do things, thinking this means they need to be independent. We believe what teachers are actually looking for is not independence but a way to have *autonomy* (or the ability to craft their job in meaningful ways) within the framework of their school community.

That being said, excess autonomy is just as bad as no autonomy (Hargreaves, 2015). With complete autonomy, the paradox of choice can paralyze people. The fear of missing out makes people bounce from one decision to another, hoping to stumble on the correct answer. This level of autonomy also leads to education inequality because choosing becomes more about an individual's decision-making skill to implement the best teaching practices (Hargreaves, 2015). That's where job crafting comes in.

The most certain way to burn out in the teaching profession is to want independence and actually get it.

According to Mitsuhashi (2018), *job crafting* consists of actions people take to make their job fit their strengths. Job crafting allows people the flexibility to modify a job while still achieving the overall requirements of the job. Job crafting is autonomy with guardrails (see figure 8.2).

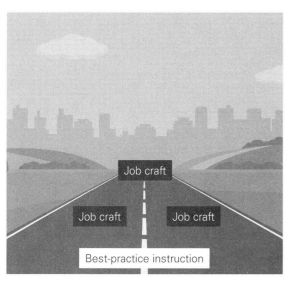 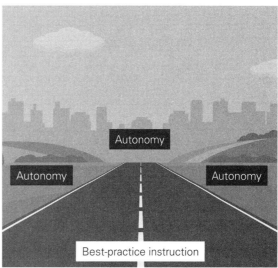

FIGURE 8.2: Job crafting and autonomy.

For example, think about how teachers use their instruction time in the classroom. Autonomy (or pure independence) allows teachers to not use best practices. A teacher who wants the autonomy to show a movie three days a week for the entire class period is not using best practices. *Job crafting* means having autonomy to decide on methods within the guardrails of best-practice instruction. Teachers should have the ability to craft their jobs while maintaining consistency in overall deliverables across the school or district. Teachers face an increasing number of mandates and constraints, and this makes job crafting difficult.

School districts and teachers must balance local concerns and issues with the growing list of government mandates. Often these are unfunded mandates with little support for implementation. In 2019, Michael Brown, director of legislative affairs for the Indiana Department of Education, sent an eight-page memo to school principals and superintendents outlining required training for school employees, which included CPR training, suicide prevention training, information on bloodborne pathogens, bullying prevention training, child abuse and neglect reporting, signs and indicators of human trafficking, criminal organization activity reporting, seizure training, and test security and integrity training (Indiana Department of Education Office of Legislative Affairs, 2019). In addition to these general items, Brown also outlined training for specific groups or individuals in each building, including "Stop the Bleed" (primary trauma care), seclusion and restraint training, lockout/tagout procedures, concussion protocols, heat preparedness training, and internal control standards training. The state of Indiana also required each district to have at least one reading specialist trained in dyslexia, homeless liaison, and school safety specialist (Indiana Department of Education Office of Legislative Affairs, 2019). The Indiana General Assembly passed thirty new bills impacting education in 2017, thirty-six in 2018, and forty-two in 2019 (Indiana State Teachers Association, n.d.a, n.d.b, 2017).

In addition, many states have explicit curriculum requirements with specific elements teachers must teach in certain grade levels or courses. For example, many state legislators have passed, or are considering passing, a law requiring all schools to teach cursive writing to specific grades (Yount, 2019). In 2019, Indiana passed a law that requires all students take the naturalization test (that is, the examination one must take to become a naturalized citizen of the United States; Murphy, 2019). In Florida, the state board of education passed a rule requiring schools to educate teachers and students about child-trafficking prevention (Florida Department of Education, 2019). At the national level, the Every Student Succeeds Act (ESSA, 2015) created additional mandates for schools and school districts. The Indiana ESSA plan includes academic assessments, programs for low-performing schools, educator evaluation, and student support (U.S. Department of Education, n.d.). That's a lot to keep up with.

The number of mandates facing educators creates a challenging environment for them to find job satisfaction. Deming states, "All anyone asks for is a chance to work with pride" (as cited in Conzemius & Morganti-Fisher, 2015). Business leaders identify the education system as a model unlikely to result in satisfaction among practitioners. State mandates, with a quantitative focus to measure the quality of a school, have led to a miserable work environment. Author, consultant, and keynote speaker Lisa McLeod (2016) states, "One need look no further than our public school system to see how focusing exclusively on numbers can suck the soul out of even the most well-intended professional" (p. 36).

With these challenges in mind, what are some practical ways for teachers to job craft? Job crafting can take many forms, and paying attention to when and where to best use it will help ensure teachers have ample opportunities.

What Job Crafting Can Look Like

The ability to craft a job has a positive impact on the way employees view their jobs, so district and building leaders should create conditions for this type of activity. There are areas of teaching where you can have lots of job crafting opportunities and then other areas where very little to no job crafting should occur. Some schools refer to this as the *loose-tight organizational structure*. The concept and importance of a loose-tight structure is crucial to the PLC process (DuFour et al., 2016). In areas that are *tight*, there is little to no job crafting; in areas that are *loose*, more job crafting can occur.

Now you might be thinking, why don't they just call it *loose-tight?* Why use the term *job crafting?* Often, leaders who use the loose-tight organizational structure consider the *loose* part smaller teams having the ability to make decisions and do things on their own. Job crafting goes one step further, as it is extremely individualized. No team consensus is necessary. It is personal. Think of doing the same thing as a whole organization as *tight*, doing things in smaller teams within the organization as *loose*, and doing things as an individual as *job crafting*.

Some job crafting might take seismic shifts in the school culture, but other, smaller changes can occur almost immediately. The company Cornerstone OnDemand discovered employees who use Firefox or Chrome internet browsers at work instead of Internet Explorer stayed in their jobs longer and had higher performance evaluations than their peers (Pinsker, 2015). The company's chief analytics officer, Michael Housman, determined this was due to employees actively downloading a browser that would help them to do their job more effectively and efficiently. Downloading a different browser was not a requirement of the job but something the employees did independently to improve their productivity and better suit their needs than the default browser (Pinsker, 2015). In many districts, teachers are unable to download new updates for software to their school computers, so analyzing different web browsers is a nonstarter—but does it have to be? Shouldn't there be a way for teachers to customize their computers to best meet their needs without locking down the entire system?

Of course, this example might well have technology directors panicking at the thought of opening the floodgates to malware and viruses—and rightfully so. Guidance and oversight are necessary guardrails. However, giving teachers a menu of options would go a long way in empowering them to use what works best for them individually.

There are countless other ways to craft a job. According to well-being expert Chase Mielke (2019), a form of crafting a job is developing new tasks or modifying undesirable tasks. Professors and coauthors Amy Wrzesniewski and Jane E. Dutton (2001) refer to this as *task crafting*. Lesson plans, for example, are tools educators develop and utilize specifically to assist teachers in creating and executing an effective lesson. Lesson plans include various required criteria to ensure teachers think through and execute a lesson well. Do a quick search for lesson-plan templates and you'll quickly realize there are thousands of ways to create one. It is impossible to have a one-size-fits-all template that fits everyone's needs. Yet, in U.S. school districts, leaders force teachers to utilize the standardized template for their school or district—not one typically designed for the benefit of the classroom teachers, but rather for the administrators looking at the lesson plans in the name of quality control or accountability.

What if leaders modified the policy to allow teachers each to organize their lesson plans in ways they felt best served their individual teaching needs? When an administrator does an observation, are the lessons going smoothly? Are teachers teaching effectively? If so, let them be! Some teachers may need assistance with the organization and execution of lesson plans. This is when someone should step in and help teachers structure plans in more helpful ways. Perhaps it is helping inexperienced teachers during teacher orientation with effective ways of creating lesson plans. Chances are they created lesson plans for their pre-service preparation program; they might feel more comfortable using that format versus the official district format.

Another way to craft a job is to craft the *why*, also called *cognitive crafting*. *Cognitive crafting* involves shifting the way someone perceives tasks (Mielke, 2019). Cognitive crafting closely associates with Csikszentmihalyi's (2008) concept of flow we discuss in chapter 3 (page 55) and assimilation in chapter 5 (page 91). Indeed, all occupations have aspects people in that profession don't like to do. Sometimes, you just have to change your mindset. However, it's important to note, the more cognitive crafting an employee needs to do, the less overall job satisfaction that employee will have. It is important for school district leaders to be mindful of the amount of cognitive crafting teachers do and limit it when possible.

The *When* and *Where* of Teacher Job Crafting

Think about four of the many key areas in teaching: (1) standards, (2) instruction, (3) assessment, and (4) grading. Teachers do a multitude of other things, but here we focus on these four main areas; in these areas, it is critical to understand the *when* and *where* of job crafting.

For example, think about standards. For essential standards, there is no job crafting (or at least we believe there shouldn't be) as long as there are a reasonable number of standards to teach and not a list that takes the typical K–12 student twenty-two years to attain. To have a guaranteed and viable curriculum, the school or district must decide (as an organization) what standards students must learn. If the district is small enough, building consensus in the entire grade-level teacher team can accomplish these decisions. In larger districts, teachers representatives may have to finalize the decisions. Teachers should review these *essential standards* regularly—at least every few years or more frequently, as needed. Under no circumstances should nonteachers, like district leaders, dictate the essential standards without teacher input. In other words, the organization is very tight on the essential standards but only after consensus from the teacher teams. It is akin to entering a social contract in political theory. All other standards (or the nice-to-know standards) are left to the individual teacher. Depending on the number and depth of these nonessential standards, teachers will cover them in varying degrees. However, it's up to teachers to determine when and to what extent they address these standards—they have opportunities here for job crafting.

When looking at instruction, a high level of job crafting can and should occur. The only guardrail in instruction must include researched best practice—or evidence-based practice. As Hattie (2009) shows through meta-analyses, dozens of practices lead to student growth. It must be left up to the professional teacher to determine the best course of action. Just as a doctor diagnoses patient needs (and each patient may need a different form of treatment), a teacher must have the same latitude. At the same time, no one wants a doctor practicing medicine by guessing or wishing something will help.

The art of instruction is best left up to the individual teacher. Teachers each know their students best and understand their needs. For job crafting to occur in its highest form—giving teachers the ability to modify the task of instruction—it is important to have strong collaborative grade-level or subject-area teams in place. Teams, the engine that drives a successful PLC, serve as a safety net if a teacher is not using best-practice instruction or misdiagnosing what a student or group of students need (DuFour et al., 2016).

This brings us to assessment. For teachers to have the ability to utilize instruction in the way they see fit, it is important for teacher teams to utilize common formative assessments. Grade-level or subject-area teams give the same assessments around the same time. Again, PLC practices are important to keep in mind here. Teachers can instruct in the way they see fit, and then it is through the common formative assessments, which focus on essential standards, team members check in with one another to see the effectiveness of their instruction. At this point, the team moves into action-research mode, where they examine results to find the instruction method most impactful for students. Individual teachers determine all the other formative assessments. And as you know, formative assessments can take a wide variety of forms.

The content on state standardized assessments involves little to no crafting and is extremely tight, not only throughout the district but also the state. The types of questions on the state assessments are also tight. No job crafting seems possible here. There may also be other required district assessments. We'll delve into this a little further in the Implications for School Leaders selection (page 154).

Finally, we come to grading. Grading for the essential standards must be as congruent as the essential standards themselves. The process and procedure for how teachers grade, measure, and report must be congruent for instructional parity. Mastery in one teacher's classroom must be congruent with mastery in another teacher's classroom. As with essential standards, the level of mastery and the process items teacher teams use to score them must be teacher driven at either the building or district level. Once teams decide the purpose and process, all teachers must follow a social contract in terms of their engagement with essential standards.

In the context of the overall school education–delivery system, teachers should feel they have the ability to choose the best activities for their students. As part of this success, the school culture should encourage data-informed decisions. The stronger the PLC process is in a district or school, the more successful and powerful this becomes; however, at times, districts or schools try to make up for a weak PLC by tightening the reins and therefore reducing the ability to job craft. The district chart in figure 8.3 illustrates where and how job crafting occurs.

	Tight	Loose	Job Crafting
Standards	Identified district essential standards	All other standards	How to integrate all other standards with district essential standards
Instruction	Science of instruction (based on best-practice research)	Art of instruction (best-practice guardrails)	
Assessment	Common formative assessment and state testing	Formative assessments	How and when to conduct formative assessments
Grading	Purpose and process	Tools to use to assist grading and feedback	

FIGURE 8.3: Job crafting in four areas of teaching.

MAKING *JOB CRAFTING* MATTER

Establishing a professional reputation as a relevant, responsive, and healthy member of your PLC is a key ingredient in making job crafting matter, especially for teachers who work with limited latitude in terms of leadership flexibility or strict pacing regimens. With the advent of professional social media outlets, more teachers than ever are garnering national if not international recognition for creativity in the classroom. With this notoriety typically comes permission to job craft, especially if doing so brings a positive spotlight on those in charge of allowing that leeway.

> School principals, curriculum directors, and other central office administrators may look more favorably toward teachers doing things their own way, especially if it helps them and the district look good. We think of the expression, *a high tide raises all ships*. Well, bring on that high tide! Bring on the recognition and accolades, and most of all, do it authentically and sustainably by bringing your own creative practices to demonstrate what works on behalf of students, teachers, teaching, and learning. And in doing so, refine, name, develop, and brand your work. Then, pitch your work to those in charge you wish to put this signature—and those similar—on much of what you do, with more good things coming if the school celebrates more job crafting. This, of course, puts pressure on you to bring your A game; however, if you are truly as resourceful as your new brand purports, you'll assuredly deserve the latitude to play the school game your own way. Everyone wins!

Implications for Teachers

Teachers must be able to identify when they are capable of making changes in their work environment. Because teachers don't have direct control over their ability to job craft, it is important for them to continually advocate the importance of this strategy to stakeholders. Frequently, teachers have the opportunity to job craft, but do not realize leaders have empowered them to do so. When teachers see an area they feel should be modified, they must feel comfortable and confident enough to ask the school and district leaders for such modifications.

It is important to dialogue with school and district leaders regarding the implications for allowing teachers to job craft. If administrators aren't familiar with job crafting or the elements of mattering, they may not see the importance of giving teachers the ability to modify their job. In fact, some administrators may think they're doing teachers a favor by streamlining processes they believe are helpful without taking into consideration the individual strengths of each teacher. It is important to remember that few people become administrators simply to make life miserable for teachers.

> When teachers see an area they feel should be modified, they must feel comfortable and confident enough to ask the school and district leaders for such modifications.

Having conversations about job crafting and the reasoning behind it can go a long way in helping leaders understand why it is necessary. Initiating these conversations before making requests may help leaders be receptive to changes and less likely see them as an attack on their leadership. Being clear on the purpose of the task is extremely important as well. There may be dictates from higher-ups or even the state that require teachers do some tasks a certain way. Often teachers may lack the big-picture view district leaders are privy to. It's important to ask clarifying questions on the purpose and outcome to ensure the way the changes being proposed will ultimately achieve the same goal.

If your district leaders focus on data and results, a good way to convince them to let teachers try job crafting is to pilot the change. Perhaps the needed change has to do with a weekly meeting or a report done a certain way; suggest allowing teachers to try a different way for a specified time. After that time, teachers can determine together if the modification was better, worse, or the same. By mutually agreeing on the effectiveness of modification beforehand, teachers can continue their job crafting. It is akin to action research involving students that teachers often engage in.

While there are some ways teachers can help facilitate job crafting, the reality is so much of it relies on others, which is why we consider it part of the external dimension. Sometimes, reframing the perception of mundane and tedious work is an important aspect of job crafting (Mitsuhashi, 2018). Job crafting can help employees create meaning in their work. Harvard professor Teresa Amabile and San Diego State University professor Steven Kramer (2011) state that meaningful work is what people want most from their jobs. Meaningful work is more significant than a salary increase or promotion (Barker, 2017). Employees deserve to work in a place where they feel supported and energized every day (Watson, 2015).

Teachers who embrace job crafting and doing things their own way (within smart parameters) can do the following.

- Step into your most confident self and say, "Because I am a teacher, I have game! I can teach any class, scale any mountain of challenges, and make differences where they're in short supply. I can be counted on to try again when students aren't learning because I'm just that good!" Then, live it. Represent! It's really all that permission slip for job crafting requires.

- Work with colleagues and your leadership team to identify areas everyone recognizes and values for job crafting. Ensure these areas smartly integrate into systems that, by design and need, must be uniform to a certain degree. In short, delimit the *whats* from the *hows*, and own the latter. Have an open and honest conversation regarding whether you agree with the job crafting chart in figure 8.3 (page 151) with respect to standards, instruction, assessment, and grading.

- Get together with your grade-level or content-area colleagues to identify one another's best practices for success. Know if your team members can identify and find value in what you produce, then others outside your organization will as well. This is the beginning of your market research. Once you identify your best practices, consider developing feedback to your job crafting repertoire, as well as your brand, which can transcend what you do with your students.

- Seek out opportunities to have conversations with colleagues about how to value individual approaches in situations where teachers must honor pacing guides. Find the loose within the tight, in other words. Pacing should not be so lockstep that it impinges on creative or professional agency. Recall again, it's not simply autonomy or independence you're championing, it's job crafting—the how, after establishing the why and what.

Implications for School Leaders

Educational leaders should welcome ideas on ways teachers can job craft. Teachers may want to tweak a process (for example), but often they do not feel empowered to do so. Administrators must be open and discuss the concept of job crafting with teachers. It may even be necessary for districts to explicitly create conditions requiring that teachers job craft in some way. For example, give teacher teams the ability to create their agenda or format for meetings (as long as this is within the school or district's established guardrails). Is it really that important for *all* teachers to use the same lesson-plan format? As long as the required components are present, does it matter? Depending on teachers' history with former school or district leaders, they may be hesitant to attempt tweaking any task for fear of reprimand. If leaders have clear guardrails on expectations, job crafting can be a powerful tool for teachers, while leaders stay focused on the overall goals of the organization. Is important for leaders to be comfortable with teachers willing to step out of their comfort zone and talk about ways to modify current practice. Leaders who don't have confidence in their leadership ability will often view teachers' requests to job craft as threats. Administrators must adopt the attitude that teachers are not questioning their authority or motives for practicing a certain way but simply want to empower themselves.

Administrators ultimately have the ability to create conditions that will enable teachers to job craft—or not. And conversely, they can create conditions where teachers feel psychologically unsafe to request job crafting. Again, not only do administrators need to recognize their power in creating a safe environment for job crafting but also openly discuss these opportunities to ensure teachers take advantage and feel empowered to make those subtle changes in the workplace. Additionally, school leaders can liaise with key stakeholders who impact the ability of teachers to job craft through local control of the district. Whenever possible, policymakers should allow local districts flexibility when implementing academic programs. When policies are rigid, without room for modifications, the ability for teachers to tweak activities to carry out the policy becomes difficult.

Administrators who are explicitly clear on what must be tight in an organization is a crucial component for making job crafting work. They should prioritize the non-negotiables. Think about it like the essential or priority standards—some content standards are more important than others. Having a loose-tight organization is similar; the organization prioritizes certain activities over others. Just as teachers will often try to argue all of the standards are equally important, some administrators believe everything they ask teachers to do is equally important—and they want all teachers to do everything the exact same way. And again, just as we advise teachers to emphasize the most important elements of what students need to know, administrators must do the same and prioritize teachers' actions. Not everything in the organization should be tight. When administrators don't differentiate between the tight and loose, teachers may believe everything must be tight and there is no flexibility for them to job craft.

School administrators are still captains of their own metaphorical ships. However, they must rely on the talents of an outstanding crew to make the voyage safely amid, at times, high seas. In fostering job crafting (smartly and within reason), school leaders should do the following.

- Create motivation, incentives, and opportunities to best allow job crafting to flourish in your school. In doing so, you encourage teachers to be malleable within established guidelines or guardrails. In short, create the administrative boundaries, then get out of the way of the teaching professionals—and enjoy what you see!

- With respect to technology, consider allowing teachers the choice between a Mac or a PC for their teacher device. Some prefer Macs, while others prefer PCs—just ask any Mac or PC user if they would want to switch platforms. Adopt a hardware-agnostic philosophy for allowing teachers the ability to choose their platform; this can significantly help teachers job craft. Having both platforms in use in the district requires tech savvy. However, since allowing this choice could help teachers with overall agency and creativity, it may be worth the effort.

- Allow teachers flexible hours on certain days. If students are not in the building (either before or after school), and there are no meetings scheduled, might teachers have the flexibility to work earlier or later as their personal needs and schedules allow? Even allowing teachers a fifteen- to twenty-minute flex to beginning and end times could have a real impact on their ability to job craft.

Conclusion

Here we'll return to Chandra's story to see how she was able to job craft.

> A month later, Chandra returned to the sushi counter, readying herself for another weekend of graduate classes. She mused at the opportunity to share one of her signature moves—as her professor would call them—she did over the past month. The principal asked teachers to facilitate a weekly advisory for purposes of ensuring each student in the building would take a more active role in setting personal goals for the coursework, something the principal learned from Hattie's (2009) Visible Learning book that impacts student achievement.
>
> While the school provided teachers a template of weekly activities and checklists for their advisories, the teachers did enjoy some latitude during this time, particularly because a veteran teacher involved in a book study proactively asked the principal at the start of the school year if she could deploy both art and science each week. "The templates and checklists are our science," she noted. "Whereas how we bring ourselves to advisory

> is the art part." Chandra liked that, and immediately thought of her professor's notion of signature moves when he was first proposed this idea.
>
> Each of the past four weeks, Chandra would think every Sunday evening, "What's going to be my signature move in advisory this week?" and then pondered, "How will my move uniquely help students?" During the first week, Chandra focused candidly and openly on her own vulnerability while with students. She wanted students to know it's OK to admit fear and ask for help. That was her signature. All the while, she handled checklists and templates her way. The second week, Chandra asked students to share their worst fears and best outcomes for the school year, not allowing others to judge or editorialize but simply thanking them for sharing their voice and vulnerability. That was her signature. She found out during lunch in the teacher's lounge that few of her colleagues thought hers was a good use of time. That was OK with her; she still did the minimum the templates and checklists required. The third week involved students talking about what they felt was important and not in the actual checklists and templates as they moved through the material. Chandra did not judge; she let students have their voice, a part of her signature. During the fourth week, Chandra found the students asking to prepare for advisory and facilitate the activities themselves—a truly student-run experience. Boom! That was as close to her signature as she could have wanted—very early on.
>
> Doing things her own way in a loose-tight system was fostering a foundational level of student engagement that would influence the larger tight goal of the overall initiative: Student agency and knowledge of what they are to accomplish and how they were doing helped them achieve success.

Job crafting is much easier to explain than do. It takes trust between teachers and administrators to pull off successful job crafting in any meaningful way. The benefit of doing so, however, is worth the time and effort it takes to create conditions that make job crafting feasible.

The responsibility heavily relies on administrator's actions and attitudes. In plenty of school districts, even the possibility of a teacher suggesting job crafting would be seen as a threat to leadership. Administrators must have a psychologically safe environment for teachers. There are no ifs, ands, or buts about it. School principals and district leaders may attempt to create some excuse or some reason as to why job crafting cannot occur, but it must.

While much is outside the control of district and building leaders, the impetus is on them to clearly articulate what areas teachers can job craft and what areas the district and school need to be tight on. Administrators must make difficult decisions but can't simply say everything must be done lockstep. Just as students are individuals, with individual strengths and talents, so are teachers. It is also imperative principals continue to work with key stakeholders to help them understand the importance of flexibility within the education system.

Now that we've discussed all eight of the elements of mattering, it's time to put them all together—and take action.

Next Steps: Chapter 8 Recap Activity

Fill in the following diagram from the chapter's beginning, this time with unique information pertinent to you and this foundational element in mattering.

The External Element of Job Crafting in Mattering	
Capability to make subtle changes to the work environment to meet individual needs	
Your Way to Conceive:	Job Crafting
Your Way to Believe:	
Your Way to Achieve:	

Ensuring Teachers Matter © 2024 Solution Tree Press • SolutionTree.com
Visit **go.SolutionTree.com/teacherefficacy** to download this free reproducible.

Your Personal Professional Development: Thought Experiment—Job Crafting

The following thought experiment gives you an opportunity to imagine a different reality. Take time to visualize the scenario. You may want to revisit these questions several times to get a complete picture. It takes practice. Find your quiet space and consider the possibilities.

Envision yourself as a consultant who has a flexible school schedule and travels the United States offering professional learning and speaking opportunities for educators. You are readying yourself for a keynote speech, turning on your lapel microphone as you ascend the steps to a stage where you will speak to a group of three thousand influencers who can change the course of what happens in U.S. schools and beyond.

Each audience member will receive a copy of your book, placed on their seats shortly before their arrival. Along with that book are five to ten sell sheets they can disseminate in their buildings. Each sell sheet includes a synopsis of your book, the cover image, and a code for immediate ordering for work friends and colleagues.

Here is what we would like you to share in this thought experiment.

First, what is the title of your book? *The title should reflect your particular expertise that is suitable for your own job crafting in your school.*

Next, what are three main takeaways audience members will learn from your speech? *Note that you can consider the takeaways as three* whats: *What three aspects of your job can you do differently?*

What one: _____

What two: _____

What three: _____

Finally, for each *what* you list, now create two or three *hows* that represent your brand or craft. *These are your distinctive ways of delivering as a teacher that make a positive difference in student learning excitement, interpersonal or behavioral well-being, and school achievement.*

What one: _____

» How a: _____

» How b: _____

» How c: _____

What two: _____

» How a: _____

» How b: _____

» How c: _____

Ensuring Teachers Matter © 2024 Solution Tree Press • SolutionTree.com
Visit **go.SolutionTree.com/teacherefficacy** to download this free reproducible.

What three: _____

> » How a: _____

> » How b: _____

> » How c: _____

Questions to ponder:

How important is job crafting to you in your workplace?

What resonates most with you about job crafting?

Do you see job crafting in your building? If so, where?

What is one small thing you can do to strengthen job crafting in yourself?

What can you do to expand job crafting opportunities for others?

CHAPTER 9

Putting It All Together: Smarter Stuff That Matters

The eight elements we describe in this book are critical to ensuring teachers matter. Mattering leads to higher career satisfaction and career longevity with fewer symptoms of depression (Flett, 2018). Teacher mattering leads to increases in collective efficacy, self-efficacy, and positive culture (Wilfong & Donlan, n.d.). All elements of mattering are essential not only for an individual's enjoyment as a teacher but also for the entire teaching profession.

There are two necessary steps to start the mattering journey. First, it is important for teachers and leaders to understand and identify the eight elements of mattering. Second, teachers must identify areas in most need of attention. The foundational elements of a mattering survey for K–12 teachers creates a quick way for teachers to determine their level of mattering to colleagues (as cited in Wilfong, 2021).

This chapter includes instructions for individual teachers and teacher leaders on how to use the survey. We also include self-reflection tools for teachers and teacher leaders as they address the sense of mattering in their school and district.

Readers may notice this chapter does not start with our conceive-believe-achieve framing device. Our intent is now to take the ideas on mattering we share throughout this book and actually put them into action. It's time to move past conceiving and believing, and get something done. You can do it!

Getting Started on Putting It All Together

Here, you'll find tools to create action items that ideally increase a sense of mattering in teachers. The foundational elements of the mattering survey and instructions on how to utilize it serve as launching points for the tools we include throughout the rest of the chapter. If you are using a tool to gauge your own sense of mattering, it is important for you to complete the survey first before moving on to any other tools. See figure 9.1 for an overview of this process. Each of the tools listed appears later in this chapter.

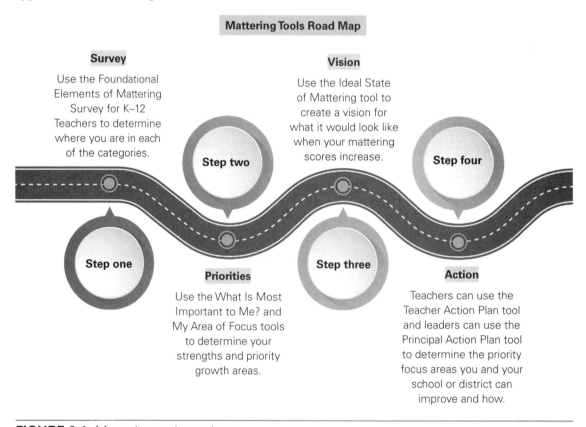

FIGURE 9.1: Mattering tools road map.

Foundational Elements of Mattering Survey for K–12 Teachers

> If school leaders understand the foundations of how or under what conditions teachers feel they matter, it could lead to a more positive work environment.

Mattering is feeling you are significant, and that others would miss you if you were gone, or *meaningful significance* (Rosenberg & McCullough, 1981). Understanding the elements that make up a teacher's sense of mattering is useful when trying to address some of the common problems educators face, including high stress levels, job dissatisfaction, and low pay. If school leaders understand the foundations of how or under what conditions teachers feel they matter, it could lead to a more positive work environment.

Putting It All Together: Smarter Stuff That Matters | 163

Following are instructions for completing the survey.

> 1. Read each statement in part one and indicate how each statement describes how you feel. Enter a score between 1–10 (1 = Never, 10 =Always).
> 2. Once you have rated each of the twenty-four questions, copy the scores into the corresponding white box in part two.
> 3. Complete the score summary box in part three by adding the scores for each column. Each column will have three scores.

See figure 9.2 for a completed survey example. Use the reproducible "Foundational Elements of Mattering Survey for K–12 Teachers" (page 172) to complete your own survey.

Foundational Elements of Mattering Survey for K–12 Teachers

Part one: Score each statement from 1 (never) to 10 (always).

	Score
1. I feel that my colleagues really care about me.	7
2. I lose track of time teaching or preparing because I am so involved in the activity.	6
3. I do not mind doing tasks that I don't like when I know it helps the overall goal.	8
4. I feel I am paid adequately for the job I do.	6
5. I am empowered to change daily routines to meet my needs as a teacher.	5
6. I feel teachers have a fairly stable job compared to the rest of society.	9
7. I believe I was called to do this job.	9
8. I can be the same person at home that I am at work.	5
9. I feel I belong among my colleagues.	4
10. When I am teaching, time seems to fly by during the day.	4
11. I don't mind doing tasks I don't like if I know it will serve a higher purpose within the organization.	5
12. I have protection from arbitrary termination.	10
13. My salary makes me feel like I am valued.	7
14. I can make changes to my job to make things run smoother.	5
15. I feel teaching is my reason for being.	3
16. I don't have to have a different image at work.	3

FIGURE 9.2: Foundational elements of mattering survey for K–12 teachers.   continued ▶

17. When I am teaching, I get totally immersed in what I am doing.		4
18. I can rely on my colleagues to help me.		6
19. I have a steady paycheck.		10
20. I don't have to compromise my feelings at work.		4
21. There are certain things I don't like doing, but the task is enjoyable because I know it will help meet our overall goals.		3
22. I am the best version of myself as a teacher.		4
23. My salary is comparable to other professions requiring the same skill level.		5
24. I am able to make adjustments to my work to be more productive.		5

Part two: Place your scores from part one in the white boxes. Place the total of those three scores in each column in the bottom row.

1. I feel that my colleagues really care about me.	7							
2. I lose track of time teaching or preparing because I am so involved in the activity.			6					
3. I do not mind doing tasks that I don't like when I know it helps the overall goal.					8			
4. I feel I am paid adequately for the job I do.						6		
5. I am empowered to change daily routines to meet my needs as a teacher.								5
6. I feel teachers have a fairly stable job compared to the rest of society.							9	
7. I believe I was called to do this job.				9				
8. I can be the same person at home that I am at work.		5						
9. I feel I belong among my colleagues.	4							
10. When I am teaching, time seems to fly by during the day.			4					
11. I don't mind doing tasks I don't like if I know it will serve a higher purpose within the organization.					5			
12. I have protection from arbitrary termination.							10	
13. My salary makes me feel like I am valued.						7		
14. I can make changes to my job to make things run smoother.								5
15. I feel teaching is my reason for being.				3				

		1	2	3	4	5	6	7	8
16. I don't have to have a different image at work.			3						
17. When I am teaching, I get totally immersed in what I am doing.					4				
18. I can rely on my colleagues to help me.		6							
19. I have a steady paycheck.									10
20. I don't have to compromise my feelings at work.			4						
21. There are certain things I don't like doing, but the task is enjoyable because I know it will help meet our overall goals.							3		
22. I am the best version of myself as a teacher.						4			
23. My salary is comparable to other professions requiring the same skill level.								5	
24. I am able to make adjustments to my work to be more productive.									5
Total:		17	12	14	16	16	18	29	15
		1	2	3	4	5	6	7	8

Part three: Summarize your scores by copying the total scores from part two in the following boxes. For example, the column 1 (Community) total in part two was 17, so you then write 17 in in the first row.

Category	Number	Element	Total Score
Interpersonal	1	Community	17
	2	Authenticity	12
	3	Flow	14
Intrapersonal	4	Purpose	16
	5	Assimilation	16
External	6	Compensation	18
	7	Stability	29
	8	Job crafting	15

Explanation of scoring:

Lower scores indicate areas that may need attention.

These scores do not have an average or mean; they are not normed. Scores are relative to the person completing the survey.

Categories with lower scores are areas in need of development, while categories with higher scores are elements stronger in the person completing the survey.

As you can see from the scores, this teacher may struggle a bit with authenticity and job crafting, while stability is very strong. It is important to remember these scores are relative to the individual, and it's difficult to compare one person's score directly with another's. It is not a normed scale—in other words, there is no established normal or average score. (Visit https://matteringk12.com for an online scale.)

Reflect on the relative importance of each element from the survey results in figure 9.2 (page 163). Use the reflection sheets included in the following sections to guide your thinking.

Teacher Reflection Tool: What Is Most Important to Me?

Everyone has different perceptions of which elements of mattering are important. Much depends on outside factors in teachers' life experiences, which shape their psychological needs.

When examining the elements of mattering, you must determine which factors are more important (and therefore need more emphasis), and which are less important. This can be difficult, so take time to reflect and thoughtfully consider these elements as they relate to you. You can refer to figure I.2 (page 10) for the eight elements.

See figure 9.3 for an example. The reproducible "Teacher Reflection Tool: What Is Most Important to Me?" (page 175) gives you the opportunity to fill in your own ideas.

Most Important Elements	Less Important Elements
Community and Stability	Purpose
Why?	Why?
I enjoy being around people and working with others.	I think I can find purpose in just about anything I do. Doing things with friends and family is more important, and I find my purpose in that.
I like the feeling of connection to others.	
I also like having a steady paycheck. I have bills to pay, and knowing I have a steady job is important!	

FIGURE 9.3: Teacher reflection tool: What is most important to me? example.

It is also important to understand because of different life experiences and situations, some elements may become more important and less important to you over time.

Teacher Reflection Tool: My Area of Focus Matrix

To help visualize how each element of mattering impacts you, see the example in figure 9.4. Ask yourself, "What is most important to me?" as your guide to complete the matrix. List the most important elements on the far left, and the less important items more toward the right on the continuum. Your score for each category will determine where you place it vertically on the chart. The reproducible "Teacher Reflection Tool: My Area of Focus Matrix" (page 176) gives you the opportunity to fill in your own ideas.

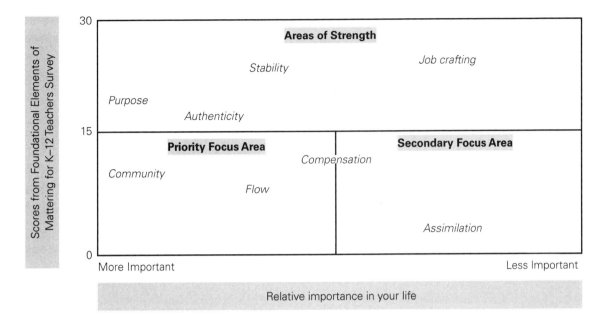

FIGURE 9.4: Teacher reflection tool: My area of focus matrix example.

The elements of mattering weigh differently in importance depending on the individual. What may be an important element for you may be less important for someone else. This makes mattering unique to everyone. In the example in figure 9.4, purpose and community are the most important elements, while job crafting and assimilation are less important. This may or may not be what your results show. In this example, the purpose score was 18, while the community score was 14. Categories in the lower left square of the matrix are the priority focus areas for this person. Even though assimilation had the lowest score, it is more important for this person to work on community and flow before concentrating on assimilation. Yours will be unique to you.

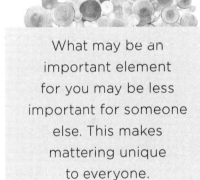

What may be an important element for you may be less important for someone else. This makes mattering unique to everyone.

Teacher Reflection Tool: The Ideal State of Mattering

Envisioning your identified priority focus areas, think about what each element would look, sound, and feel like if it would move from a low score to a high score. This is perhaps one of the most challenging tools to complete because it requires you to visualize and anticipate how things can change from your current reality. Take your time completing this activity. You may want to work on it, then let it sit for a few days before you come back to work on it again.

Do not let thinking something is impossible or unlikely to happen consume you. This is the time to focus on what each element would look like in a perfect situation. Not everything is going to be within your control, and for right now that's OK. Now is the time for dreaming (the *doing* comes next)! See the example in figure 9.5 (page 168) to imagine this ideal situation. The reproducible "Teacher Reflection Tool: The Ideal State of Mattering" (page 177) gives you the opportunity to fill in your own ideas.

Focus Priority: Community
Why is this a focus priority? What is missing from your current reality?
Community is very important to me. Being able to work with others collaboratively to bring about change is energizing. There is nothing better than accomplishing something worthwhile with others.
My team, and many people in my building, don't like working together as much as I do. I would rather co-plan with a team. We all get along and are friendly to one another but we don't really have meaningful conversations about teaching with one another. At my other school, we were not afraid to call out one another when we saw someone doing something they shouldn't, or we would give one another advice to help everyone improve. Here people are friendly, but they don't want to rock the boat or give suggestions on how to do something better because I think they are afraid others might not like them. We are a friendly bunch as long as we don't discuss anything to do with school.
Think about the focus priority in the ideal state. What would be different?
When we have conversations with one another about teaching, it's an effort to improve not just give one another a pat on the back (which is also sometimes deserved). If we were a true community, we would work to improve one another and discuss ways we could get better as a team. We would be willing to share our successes and failures to improve.
What would you and your colleagues be doing differently?
We would have conversations about how to help students (not just complain about them) and talk about how we teach—what works and what doesn't.
How would you feel?
I think I would feel more energetic about teaching. I would become more of a lab tester rather than just someone going through the motions. It would also give me something in common to talk about. Right now, everyone talks about their weekend plans with their families. I like to do online gaming, but no one is interested in that, so I feel left out. I know some teachers have been doing some great things, and I could really learn from them.
How would it sound?
Our discussions in the lunchroom would include some of the ways we are teaching and what works. You might hear someone say, "Hey does anyone have an idea on how to help a student who keeps blurting out answers?" Instead of getting a sarcastic answer, we would actually have a meaningful conversation about strategies. Everyone would benefit!
Think about your preceding statements—what would have to change to accomplish them?
I think people are afraid to be collegial because in this school, it isn't cool to be vulnerable and ask questions. The last principal would use your questions against you on the evaluation. People would need to feel safe to say things that might make others uncomfortable. Right now, people do everything they can to talk about anything but teaching and school. It just seems so fake to me.

FIGURE 9.5: Teacher reflection tool: The ideal state of mattering example.

Teacher Action Plan

Now is the time for action!

Use your answers from the Ideal State of Mattering Reflection Tool (see figure 9.5) as a guide to complete your action plan (see figure 9.6).

Take your answers from the question, What would have to change in order to accomplish this? And break them down into the most basic elements in the first column. You may need to use multiple rows for one statement.

What needs to change?	Who is responsible?	What will I do to move toward this change?	When will I do it?	What will progress in this area look like (success criteria)?
Psychological safety	Principal and building leadership team	Talk to the new principal about my concerns and see if she is aware of the culture.	Next week	Discussion with the principal leads to an actionable step.
Psychological safety	Grade-level team	Talk to my team and see what they think about discussions.	Right after I talk to the principal	My team sets aside time to talk about being vulnerable and what that looks like.
Difficult conversations	My work bestie (Allison) and me	I need to be more willing to step out of my comfort zone and have conversations about teaching with other people. I'm going to talk to Allison about teaming with me to get this done!	In the lunchroom at the start of next semester (three weeks away). Allison and I will hatch a plan together!	Allison and I start a conversation in the lunchroom every day or two to three times a week to get advice on how to deal with something going on in the classroom. If the conversation goes negative (which it usually does), we will be ready with a redirect to bring the conversation back to focusing on a solution.
Getting more on board	My work bestie (Allsion) and me (with funding from the principal)	Allsion and I are going to start a book study for one hour after work, every other week. The principal will provide the books on a topic about best-practice instruction. Once I get some others interested, we will pick the book together.	Two weeks after the semester starts	Allison and I will have our book study meet six times to discuss a book and things we implemented in class. We will set up norms to make sure the group stays on track.

FIGURE 9.6: Teacher action plan example.

In the next column, identify who is responsible for this particular action; it could be you, the principal, the superintendent, or someone else. The third column is the action step. Regardless of who is responsible, what are you going to do to move toward this change? For example, if the principal is responsible for the action step, you might write your plan to bring it up in a meeting with the principal or, if you think this action will impact the entire staff, at a principal leadership meeting.

Next, determine your deadline to take action. Be realistic. Do not try to address each item at the same time. Finally, create your success criteria with the goal to make progress in the far-right column. What will progress look like when you see positive change occurring? Chances are you will never get to the perfect state, yet you most assuredly can move toward the ideal.

What do you list first? Start with tasks easiest to accomplish quickly and then move to the most difficult tasks. Do not create too many items for the What needs to change? column. You may have fifty things to change, but that's overwhelming. Stick to a few items at one time and then, as you progress, revisit and add to the list (see figure 9.6). The reproducible "Teacher Action Plan" (page 178) gives you the opportunity to fill in your own ideas.

Principal Action Plan

If you would like to address teacher mattering schoolwide, do the following.

- Ask teachers to complete the Foundational Elements of Mattering Survey for K–12 Teachers (page 172).
- Encourage teachers to complete the Teacher Reflection Tool: My Area of Focus Matrix (page 176).
- Survey teachers anonymously to report their areas of focus categories.
- Use the results from the survey (page 172) to address teacher mattering in your school.

It may be tempting to give teachers the survey and use those results to determine the school's areas of focus. However, it is important to remember that each individual weighs the elements of mattering differently. Overall, a staff might score a particular element low; however, if the element is not that important to those individuals compared to other elements, it may not be as impactful when changes occur. By identifying the priority focus for individuals and using them as your starting point, you are more likely to make a bigger impact on teachers' sense of mattering. For example, the staff may score the element of flow low, but they might also rank flow as less important—so even big changes in flow might not bring the impact you hope for. As a leader, you must find the right combination of what needs to improve and the importance of the element among the teachers.

Use a chart with your teacher leadership team (or other designated group of teachers) to create the Principal Action Plan to address the priority focus area (see figure 9.7 for an example). The reproducible "Principal Action Plan" (page 197) gives you the opportunity to fill in your own ideas. When completing this chart, be sure to consider quick wins that can make a difference. This will give your team momentum to carry out more difficult changes. You will also want to have a mix of short- and long-term actions.

What area do teachers score with the most need based on the survey results? *Community*				
What needs to change?	Who is responsible?	What will I do to move toward this change?	When will I do it?	What will progress in this area look like (success criteria)?
A better balance between collegial and congenial conversations	Me, leadership team members, and the teachers, but mostly me —at least to get the ball rolling	Talk to leadership team members about having more collegial conversations and what that looks like. Ask, "We have collegial conversations in our meetings, why can't we expand that to the rest of the teachers?"	Our next leadership team meeting (next week)	The team will create some ideas on how we can accomplish this.
Psychological safety	Me	The staff didn't trust the previous principal. I'm new, so the teachers don't know me—yet. I need to be clear, consistent, and open in my communications with teachers.	Now!	My weekly newsletter to the staff will include various things I am doing, why these things are happening, and a new process to open communication.
Understanding how an effective PLC operates	Leadership team members and me	Leadership team members and I will model the PLC process during our next professional learning and discuss "PLC right" versus "PLC light."	Second Monday of the month	The leadership team and I will demonstrate a collaborative team meeting with teachers observing our discussion.
Building the PLC process	The building leadership team and me	Ongoing professional learning around the PLC process and how that can translate to student success.	Ongoing	By the end of the year, teachers will have a better understanding of the PLC process and will want to continue developing the system.
Celebrate!	Me and leadership team members	Celebrate the success of teachers and students—not just the obvious but little successes. leadership team members are going to brainstorm with me to figure out the things we can celebrate together.	Ongoing	The entire school will celebrate something we accomplish at least once a month (hopefully more!).

FIGURE 9.7: Principal action plan example.

We hope the tools in this chapter help take mattering from a nebulous concept to actions you can take in your school. Teachers need to matter, and students need teachers who feel they matter.

Foundational Elements of Mattering Survey for K–12 Teachers

Part one: Score each statement from 1 (never) to 10 (always).

		Score
1.	I feel that my colleagues really care about me.	
2.	I lose track of time teaching or preparing because I am so involved in the activity.	
3.	I do not mind doing tasks that I don't like when I know it helps the overall goal.	
4.	I feel I am paid adequately for the job I do.	
5.	I am empowered to change daily routines to meet my needs as a teacher.	
6.	I feel teachers have a fairly stable job compared to the rest of society.	
7.	I believe I was called to do this job.	
8.	I can be the same person at home that I am at work.	
9.	I feel I belong among my colleagues.	
10.	When I am teaching, time seems to fly by during the day.	
11.	I don't mind doing tasks I don't like if I know it will serve a higher purpose within the organization.	
12.	I have protection from arbitrary termination.	
13.	My salary makes me feel like I am valued.	
14.	I can make changes to my job to make things run smoother.	
15.	I feel teaching is my reason for being.	
16.	I don't have to have a different image at work.	
17.	When I am teaching, I get totally immersed in what I am doing.	
18.	I can rely on my colleagues to help me.	
19.	I have a steady paycheck.	
20.	I don't have to compromise my feelings at work.	
21.	There are certain things I don't like doing, but the task is enjoyable because I know it will help meet our overall goals.	
22.	I am the best version of myself as a teacher.	
23.	My salary is comparable to other professions requiring the same skill level.	
24.	I am able to make adjustments to my work to be more productive.	

Part two: Place your scores in the white boxes. Place the total of those three scores in each column in the bottom row.

1.	I feel that my colleagues really care about me.								
2.	I lose track of time teaching or preparing because I am so involved in the activity.								
3.	I do not mind doing tasks that I don't like when I know it helps the overall goal.								
4.	I feel I am paid adequately for the job I do.								
5.	I am empowered to change daily routines to meet my needs as a teacher.								
6.	I feel teachers have a fairly stable job compared to the rest of society.								
7.	I believe I was called to do this job.								
8.	I can be the same person at home that I am at work.								
9.	I feel I belong among my colleagues.								
10.	When I am teaching, time seems to fly by during the day.								
11.	I don't mind doing tasks I don't like if I know it will serve a higher purpose within the organization.								
12.	I have protection from arbitrary termination.								
13.	My salary makes me feel like I am valued.								
14.	I can make changes to my job to make things run smoother.								
15.	I feel teaching is my reason for being.								
16.	I don't have to have a different image at work.								
17.	When I am teaching, I get totally immersed in what I am doing.								
18.	I can rely on my colleagues to help me.								
19.	I have a steady paycheck.								
20.	I don't have to compromise my feelings at work.								
21.	There are certain things I don't like doing, but the task is enjoyable because I know it will help meet our overall goals.								
22.	I am the best version of myself as a teacher.								
23.	My salary is comparable to other professions requiring the same skill level.								
24.	I am able to make adjustments to my work to be more productive.								
Total:									
		1	2	3	4	5	6	7	8

Ensuring Teachers Matter © 2024 Solution Tree Press • SolutionTree.com
Visit **go.SolutionTree.com/teacherefficacy** to download this free reproducible.

Part three: Summarize your scores by copying the total scores from part two in the following boxes.

For example, so if the column 1 (Community) total in part two was 17, you would then write 17 in the first row.

Category	Number	Element	Total Score
Interpersonal	1	Community	
Interpersonal	2	Authenticity	
Interpersonal	3	Flow	
Intrapersonal	4	Purpose	
Intrapersonal	5	Assimilation	
External	6	Compensation	
External	7	Stability	
External	8	Job crafting	

Explanation of scoring:

Lower scores indicate areas that may need attention.

These scores do not have an average or mean; they are not normed. Scores are relative to the person completing the survey.

Categories with lower scores are areas in need of development, while categories with higher scores are elements stronger in the person completing the survey.

Teacher Reflection Tool: What Is Most Important to Me?

Most Important Elements	Less Important Elements
Why?	Why?

Ensuring Teachers Matter © 2024 Solution Tree Press • SolutionTree.com
Visit **go.SolutionTree.com/teacherefficacy** to download this free reproducible.

Teacher Reflection Tool: My Area of Focus Matrix

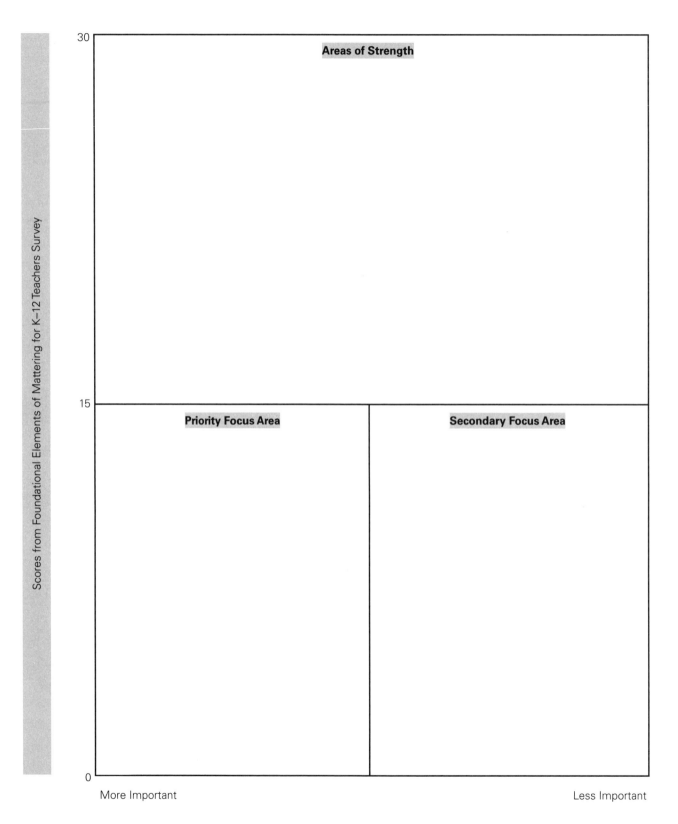

Teacher Reflection Tool: The Ideal State of Mattering

Focus Priority: _____

Why is this a focus priority? What is missing from your current reality?

Think about the focus priority in the ideal state. What would be different?   What would you and your colleagues be doing differently?   How would you feel?   How would it sound?

Think about the preceding statements—what would have to change to accomplish them?

Ensuring Teachers Matter © 2024 Solution Tree Press • SolutionTree.com
Visit **go.SolutionTree.com/teacherefficacy** to download this free reproducible.

Teacher Action Plan

What needs to change?	Who is responsible?	What will I do to move toward this change?	When will I do it?	What will progress in this area look like (success criteria)?

Ensuring Teachers Matter © 2024 Solution Tree Press • SolutionTree.com
Visit **go.SolutionTree.com/teacherefficacy** to download this free reproducible.

Principal Action Plan

What area do teachers score with the most need based on the survey results? _____

What needs to change?	Who is responsible?	What will I do to move toward this change?	When will I do it?	What will progress in this area look like (success criteria)?

Epilogue:
A Fair Adieu

We end our book near where we began, with encouragement to reframe the way you think about the other adults in your school, and what you must first do for teachers to tend most to the needs of students. First, ensure teachers matter to one another. That aspect of mattering is in addition to other ways teachers matter, such as for what they do for students, learning, families, and the community.

Adults' perspectives regarding other adults in schools are powerful. Ties of teachers to other members of their team provide synergy, allowing energy to do one of life's most challenging tasks—make a positive difference in the lives of students (who, by the way, are not coming to school any easier to educate). Society's competing influences, whether social media's instantaneous gratification or narratives countering the benefits of long-term educational investment, are enough to make teaching, well, arduous at the minimum, and at most, a necessary team sport, if done well.

> There is a special place for mattering among teachers. As a group, teachers complete tasks each day with a difficulty level continuously dialed up due to factors outside their immediate control.

This brings up a question, Why teachers? Why is mattering so important in the education profession, and are the same needs present in other professions? Think about accountants, social workers, or mid-level managers in corporate settings—Does mattering matter to them as well? Most likely. However, there is a special place for mattering among teachers. As a group, teachers complete tasks each day with a difficulty level continuously dialed up due to factors outside their immediate control. Also, when operating in full view of others—or at least in having one's outcomes public—mattering *matters*!

So where do we go, in terms of our fair adieu? What might we leave with you as this book's conclusion?

It's this.

Understand that in schools, it's not just about the students. It never has been, and it never will be. Remember the tree we talked about in the introduction? It's never just about the leaves, the branches, and all else that flourishes upon it. It never has been. It never will be. Something more deeply rooted matters in schools. Something much more foundational is providing life, sustenance, and potential for all the good and all the growth to take place. In our case, it's teacher mattering. And in situations where leaders, pundits, and policymakers profess otherwise, just give it time, and turnover and burnout will come knocking. Residually and directly, students will end up suffering if the adults in their school do not take care of one another.

School is first about the adults, those putting their craft on the line, making a difference for the students they love, in full view of others, and bearing the burden of all society's shortfalls because of a perplexing combination of societal abrogation locally, and larger state and national narratives perpetuating a need to blame teachers. Isn't it interesting how many educators fall prey to this storyline, thinking fondly of their own schools while all too eager to point the finger at others?

Instead, reframe the finger-pointing with a new and long-overdue self-utterance: "Teachers matter; teachers deserve to take care of themselves *first*, so they can best take care of the students in all local communities *most*." Doing so will ensure more positive pathways of teacher retention, satisfaction, and success. Teachers will talk their own students into following in their footsteps once again—and similarly do so returning home each evening, around the dinner table, with their own children.

References and Resources

Agyapong, B., Obuobi-Donkor, G., Burback, L., & Wei, Y. (2022). Stress, burnout, anxiety and depression among teachers: A scoping review. *International Journal of Environmental Research and Public Health*, *19*(17), 10706. https://doi.org/10.3390/ijerph191710706

Allegretto, S. (2022, August 16). *The teacher pay penalty has hit a new high: Trends in teacher wages and compensation through 2021.* Washington, DC: Economic Policy Institute. Accessed at https://files.epi.org/uploads/251657.pdf on April 18, 2023.

Allegretto, S., & Mishel, L. (2016, August 9). *The teacher pay gap is wider than ever: Teachers' pay continues to fall further behind pay of comparable workers.* Washington, DC: Economic Policy Institute. Accessed at https://files.eric.ed.gov/fulltext/ED568892.pdf on April 18, 2023.

Allegretto, S., & Mishel, L. (2018, September 5). *The teacher pay penalty has hit a new high: Trends in the teacher wage and compensation gaps through 2017.* Washington, DC: Economic Policy Institute. Accessed at https://files.eric.ed.gov/fulltext/ED593401.pdf on April 18, 2023.

Amabile, T., & Kramer, S. (2011). *The progress principle: Using small wins to ignite joy, engagement, and creativity at work.* Boston: Harvard Business Review Press.

American Federation of Teachers. (2017). *2017 educator quality of work life survey.* Washington, DC: Author. Accessed at www.aft.org/sites/default/files/2017_eqwl_survey_web.pdf on April 18, 2023.

Amundson, N. E. (1993). Mattering: A foundation for employment counseling and training. *Journal of Employment Counseling, 30*(4), 146–152. https://doi.org/10.1002/j.2161-1920.1993.tb00173.x

Anderson, K. N., Swedo, E. A., Trinh, E., Ray, C. M., Krause, K. H., Verlenden, J. V., et al. (2022). Adverse childhood experiences during the COVID-19 pandemic and associations with poor mental health and suicidal behaviors among high school students—Adolescent Behaviors and Experiences Survey, United States, January–June 2021. *Morbidity and Mortality Weekly Report, 71*(41), 1301–1305.

Anderson, M. (2010). *The well-balanced teacher: How to work smarter and stay sane inside the classroom and out.* Alexandria, VA: ASCD.

Aragon, S. (2016, May). *Teacher shortages: What we know.* Denver, CO: Education Commission of the States. Accessed at https://files.eric.ed.gov/fulltext/ED565893.pdf on April 18, 2023.

Ashforth, B. E., & Schinoff, B. S. (2016). Identity under construction: How individuals come to define themselves in organizations. *Annual Review of Organizational Psychology and Organizational Behavior, 3*(1), 111–137.

Autonomy. (n.d.) In *Online Etymology Dictionary.* Accessed at https://etymonline.com/word/autonomy on June 2, 2023.

Bailey, J. P., & Hess, F. M. (2020, May). *A blueprint for back to school.* Washington, DC: American Enterprise Institute. Accessed at https://cace.org/wp-content/uploads/2020/05/A-Blueprint-for-Back-to-School.pdf on April 18, 2023.

Baker, B. D. (2017, December). *How money matters for schools.* Palo Alto, CA: Learning Policy Institute. Accessed at https://learningpolicyinstitute.org/media/384/download?inline&file=How_Money_Matters_REPORT.pdf on April 18, 2023.

Bandura, A. (1977). Self-efficacy: Toward a unifying theory of behavioral change. *Psychological Review, 84*(2), 191–215. https://doi.org/10.1037/0033-295X.84.2.191

Barker, E. (2017). *Barking up the wrong tree: The surprising science behind why everything you know about success is (mostly) wrong.* New York: HarperOne.

Barnum, M. (2023, March 6). *Teacher turnover hits new highs across the U.S.* Accessed at https://chalkbeat.org/2023/3/6/23624340/teacher-turnover-leaving-the-profession-quitting-higher-rate on July 10, 2023.

Baron, E. J., Hyman, J. M., & Vasquez, B. N. (2022, March). *Public school funding, school quality, and adult crime* (EdWorkingPaper 29855). Accessed at https://nber.org/papers/w29855 on July 19, 2023.

Barrett, K. (2018, August 1). *The evidence is clear: More money for schools means better student outcomes.* Accessed at www.nea.org/nea-today/all-news-articles/evidence-clear-more-money-schools-means-better-student-outcomes on August 16, 2023.

Barth, R. S. (2006, March 1). Improving relationships within the schoolhouse. *Educational Leadership, 63*(6), 8. Accessed at https://ascd.org/publications/educational-leadership/mar06/vol63/num06/Improving-Relationships-Within-the-Schoolhouse.aspx on April 18, 2023.

Behrstock-Sherratt, E. (2016, June). *Creating coherence in the teacher shortage debate: What policy leaders should know and do.* Arlington, VA: American Institutes for Research.

Benisek, A. (2022, September 26). *What is frequency illusion?* Accessed at https://webmd.com/mental-health/what-is-frequency-illusion on July 19, 2023.

Bennis, W., & Biederman, P. W. (2007). *Organizing genius: The secrets of creative collaboration* [Kindle version]. New York: Basic Books.

Berman, E. M., West, J. P., & Richter, M. N., Jr. (2002). Workplace relations: Friendship patterns and consequences (according to managers). *Public Administration Review, 62*(2), 217–230. https://doi.org/10.1111/0033-3352.00172

Bethell, C. D., Davis, M. B., Gombojav, N., Stumbo, S., & Powers, K. (2017, October). *Issue brief: A national and across-state profile on Adverse Childhood Experiences among U.S. children and possibilities to heal and thrive.* Baltimore, MD: Johns Hopkins Bloomberg School of Public Health. Accessed at https://greatcircle.org/images/pdfs/aces-brief-101717.pdf on April 18, 2023.

Black, J. S., & Gregersen, H. B. (2002). *Leading strategic change: Breaking through the brain barrier.* Hoboken, NJ: Prentice Hall.

Bleiberg, J., Brunner, E., Harbatkin, E., Kraft, M. A., & Springer, M. G. (2021). *The effect of teacher evaluation on achievement and attainment: Evidence from statewide reforms* [EdWorkingPaper 21–496]. Providence, RI: Annenberg Institute. Accessed at https://edworkingpapers.com/sites/default/files/ai21-496.pdf on April 18, 2023.

Bloom, B. S. (Ed.). (1956). *Taxonomy of educational objectives: The classification of educational goals, Handbook I: Cognitive domain.* New York: McKay.

Bohannon, L. F. (2019). *Beginner's pluck: Build your life of purpose and impact now.* Grand Rapids, MI: Baker.

Boogren, T. H. (2020). *180 days of self-care for busy educators.* Bloomington, IN: Solution Tree Press.

Boser, U., & Straus, C. (2014, July 23). *Mid- and late-career teachers struggle with paltry incomes.* Washington, DC: Center for American Progress. Accessed at https://americanprogress.org/issues/education-K-12/reports/2014/07/23/94168/mid-and-late-career-teachers-struggle-with-paltry-incomes on April 18, 2023.

Bruno, R. (2018, June 20). *When did the U.S. stop seeing teachers as professionals?* Accessed at https://hbr.org/2018/06/when-did-the-u-s-stop-seeing-teachers-as-professionals on July 19, 2023.

Bryant, J., Ram, S., Scott, D., & Williams, C. (2023, March 2). *K–12 teachers are quitting. What would make them stay?* Accessed at https://mckinsey.com/industries/education/our-insights/k-12-teachers-are-quitting-what-would-make-them-stay on July 19, 2023.

Busser, C. (2019, April 29). *Average teacher salary down 4.5 percent, NEA report finds* [Press release]. Accessed at https://nea.org/about-nea/media-center/press-releases/average-teacher-salary-down-45-percent-nea-report-finds on July 20, 2023.

Campbell, D. E. (2006). What is education's impact on civic and social engagement? In R. Desjardins & T. Schuller (Eds.), *Measuring the effects of education on health and civic engagement: Proceedings of the Copenhagen Symposium* (pp. 25–126). Accessed at https://oecd.org/education/innovation-education/37437718.pdf on July 19, 2023.

Chapman, G., & White, P. (2019). *The five languages of appreciation in the workplace: Empowering organizations by encouraging people* (Updated ed.). Chicago: Northfield.

Cheng, A., Henderson, M. B., Peterson, P. E., & West, M. R. (2019). *Public support climbs for teacher pay, school expenditures, charter schools, and universal vouchers: Results from the 2018 EdNext poll*. Accessed at www.educationnext.org/public-support-climbs-teacher-pay-school-expenditures-charter-schools-universal-vouchers-2018-ednext-poll on May 31, 2023.

Community. (n.d.). In *Oxford English Dictionary*. Accessed at https://oed.com/viewdictionaryentry/Entry/37337 on July 10, 2023.

Conzemius, A. E., & Morganti-Fisher, T. (2015, April 24). *Choosing pride over fear* [Blog post]. Accessed at https://solutiontree.com/blog/choosing-pride-over-fear on April 18, 2023.

Corna, H. M. (2021, April 13). *Is money the biggest motivator for employees?* Accessed at https://linkedin.com/pulse/money-biggest-motivator-employees-hilary-m-corna on July 19, 2023.

Costin, V., & Vignoles, V. L. (2020). Meaning is about mattering: Evaluating coherence, purpose, and existential mattering as precursors of meaning in life judgments. *Journal of Personality and Social Psychology, 118*(4), 864–884.

Crum, A. J., Salovey, P., & Achor, S. (2013). Rethinking stress: The role of mindsets in determining the stress response. *Journal of Personality and Social Psychology, 104*(4), 716–733. https://doi.org/10.1037/a0031201

Csikszentmihalyi, M. (2008). *Flow: The psychology of optimal experience*. New York: Harper Perennial.

Curry, J. R., & Bickmore, D. (2012). School counselor induction and the importance of mattering. *Professional School Counseling, 15*(3), 110–122. https://doi.org/10.1177/2156759X1201500301

Dahlgren, R., Hyaatt, J., & Dobbins, C. (2007). *Time to teach: Encouragement, empowerment, and excellence in every classroom.* Washington, DC: Center for Teacher Effectiveness.

Darling-Hammond, L., Furger, R., Shields, P. M., & Sutcher, L. (2016). *Addressing California's emerging teacher shortage: An analysis of sources and solutions.* Palo Alto, CA: Learning Policy Institute. Accessed at https://learningpolicyinstitute.org/sites/default/files/product-files/LPI-Report-AddressingCA_TeacherShortage.pdf on April 19, 2023.

Darling-Hammond, L., & Podolsky, A. (2019). Breaking the cycle of teacher shortages: What kind of policies can make a difference? *Education Policy Analysis Archives, 27*(34). Accessed at https://epaa.asu.edu/ojs/article/download/4633/2226 on April 19, 2023.

Davies, T. (2019, July 11). *Indiana's state budget reserve jumps to $2.3 billion.* Accessed at https://apnews.com/article/a697238133344cbbb59a6d58e0d5c26b on May 31, 2023.

Denver Classroom Teachers Association. (n.d.). *The $100,000 teacher plan.* Accessed at https://denverteachers.org/the-100000-teacher-plan on April 19, 2023.

Dhiman, S. (2007). Personal mastery: Our quest for self-actualization, meaning, and highest purpose. *Interbeing, 1*(1), 25–35.

Donlan, R. (2022). *All other duties as assigned: The assistant principal's critical role in supporting schools inside and out.* Bloomington, IN: Solution Tree Press.

Donohoo, J., Hattie, J., & Eells, R. (2018, March 1). The power of collective efficacy. *Educational Leadership, 75*(6). Accessed at https://ascd.org/el/articles/the-power-of-collective-efficacy on July 24, 2023.

Duckworth, A. (2016). *Grit: The power of passion and perseverance.* New York: Scribner.

DuFour, R. (2004, May). *What is a "professional learning community"?* Accessed at https://allthingsplc.info/files/uploads/DuFourWhatIsAProfessionalLearningCommunity.pdf on July 17, 2023.

DuFour, R., DuFour, R., Eaker, R., & Many, T. W. (2010). *Learning by doing: A handbook for Professional Learning Communities at Work* (2nd ed.). Bloomington, IN: Solution Tree Press.

DuFour, R., DuFour, R., Eaker, R., Many, T. W., & Mattos, M. (2016). *Learning by doing: A handbook for Professional Learning Communities at Work* (3rd ed.). Bloomington, IN: Solution Tree Press.

DuFour, R., DuFour, R., Eaker, R., Mattos, M., & Muhammad, A. (2021). *Revisiting Professional Learning Communities at Work: Proven insights for sustained, substantive school improvement* (2nd ed.). Bloomington, IN: Solution Tree Press.

Duhigg, C. (2014). *The power of habit: Why we do what we do in life and business.* New York: Random House.

Education Resource Strategies. (2023, May 11). *Examining school-level teacher turnover trends: A new angle on a pervasive issue.* Accessed at https://erstrategies.org/tap/teacher_turnover_trends_analysis on July 19, 2023.

Elliott, G., Kao, S., & Grant, A.-M. (2004). Mattering: Empirical validation of a social-psychological concept. *Self and Identity, 3*(4), 339–354. https://doi.org/10.1080/13576500444000119

Elmore, R. F. (Ed.). (2011). *I used to think . . . and now I think . . . : Twenty leading educators reflect on the work of school reform.* Cambridge, MA: Harvard Education Press.

Felitti, V. J., Anda, R. F., Nordenberg, D., Williamson, D. F., Spitz, A. M., Edwards, V., et al. (1998). Relationship of childhood abuse and household dysfunction to many of the leading causes of death in adults: The Adverse Childhood Experiences (ACE) study. *American Journal of Preventive Medicine, 14*(4), 245–258. https://doi.org/10.1016/s0749-3797(98)00017-8

Flett, G. L. (2018). *The psychology of mattering: Understanding the human need to be significant.* San Diego, CA: Academic Press.

Florida Department of Education. (2019, September 30). *Florida first state in nation to teach K–12 child trafficking prevention* [Press release]. Accessed at https://fldoe.org/newsroom/latest-news/florida-first-state-in-nation-to-teach-k-12-child-trafficking-prevention.stml on May 31, 2023.]

Frankl, V. E. (1992). *Man's search for meaning: An introduction to logotherapy* (4th ed.). Boston: Beacon Press.

Frankl, V. E. (2006). *Man's search for meaning.* Boston: Beacon Press.

Friend. (n.d.). In *Merriam-Webster's online dictionary.* Accessed at https://merriam-webster.com/dictionary/friend on May 30, 2023.

Gagné, M., Forest, J., Gilbert, M.-H., Aubé, C., Morin, E., & Malorni, A. (2010). The motivation at work scale: Validation evidence in two languages. *Educational and Psychological Measurement, 70*(4), 628–646. https://doi.org/10.1177/0013164409355698

García, H., & Miralles, F. (2017). *Ikigai: The Japanese secret to a long and happy life* (H. Cleary, Trans.). New York: Penguin.

George, L. S., & Park, C. L. (2016). Meaning in life as comprehension, purpose, and mattering: Toward integration and new research questions. *Review of General Psychology, 20*(3), 205–220. https://doi.org/10.1037/gpr0000077

Glazerman, S., & Seifullah, A. (2012, March 7). *An evaluation of the Chicago Teacher Advancement Program (Chicago TAP) after four years.* Washington, DC: Mathematica Policy Research. Accessed at https://mathematica.org/publications/an-evaluation-of-the-chicago-teacher-advancement-program-chicago-tap-after-four-years on April 19, 2023.

Gmelch, W. H. (1983). Stress for success: How to optimize your performance. *Theory Into Practice, 22*(1), 7–14. https://doi.org/10.1080/00405848309543031

Godin, S. (2008). *Tribes: We need you to lead us.* New York: Portfolio.

Goldstein, D. (2015). *The teacher wars: A history of America's most embattled profession*. New York: Anchor Books.

Gould, E. (2019, October 10). *Back-to-school jobs report shows a continued shortfall in public education jobs*. Accessed at https://epi.org/publication/back-to-school-jobs-report-shows-a-continued-shortfall-in-public-education-jobs on April 19, 2023.

GovTrack.us. (2023). *H.R. 1532—112th Congress: Race to the Top Act of 2011*. Accessed at www.govtrack.us/congress/bills/112/hr1532 on April 19, 2023.

Grandey, A., Foo, S. C., Groth, M., & Goodwin, R. E. (2012). Free to be you and me: A climate of authenticity alleviates burnout from emotional labor. *Journal of Occupational Health Psychology*, *17*(1), 1–14.

Greene, C. M., Morgan, J. C., Traywick, L. S., & Mingo, C. A. (2017). Evaluation of a laughter-based exercise program on health and self-efficacy for exercise. *The Gerontologist*, *57*(6), 1051–1061. https://doi.org/10.1093/geront/gnw105

Guillebeau, C. (2014). *The happiness of pursuit: Finding the quest that will bring purpose to your life*. New York: Harmony Books.

Haig, M. (2021). *The comfort book*. New York: Penguin Life.

Haim-Litevsky, D., Komemi, R., & Lipskaya-Velikovsky, L. (2023). Sense of belonging, meaningful daily life participation, and well-being: Integrated investigation. *International Journal of Environmental Research and Public Health*, *20*(5), 4121. http://dx.doi.org/10.3390/ijerph20054121

Hargreaves, A. (2015). Autonomy and transparency: Two good ideas gone bad. In J. Evers & R. Kneyber (Eds.), *Flip the system: Changing education from the ground up* (pp. 120–133). New York: Routledge.

Hargreaves, A., & O'Connor, M. T. (2017). Cultures of professional collaboration: Their origins and opponents. *Journal of Professional Capital and Community*, *2*(2), 74–85. https://doi.org/10.1108/jpcc-02-2017-0004

Hart Research Associates (2022). *Under siege: The outlook of AFT members* [Slide presentation]. Accessed at https://aft.org/sites/default/files/media/2022/de-14326_aft_member_survey.pdf on July 19, 2023.

Hattie, J. (2003, October). *Teachers make a difference: What is the research evidence?* [Conference presentation]. Presented at the Building Teacher Quality: What Does the Research Tell Us ACER Research Conference, Melbourne, Australia. Accessed at https://research.acer.edu.au/cgi/viewcontent.cgi?article=1003&context=research_conference_2003 on April 19, 2023.

Hattie, J. (2009). *Visible learning: A synthesis of over 800 meta-analyses relating to achievement*. New York: Routledge.

Hayton, J. C., Carnabuci, G., & Eisenberger, R. (2012). With a little help from my colleagues: A social embeddedness approach to perceived organizational support. *Journal of Organizational Behavior*, *33*(2), 235–249. https://doi.org/10.1002/job.755

Heath, C., & Heath, D. (2010). *Switch: How to change things when change is hard*. New York: Broadway Books.

Heath, C., & Heath, D. (2017). *The power of moments: Why certain experiences have extraordinary impact*. New York: Simon & Schuster.

Hemphill, A. (2018, July). *How teachers in the U.S. and Finland see their jobs*. Alexandria, VA: Center for Public Education. Accessed at https://files.eric.ed.gov/fulltext/ED608846.pdf on April 19, 2023.

Herron, A. (2019, May 10). Indiana's May school referendums failed at their highest rate in eight years. Here's why that might be. *IndyStar*. Accessed at https://indystar.com/story/news/education/2019/05/10/indiana-school-referendumsprimary-election-proposals-pass-lowest-rate-8-years/1140740001 on April 19, 2023.

Howes, L. M., & Goodman-Delahunty, J. (2015). Teachers' career decisions: Perspectives on choosing teaching careers, and on staying or leaving. *Issues in Educational Research, 25*(1), 18–35. Accessed at https://iier.org.au/iier25/howes.pdf on April 19, 2023.

Hughes, G. D. (2012). Teacher retention: Teacher characteristics, school characteristics, organizational characteristics, and teacher efficacy. *The Journal of Educational Research, 105*(4), 245–255. https://doi.org/10.1080/00220671.2011.584922

Hülsheger, U. R., & Schewe, A. F. (2011). On the costs and benefits of emotional labor: A meta-analysis of three decades of research. *Journal of Occupational Health Psychology, 16*(3), 361–389. https://doi.org/10.1037/a0022876

Hunter, J. (2015, February 26). *A bad system will beat a good person every time*. Accessed at https://deming.org/a-bad-system-will-beat-a-good-person-every-time on April 19, 2023.

Imonitie, D. (2020). *Conceive believe achieve: Create a burning desire master the skills to win work in faith*. Houston, TX: Di Angelo.

Indiana Department of Education Office of Legislative Affairs. (2019). *UPDATED—Required trainings for school employees*. Accessed at https://in.gov/doe/files/Educator-Training-2022.6.24b.pdf on July 19, 2023.

Indiana State Teachers Association. (n.d.a). *ISTA 2017 legislative review*. Accessed at https://ista-in.org/uploads/2017-Legislative-Review.pdf on April 19, 2023.

Indiana State Teachers Association. (n.d.b). *Legislative summary 2019*. Accessed at https://ista-in.org/uploads/2019-Legislative-Summary.pdf on April 19, 2023.

Indiana State Teachers Association. (2017, April 26). *2017 legislative review*. Accessed at https://ista-in.org/2017-legislative-review on April 19, 2023.

Ingersoll, R. M., & Collins, G. J. (2018). The status of teaching as a profession. In J. H. Ballantine, J. Z. Spade, & J. M. Stuber (Eds.), *Schools and society: A sociological approach to education* (6th ed., pp. 199–212). Thousand Oaks, CA: SAGE.

Institute of Education Sciences. (2022, May). *School pulse panel—Student behavior.* Accessed at https://ies.ed.gov/schoolsurvey/spp on July 10, 2023.

Jaramillo, S. (2019, August 23). *Finding ikigai through engaging work.* Accessed at https://ibj.com/articles/finding-ikigai-through-engaging-work on July 19, 2023.

Jennings, R. E., Lanaj, K., Koopman, J., & McNamara, G. (2022). Reflecting on one's best possible self as a leader: Implications for professional employees at work. *Personnel Psychology, 75*(1), 69–90.

Joseph, S. (2019, January 2). *What is eudaimonic happiness? How and why positive psychologists are learning from Aristotle* [Blog post]. Accessed at https://psychologytoday.com/us/blog/what-doesnt-kill-us/201901/what-is-eudaimonic-happiness on July 19, 2023.

Jung, A.-K. (2015). Interpersonal and societal mattering in work: A review and critique. *The Career Development Quarterly, 63*(3), 194–208. https://doi.org/10.1002/cdq.12013

Kaado, B. (2023, March 17). *Money isn't enough: Six incentives to motivate your employees.* Accessed at https://businessnewsdaily.com/10731-money-not-enough.html on July 19, 2023.

Kahler, T. (2008). *The process therapy model: The six personality types with adaptations.* Little Rock, AR: Author.

Kanold, T. D. (2017). *HEART! Fully forming your professional life as a teacher and leader.* Bloomington, IN: Solution Tree Press.

Kanold, T. D. (2021). *SOUL! Fulfilling the promise of your professional life as a teacher and leader.* Bloomington, IN: Solution Tree Press.

Kanold, T. D., & Boogren, T. H. (2022). *Educator wellness: A guide for sustaining physical, mental, emotional, and social well-being.* Bloomington, IN: Solution Tree Press.

Kenworthy, J., Fay, C., Frame, M., & Petree, R. (2014). A meta-analytic review of the relationship between emotional dissonance and emotional exhaustion. *Journal of Applied Social Psychology, 44*(2), 94–105.

Kim, J., Shin, Y., Tsukayama, E., & Park, D. (2020). Stress mindset predicts job turnover among preschool teachers. *Journal of School Psychology, 78*(5), 13–22. https://doi.org/10.1016/j.jsp.2019.11.002

Kirkhus, D. K. (2011). *Contributory factors to teachers' sense of community in public urban elementary schools* [Unpublished doctoral dissertation]. Seton Hall University.

Kirst, M. W. (2010). The political and policy dynamics of K–12 education reform from 1965 to 2010: Implications for changing postsecondary education. *Research Priorities for Broad Access Higher Education.* Accessed at https://cepa.stanford.edu/content/political-and-policy-dynamics-k-12-education-reform-1965-2010-implications-changing-postsecondary-education on July 24, 2023.

Kraft, M. A., Brunner, E. J., Dougherty, S. M., & Schwegman, D. J. (2020). Teacher accountability reforms and the supply and quality of new teachers. *Journal of Public Economics, 188*, 104212.

Kreber, C., Klampfleitner, M., McCune, V., Bayne, S., & Knottenbelt, M. (2007). What do you mean by "authentic"? A comparative review of the literature on conceptions of authenticity in teaching. *Adult Education Quarterly, 58*(1), 22–43.

Kruger, J., & Dunning, D. (1999). Unskilled and unaware of it: How difficulties in recognizing one's own incompetence lead to inflated self-assessments. *Journal of Personality and Social Psychology, 77*(6), 1121–1134.

Kyriacou, C. (2011). Teacher stress: From prevalence to resilience. In J. Langan-Fox & C. L. Cooper (Eds.), *Handbook of stress in the occupations* (pp. 161–173). Northampton, MA: Elgar.

Lankford, H., Loeb, S., McEachin, A., Miller, L. C., & Wyckoff, J. (2014). Who enters teaching? Encouraging evidence that the status of teaching is improving. *Educational Researcher, 43*(9), 444–453. https://doi.org/10.3102/0013189X14563600

Leachman, M. (2017, November 29). *K–12 funding in some states still far below pre-recession levels* [Blog post]. Accessed at https://cbpp.org/blog/K-12-funding-in-some-states-still-far-below-pre-recession-levels on April 19, 2023.

Lee, S.-L., Chan, H.-S., Tong, Y.-Y., & Chiu, C.-Y. (2023). Growth mindset predicts teachers' life satisfaction when they are challenged to innovate their teaching. *Journal of Pacific Rim Psychology, 17.* https://doi.org/10.1177/18344909231167533

Lilly Endowment. (n.d.). *Teacher Creativity Fellowship: A program for personal renewal of Indiana educators*. Accessed at https://lillyendowment.org/for-grantseekers/renewal-programs/teacher-creativity on July 31, 2023.

Lundin, S. C., Paul, H., & Christensen J. (2000). *Fish! A proven way to boost morale and improve results*. New York: Hachette Books.

Mackay, H. (1997). *Dig your well before you're thirsty: The only networking book you'll ever need*. New York: Currency/Doubleday.

Marie, R. (2022). *Turning stress into success: Changing beliefs about stress using neuroscience-informed stress education during adolescence* [Doctoral dissertation, James Cook University]. Accessed at https://researchonline.jcu.edu.au/75538/1/JCU_75538_Marie_2022_thesis.pdf on July 19, 2023.

Marzano, R. J. (2007). *The art and science of teaching: A comprehensive framework for effective instruction*. Alexandria, VA: ASCD.

Maslow, A. H. (1943). A theory of human motivation. *Psychological Review, 50*(4), 370–396.

Mattos, M. (2022, August 1). *The urgency of the moment* [Keynote address]. PLC at Work Institute, Lincolnshire, IL.

McCarthy, C. J., Blaydes, M., Weppner, C. H., & Lambert, R. G. (2022). Teacher stress and COVID-19: Where do we go from here? *Phi Delta Kappan, 104*(1), 12–17. https://doi.org/10.1177/00317217221123643

McCluney, C. L., Robotham, K., Lee, S., Smith, R., & Durkee. M. (2019, November 15). *The costs of code-switching.* Accessed at https://hbr.org/2019/11/the-costs-of-codeswitching on May 30, 2023.

McKeown, G. (2021). *Effortless: Make it easier to do what matters most.* New York: Currency.

McLeod, L. E. (2016). *Leading with noble purpose: How to create a tribe of true believers.* Hoboken, NJ: Wiley.

MetLife. (2013, February). *The MetLife survey of the American teacher: Challenges for school leadership—A survey of teachers and principals.* New York: Author. Accessed at https://metlife.com/content/dam/microsites/about/corporate-profile/MetLife-Teacher-Survey-2012.pdf on April 19, 2023.

Michael, M. (2022). *From burnt out to fired up: Reigniting your passion for teaching.* Bloomington, IN: Solution Tree Press.

Mielke, C. (2019). *The burnout cure: Learning to love teaching again.* Alexandria, VA: ASCD.

Miller, J., & Adkins, A. (2016, December 14). *Women want close relationships at work.* Accessed at https://news.gallup.com/businessjournal/199349/women-close-relationships-work.aspx on July 10, 2023.

Mitra, D. (2011). *Pennsylvania's best investment: The social and economic benefits of public education.* Accessed at https://elc-pa.org/wp-content/uploads/2011/06/BestInvestment_Full_Report_6.27.11.pdf on July 20, 2023.

Mitsuhashi, Y. (2018). *Ikigai: The Japanese art of a meaningful life.* London: Octopus Books.

Morrison, N. (2022, December 30). *The biggest challenge for schools in 2023 is keeping hold of teachers.* Accessed at https://forbes.com/sites/nickmorrison/2022/12/30/the-biggest-challenge-for-schools-in-2023-is-keeping-hold-of-teachers on July 20, 2023.

Murphy, P. P. (2019, April 26). *New law will require Indiana high schoolers to take the US citizenship test. Can you pass it?* Accessed at https://cnn.com/2019/04/26/us/citizenship-test-naturalization-indiana-trnd/index.html on April 19, 2023.

Murray, K. (2017). *People with purpose: How great leaders use purpose to build thriving organizations.* New York: Kogan Page.

National Commission on Excellence in Education. (1983, April). *A nation at risk: The imperative for educational reform.* Accessed at https://edreform.com/wp-content/uploads/2013/02/A_Nation_At_Risk_1983.pdf on April 19, 2023.

Neumerski, C. M., Grissom, J. A., Goldring, E., Rubin, M., Cannata, M., Schuermann, P., et al. (2018). Restructuring instructional leadership: How multiple-measure teacher evaluation systems are redefining the role of the school principal. *The Elementary School Journal*, *119*(2), 270–297.

Nevins, M. (2023, January 5). *How to get stuff done: The Eisenhower matrix (a.k.a. the urgent vs the important)*. Accessed at https://forbes.com/sites/hillennevins/2023/01/05/how-to-get-stuff-done-the-eisenhower-matrix-aka-the-urgent-vs-the-important on July 20, 2023.

Nguyen, T. D., Lam, C. B., & Bruno, P. (2022, August). *Is there a national teacher shortage? A systematic examination of reports of teacher shortages in the United States* (EdWorkingPaper: 22-631). https://doi.org/10.26300/76eq-hj32

No Child Left Behind (NCLB) Act of 2001, Pub. L. No. 107–110, § 115, Stat. 1425 (2002).

O'Brien, E., & Linehan, C. (2019). Problematizing the authentic self in conceptualizations of emotional dissonance. *Human Relations*, *72*(9), 1530–1556.

Organisation for Economic Co-operation and Development. (2014, June 25). *Teachers love their job but feel undervalued, unsupported, and unrecognised, says OECD*. Accessed at https://oecd.org/newsroom/teachers-love-their-job-but-feel-undervalued-unsupported-and-unrecognised.htm on April 19, 2023.

Palmer, P. J. (2000). *Let your life speak: Listening for the voice of vocation*. San Francisco: Jossey-Bass.

Pausch, R. (2008). *The last lecture*. London: Hachette.

PDK Poll. (2019, September). *Frustration in the schools: Teachers speak out on pay, funding, and feeling valued*. Accessed at https://pdkpoll.org/wp-content/uploads/2020/05/pdkpoll51-2019.pdf on April 19, 2023.

Peetz, C. (2022, November 15). *The status of teaching is at a fifty-year low. What can we do about it?* Accessed at https://edweek.org/teaching-learning/the-status-of-the-teaching-profession-is-at-a-50-year-low-what-can-we-do-about-it/2022/11 on July 10, 2023.

Petrilli, M. J. (2022, August 25). *The evolving education reform agenda* [Blog post]. Accessed at https://educationnext.org/the-evolving-education-reform-agenda-classroom-instruction on July 20, 2023.

Pink, D. H. (2009). *Drive: The surprising truth about what motivates us*. New York: Riverhead Books.

Pink, D. H. (2018). *When: The scientific secrets of timing*. New York: Riverhead Books.

Pinsker, J. (2015, March 16). *People who use Firefox or Chrome are better employees*. Accessed at https://theatlantic.com/business/archive/2015/03/people-who-use-firefoxor-chrome-are-better-employees/387781 on April 19, 2023.

Podolsky, A., Kini, T., Bishop, J., & Darling-Hammond, L. (2016, September 15). *Solving the teacher shortage: How to attract and retain excellent educators*. Palo Alto, CA: Learning Policy Institute.

Pratt, M. G. (2000). The good, the bad, and the ambivalent: Managing identification among Amway distributors. *Administrative Science Quarterly, 45*(3), 456–493.

Prilleltensky, I. (2014). Meaning-making, mattering, and thriving in community psychology: From co-optation to amelioration and transformation. *Psychosocial Intervention, 23*(2), 151–154. https://doi.org/10.1016/j.psi.2014.07.008

Pronko, R. B. (2019, June 28). *Backwards and in high heels: Despite challenges, women are making their mark in law*. Accessed at https://pabusinesscentral.com/articles/backwards-and-in-high-heels on August 1, 2023.

Pryce-Jones, J. (2010). *Happiness at work: Maximizing your psychological capital for success*. Hoboken, NJ: Wiley.

Rayle, A. D. (2006). Mattering to others: Implications for the counseling relationship. *Journal of Counseling and Development, 84*(4), 483–487. https://doi.org/10.1002/j.1556-6678.2006.tb00432.x

Reeve, J. (2018). *Understanding motivation and emotion* (7th ed.). Hoboken, NJ: Wiley.

Regier, N. (2020). *Seeing people through. Unleash your leadership potential with the process communication model*. Oakland, CA: Berrett-Kohler.

Robbins, M. (2007). *Focus on the good stuff: The power of appreciation*. San Francisco: Jossey-Bass.

Robinson, K. (2009). *The element: How finding your passion changes everything*. New York: Penguin.

Rogerson, L. (2004). *The importance of the emotional climate in schools: Linking teachers' sense of belonging to school community with student outcomes* [Honours thesis, Edith Cowan University]. ECU Research Online Institutional Repository. Accessed at https://ro.ecu.edu.au/theses_hons/957 on May 31, 2023

Rosenberg, M., & McCullough, B. C. (1981). Mattering: Inferred significance and mental health among adolescents. *Research in Community and Mental Health, 2*, 163–182. Accessed at https://psycnet.apa.org/record/1983-07744-001 on April 19, 2023.

Ross, B. (Host, Creator). (1983–1994). *The joy of painting* [TV series]. Arlington, VA: Public Broadcasting Service.

Rumens, N. (2017). Researching workplace friendships: Drawing insights from the sociology of friendship. *Journal of Social and Personal Relationships, 34*(8), 1149–1167. https://doi.org/10.1177/0265407516670276

Ryan, R. M., & Deci, E. L. (2000). Self-determination theory and the facilitation of intrinsic motivation, social development, and well-being. *American Psychologist, 55*(1), 68–78. Accessed at https://selfdeterminationtheory.org/SDT/documents/2000_RyanDeci_SDT.pdf on April 20, 2023.

Ryff, C. D., & Singer, B. (2000). Interpersonal flourishing: A positive health agenda for the new millennium. *Personality and Social Psychology Review, 4*(1), 30–44.

Sawchuk, S. (2020, March 20). *When schools shut down, we all lose.* Accessed at https://edweek.org/ew/articles/2020/03/20/when-americas-schools-shut-down-we-all.html on April 20, 2023.

Šćepanović, S., Constantinides, M., Quercia, D., & Kim, S. (2023). Quantifying the impact of positive stress on companies from online employee reviews. *Scientific Reports, 13*(1), 1603.

Schaffer, O. (2013, May). *Crafting fun user experiences: A method to facilitate flow* [White paper]. Accessed at https://researchgate.net/publication/272181532_Crafting_Fun_User _Experiences_A_Method_to_Facilitate_Flow on May 30, 2023.

Scholastic. (2012). *Primary sources 2012: America's teachers on the teaching profession.* Accessed at chrome-extension://efaidnbmnnnibpcajpcglclefindmkaj/https://www.scholastic.com /primarysources/pdfs/Gates2012_full.pdf on July 26, 2023.

Shughart, W. F., II, Thomas, D. W., & Thomas, M. D. (2020). Institutional change and the importance of understanding shared mental models. *Kyklos, 73*(3), 371–391. https://dx.doi.org/10.1111/kykl.12245

Simon, N. S., Johnson, S. M., & Reinhorn, S. K. (2015, July). *The challenge of recruiting and hiring teachers of color: Lessons from six high-performing, high-poverty, urban schools.* Accessed at https://projectngt.gse.harvard.edu/files/gse-projectngt/files/the_challenge_of_recruiting _and_hiring_teachers_of_color_diversity_july_2015.pdf on July 20, 2023.

Sinek, S. (2009). *Start with why: How great leaders inspire everyone to take action.* New York: Portfolio.

Sinek, S. (2020). *The infinite game.* New York: Portfolio/Penguin.

Skaalvik, E., & Skaalvik, S. (2015). Job satisfaction, stress, and coping strategies in the teaching profession—What do teachers say? *International Education Studies, 8*(3), 181–192. https://dx.doi.org/10.5539/ies.v8n3p181

Smith, A. (2012). *Innovative applications of logotherapy for military-related PTSD* [Article 5]. Accessed at https://counseling.org/docs/default-source/vistas/vistas_2012_article_5.pdf?sfvrsn=2985355c_14 on July 20, 2023.

Smith, E. N., Young, M. D., & Crum, A. J. (2020). Stress, mindsets, and success in Navy SEALs special warfare training. *Frontiers in Psychology, 10* (2962). https://doi.org/10.3389/fpsyg.2019.02962

Sokal, L., Trudel, L. E., & Babb, J. (2020). It's okay to be okay too. Why calling out teachers' "toxic positivity" may backfire. *EdCan, 60*(3). Accessed at https://winnspace.uwinnipeg.ca/bitstream/handle/10680/1873/It's%20ok%20to%20be%20okay%20too.pdf?sequence=1 on April 20, 2023.

Soldner, L. B. (2002). Why I continue to teach: Reflections of a mid-career developmental literacy educator. *Journal of College Literacy and Learning, 31*, 71–78.

Stice, J. (n.d.). *Both educators and students are more stressed than ever, according to new studies.* Accessed at https://educationworld.com/a_news/both-educators-and-students-are-more-stressed-ever-according-new-studies-5488152 on April 20, 2023.

Strauss, V. (2016, December 23). Teacher: A one-size-fits-all approach to instruction is stifling our classrooms. *The Washington Post.* Accessed at https://washingtonpost.com/news/answer-sheet/wp/2016/12/23/teacher-a-one-size-fits-all-approach-to-instruction-is-stifling-our-classrooms on April 20, 2023.

Sutcher, L., Darling-Hammond, L., & Carver-Thomas, D. (2019). Understanding teacher shortages: An analysis of teacher supply and demand in the United States. *Education Policy Analysis Archives, 27*(35), 2–40. https://doi.org/10.14507/epaa.27.3696

Tanzer, J. R. (2019). Developing authentic happiness: Growth curve models to assess lifelong happiness. *The Journal of Positive Psychology, 16*(1), 11–19. https://doi.org/10.1080/17439760.2019.1689419

Taylor, J., & Turner, R. J. (2001). A longitudinal study of the role and significance of mattering to others for depressive symptoms. *Journal of Health and Social Behavior, 42*(3), 310–325. https://doi.org/10.2307/3090217

Trespicio, T. (2015) *Stop searching for your passion* [Video file]. Accessed at https://youtube.com/watch?v=6MBaFL7sCb8 on July 20, 2023.

U.S. Bureau of Labor Statistics. (n.d.). *BLS data viewer* [Time Period: Start Year 2009, End Year 2023]. Accessed at https://beta.bls.gov/dataViewer/view/timeseries/LAUCN180390000000003 on July 19, 2023.

U.S. Census Bureau. (2023, February 9). *CPS historical time series tables.* Accessed at https://census.gov/data/tables/time-series/demo/educational-attainment/cps-historical-time-series.html on April 20, 2023.

U.S. Department of Education. (n.d.). *State template for the consolidated state plan under the Every Student Succeeds Act.* Washington, DC: Author. Accessed at https://in.gov/doe/files/essa-plan-draft-two.pdf on April 19, 2023.

Victor Frankl Institute of Logotherapy. (n.d.). *Logotherapy is both a life philosophy and treatment modality.* Accessed at https://viktorfranklinstitute.org/about-logotherapy on July 19, 2023.

Vygotsky, L. S. (1978). *Mind in society: The development of higher psychological processes.* Cambridge, MA: Harvard University Press.

Warren, R. (2012). *The purpose driven life: What on earth am I here for?* (Expanded ed.). Grand Rapids, MI: Zondervan.

Watson, A. (2015). *Unshakeable: Twenty ways to enjoy teaching every day . . . no matter what.* Tamiment, PA: Due Season Press and Educational Services.

Watson, A. (2019). *Fewer things, better: The courage to focus on what matters most.* Tamiment, PA: Due Season Press and Educational Services.

Watson, J. C., Harper, S., Ratliff, L., & Singleton, S. (2010). Holistic wellness and perceived stress: Predicting job satisfaction among beginning teachers. *Research in the Schools*, *17*(1), 29–37.

Wei, H., Corbett, R. W., Ray, J., & Wei, T. L. (2019). A culture of caring: The essence of healthcare interprofessional collaboration. *Journal of Interprofessional Care*, *34*(3), 324–331. https://doi.org/10.1080/13561820.2019.1641476

Wilfong, S. (2021). *The mattering model: The foundational elements of mattering for K–12 educators* [Doctoral dissertation, Indiana State University]. ProQuest Dissertations. Accessed at https://proquest.com/openview/e478d40e11c4f9261fd17c26b6ca3528/1?pq-origsite=gscholar&cbl=18750&diss=y on July 25, 2023.

Wilfong, S., & Donlan, R. (n.d.). *Does mattering matter? Perceptions of whether I matter as a teacher and connections to individual and collective teacher efficacy, perspectives on change, school culture, and organizational health* [Unpublished manuscript].

Will, M. (2022, April 14). *Teacher job satisfaction hits an all-time low.* Accessed at https://edweek.org/teaching-learning/teacher-job-satisfaction-hits-an-all-time-low/2022/04 on July 20, 2023.

WorkHuman Research Institute. (2017). *Bringing more humanity to recognition, performance, and life at work* [Survey report]. Accessed at https://workhuman.com/wp-content/uploads/2017/10/WHRI_2017SurveyReportA.pdf on July 20, 2023.

Wrzesniewski, A., & Dutton, J. E. (2001). Crafting a job: Revisioning employees as active crafters of their work. *The Academy of Management Review*, *26*(2), 179–201. https://doi.org/10.2307/259118

Yan, H., Chiaramonte, T., & Lagamayo, A. (2019, October 6). *Desperate to fill teacher shortages, US schools are hiring teachers from overseas.* Accessed at https://cnn.com/2019/10/06/us/international-teachers-us-shortage/index.html on April 20, 2023.

Yount, B. (2019, October 10). *Lawmaker pitches cursive requirement for public schools.* Accessed at https://thecentersquare.com/wisconsin/lawmaker-pitches-cursive-requirement-for-public-schools/article_165dc886-eb57-11e9-848f-d797a8a65ff1.html on April 20, 2023.

Index

A

Achor, S., 99
adversarial relationships, 22. *See also* community
adverse childhood experiences (ACEs), 97–98
Ashforth, B., 42
assessment and job crafting, 150–151
assimilation
    about, 91–92, 94–95
    conclusion, 104–105
    and foundational elements of mattering for K-12 teachers, 10
    getting started with, 95–100
    implications for school leaders, 102–104
    implications for teachers, 100–102
    intrapersonal element of assimilation in mattering, 95
    making assimilation matter, 100
    positivity and, 96–97
    reproducibles for, 106–108
    stress and, 97–100
    vignette for, 92–94, 104–105
attention, 6
authenticity
    about, 39–41
    conclusion, 50–51
    and foundational elements of mattering for K-12 teachers, 10
    getting started with, 41–45
    implications for school leaders, 48–50
    implications for teachers, 46–48
    interpersonal element of authenticity in mattering, 41
    making authenticity matter, 45–46
    reproducibles for, 52–54
    sensebreaking and, 44–45
    vignette for, 39–40, 50
autonomy
    job crafting and, 15, 143, 146–147
    job dissatisfaction and, 8
    making compensation matter and, 117
    public perception of teaching and, 113

B

Babb, J., 96–97
Bayne, S., 42
behavior, student misbehavior and flow, 65
being your authentic self, 42. *See also* authenticity
belonging. *See also* community
    about, 23–24
    from belonging to workplace health in adults, 25–26
    creating belonging, 24
    mattering and, 5
bias

cognitive bias, 5
implicit bias, 50
budgets
compensation and, 112–113, 117
reduction in force (RIF) and, 130
stability and forced transfers and, 131
teacher employment gap and, 8

C

celebrating the team, not just the score: community.
    See community
challenges, perceiving significant, 62
change
    authenticity and, 48–49
    flow and, 59
    optimism and, 97
    stability and forced transfers and, 131–132
check-in questions, 31
choosing the right pond, 24, 29, 47, 81. See also community
classroom management and flow, 65
classroom visits, 66
climate committee, 30
code-switching, 14, 41, 43, 46–47
cognitive bias, 5. See also bias
cognitive crafting, 149
collegial relationships, 22. See also community
communication and authenticity, 49
community
    about, 19–21
    belonging and, 23–26
    components of, 22–23
    conclusion, 34–35
    and foundational elements of mattering for K–12
        teachers, 10
    getting started with, 21–26
    implications for school leaders, 30–34
    implications for teachers, 28–30
    interpersonal element of community in mattering, 21
    making community matter, 26–27
    reproducibles for, 36–38
    vignette for, 19–20, 35
compartmentalization, 117
compensation
    about, 109, 111
    conclusion, 122–123
    external element of compensation in mattering, 111
    and foundational elements of mattering for K–12
        teachers, 10
    getting started with, 112–116
    implications for school leaders, 120–121
    implications for teachers, 118–119
    making compensation matter, 116–118
    meaning as, 115–116
    reproducibles for, 124–125
    stability and, 130
    vignette for, 109–111, 122
confluence, 116
congenial relationships, 22. See also community
core values
    changing, 47
    evaluations and, 32
    implications for school leaders, 48, 49
    implications for teachers, 46
creating a synchronized moment, 24
Crum, A., 99

D

Deci, E., 91
Deming, W., 7, 23, 148
deprofessionalization, 113
distractions
    embracing and minimizing distractions, 62–63
    school schedule and, 66
Dunning-Kruger effect, 66

E

efficacy
    flow and, 57
    implications for teachers, 64
    mattering and, 10, 11, 161
    perceiving significant challenges and, 62
    validation and, 116
Eisenhower matrix, 59
element, the, 57
embracing and minimizing distractions, 62–63
embracing what you see, that's a whole lot of me: authenticity.
    See authenticity
emotional dissonance
    authenticity and, 43
    implications for school leaders, 48, 49
    implications for teachers, 47
    surface acting and, 43–44
equity over equality, 121, 135
essential standards and job crafting, 150, 151
eudaemonia/eudaemonic well-being, 77
eustress, 99
evaluations, 32, 132–133, 135
existential flexibility, 44
extrinsic motivation, 116. See also motivation

F

Fay, C., 43
feedback and flow, 66
flow

about, 55, 57
cognitive crafting and, 149
conclusion, 67–68
and foundational elements of mattering for K-12 teachers, 10
getting started with, 57–63
implications for school leaders, 65–67
implications for teachers, 64–65
interpersonal element of flow in mattering, 57
making flow matter, 63–64
reproducibles for, 69–72
vignette for, 55–57, 67–68
flywheel effect, 64
Foo, S., 44
forced transfers, 131–132. *See also* stability
foundational elements of mattering for K–12 teachers. *See also* mattering
about, 9–10
example foundational elements of mattering survey for K-12 teachers, 163–165
reproducibles for, 172–174
use of survey, 162–163, 166
Frame, M., 43
Frankl, V., 100
"Free to Be You and Me: A Climate of Authenticity" (Grandey, Foo, Groth, and Goodwin), 44
freedom of will, 100
frequency illusions, 5
friendship and professionalism, 27–28. *See also* community
fulfillment of needs, 21

G

García, L., 112
getting lost in the moment, with a good crowd around: flow. *See* flow
getting real with how educators stack up: compensation. *See* compensation
goals and purpose, 76
Golden Circle, 96
Goldilocks zone, 62, 99
Goodwin, R., 44
grading and job crafting, 151
Grandey, A., 44
great groups, 23. *See also* community
Great Recession, 7, 112, 113
Groth, M., 44
growth mindset, 99

H

Hattie, J., 1
hedonic treadmill, 115
how, the, 96

I

"Identity Under Construction: How Individuals Come to Define Themselves in Organizations" (Ashforth and Schinoff), 42
ikigai, 78
implicit bias, 50. *See also* bias
importance, 6
incentives
assimilation and, 104
impact of, 32
job crafting and, 155
making compensation matter and, 117
purpose and, 83
infinite games, 61
influence, 21
instruction and job crafting, 150, 151
intrinsic motivation, 116. *See also* motivation
introduction
about teacher needs, 1–2
about this book, 14–17
contemporary challenges for teachers, 7–9
foundational elements of mattering for K-12 teachers, 9–10
obligation of school leaders in mattering, 12–14
role of teachers in mattering, 11–12
vignette for, 3–4
what is mattering, 2–7
"It's Okay to Be Okay Too: Why Calling Out Teachers' 'Toxic Positivity' May Backfire" (Sokal, Trudel, and Babb), 96–97

J

job crafting
about, 143, 145–146
autonomy and, 147
conclusion, 155–157
external element of job crafting in mattering, 145
and foundational elements of mattering for K-12 teachers, 10
getting started with, 146–151
implications for school leaders, 154–155
implications for teachers, 152–153
making job crafting matter, 151–152
reproducibles for, 158–160
vignette for, 143–145, 155–156
what job crafting can look like, 148–149
when and where of teacher job crafting, 150–151
job swapping, 84
just cause, 61

K

Kanold, T., 79
Kenworth, J., 43
Kim, J., 99

Klampfleitner, M., 42
Knottenbelt, M., 42
knowing how to do it, 59–60. *See also* flow
knowing how well you are doing it, 60–61. *See also* flow
knowing what to do, 58–59. *See also* flow
knowing what's necessary to accomplish to consider the task done, 61–62. *See also* flow
Kreber, C., 42

L

laughter, 102
layoffs, 129–130
legislation
    compensation and, 119
    impacting education requirements, 147–148
    implications for school leaders, 33, 137
    making stability matter and, 133–134
    public perception of teaching and, 114
Let Your Life Speak (Palmer), 78
letting things be loose or tight: job crafting. *See* job crafting; loose-tight structure
Linehan, C., 43
logotherapy, 77
loose-tight structure, 33, 148, 154. *See also* job crafting

M

Marzano, R., 1
Maslow's hierarchy of needs, 137
mattering
    external element of compensation in, 111
    external element of job crafting in, 145
    external element of stability in, 129
    foundational elements of mattering for K–12 teachers, 9–10
    foundational elements of mattering survey for K–12 teachers, 162–166
    interpersonal element of authenticity in, 41
    interpersonal element of community in, 21
    interpersonal element of flow in, 57
    intrapersonal element of assimilation in, 95
    intrapersonal element of purpose in, 76
    mattering tools roadmap, 162
    significance and, 5–6
    social integration and, 14
    teacher reflection tool: the ideal state of mattering, 167–168
    what is mattering, 2–7
McCullough, B., 14
McCune, V., 42
McLeod, L., 148
meaning as compensation, 115–116
meaningful significance, 5, 6, 162. *See also* significance and mattering
measuring the effectiveness of teaching and learning, 60

membership, 21. *See also* community
"Meta-Analytic Review of the Relationship Between Emotional Dissonance and Emotional Exhaustion, A" (Kenworthy, Fay, Frame, and Petree), 43
mission
    assimilation and, 96
    implications for school leaders, 48, 49, 83
    implications for teachers, 46, 80, 82, 119
    purpose and, 73
moai, 23
motivation
    assimilation and, 91, 95–96
    job crafting, implications for school leaders, 155
    meaning as compensation and, 115, 116

N

needs
    about teacher needs, 1–2
    fulfillment of needs and community, 21
    Maslow's hierarchy of needs, 137

O

O'Brien, E., 43
optimism, 96–97
organizational support, 24
outliers, 50

P

Palmer, O., 78
parallel play, 22
Park, D., 99
passion and purpose, 77
perception
    perceiving significant challenges, 62
    perceiving significant skills, 62
    public perception of teaching, 113–115
performance evaluations, 132–133
Petree, R., 43
Phi Delta Kappa, 117
Pink, D., 24
positivity, 96–97
principal action plan. *See also* school leaders
    putting it all together, 170–171
    reproducibles for, 179
priorities/knowing what to do, 58–59
"Problematizing the Authentic Self in Conceptualizations of Emotional Dissonance" (O'Brien and Linehan), 43
professional learning
    embracing and minimizing distractions and, 63
    implications for school leaders, 34, 65, 66–67
    implications for teachers, 64

Professional Learning Communities (PLCs)
    community and, 14, 21, 22
    implications for school leaders, 33, 34
    job crafting and, 150, 151
    loose-tight structure and, 148
professionalism and friendships, 27–28. *See also* community
psychological safety, 44, 64, 66
purpose
    about, 73, 75–76
    assimilation and, 95
    conclusion, 85–86
    and foundational elements of mattering for K–12 teachers, 10
    getting started with, 76–79
    Golden Circle and, 96
    implications for school leaders, 83–85
    implications for teachers, 80–82
    intrapersonal element of purpose in mattering, 76
    making purpose matter, 79–80
    passion and, 77
    reproducibles for, 87–90
    vignette for, 73–75, 85–86
    work and, 77–79
putting it all together: smarter stuff that matters
    about, 161
    foundational elements of mattering survey for K–12 teachers, 162–166
    getting started on, 162
    mattering tools roadmap, 162
    principal action plan, 170–171
    reproducibles for, 172–179
    teacher action plan, 168–170
    teacher reflection tool: my area of focus matrix, 166–167
    teacher reflection tool: the ideal state of mattering, 167–168
    teacher reflection tool: what is most important to me, 166

R

reduction in force (RIF), 130, 132
reliance, 6
reproducibles for
    foundational elements of mattering survey for K–12 teachers, 172–174
    next steps: chapter 1 recap activity, 36
    next steps: chapter 2 recap activity, 52
    next steps: chapter 3 recap activity, 69
    next steps: chapter 4 recap activity, 87
    next steps: chapter 5 recap activity, 106
    next steps: chapter 6 recap activity, 124
    next steps: chapter 7 recap activity, 139
    next steps: chapter 8 recap activity, 158
    principal action plan, 179
    teacher action plan, 178
    teacher reflection tool: my area of focus matrix, 176
    teacher reflection tool: the ideal state of mattering, 177
    teacher reflection tool: what is most important to me, 175
    your personal professional development: thought experiment—assimilation, 107–108
    your personal professional development: thought experiment—authenticity, 53–54
    your personal professional development: thought experiment—community, 37–38
    your personal professional development: thought experiment—compensation, 125
    your personal professional development: thought experiment—flow, 70–72
    your personal professional development: thought experiment—job crafting, 159–160
    your personal professional development: thought experiment—purpose, 88–90
    your personal professional development: thought experiment—stability, 140–141
response to intervention (RTI), 7
Robinson, K., 24, 57
Rosenberg, M., 14
Ryan, R., 91

S

Salovey, P., 99
schedules and distractions, 66. *See also* flow
Schinoff, B., 42
school leaders
    assimilation and implications for, 102–104
    authenticity and implications for, 48–50
    community and implications for, 30–34
    compensation and implications for, 120–121
    flow and implications for, 65–67
    job crafting and implications for, 154–155
    obligation of school leaders in mattering, 12–14
    principal action plan, 170–171, 179
    purpose and implications for, 83–85
    stability and implications for, 136–137
seeing the downside as a necessary upside: assimilation. *See* assimilation
self and authenticity, 42
self-determination theory, 91
self-fulness, 43
self-regulation, 91
sensebreaking, 43, 44–45
shared emotional connection, 21
Shin, Y., 99
significance and mattering, 5–6. *See also* meaningful significance
skills, perceiving significant, 62
Sokal, L., 96–97
SOUL! (Kanold), 79
stability
    about, 127–129
    conclusion, 137–138
    external element of stability in mattering, 129
    forced transfers and, 131–132

and foundational elements of mattering for K–12
teachers, 10
getting started with, 129–133
implications for school leaders, 136–137
implications for teachers, 135–136
making stability matter, 133–134
meaning as compensation and, 116
performance evaluations and, 132–133
reproducibles for, 139–141
vignette for, 127–128, 137–138
working a second job and, 130–131
staying the course, en route to my why: purpose. *See* purpose
stress
assimilation and, 97–100
friendship and professionalism and, 27
implications for teachers, 101
positivity and, 96–97
teacher stress, 25
surface acting. *See also* authenticity
code-switching and, 41
emotional dissonance and, 43–44
implications for school leaders, 49
implications for teachers, 46, 47
mattering and, 45
surveys
example foundational elements of mattering survey for K–12 teachers, 163–165
foundational elements of mattering survey for K–12 teachers, 162–163, 166
mattering tools roadmap, 162
public perception of teaching and, 114
reproducibles for, 172–174
synchronization, 24

T

taking care to take care: stability. *See* stability
task crafting, 149. *See also* job crafting
teacher action plan
example teacher action plan, 169–170
putting it all together, 168–170
reproducibles for, 178
teacher employment gap, 8
teacher evaluations, 32, 132–133, 135
teacher reflection tools. *See also* putting it all together: smarter stuff that matters
reproducibles for, 175, 176, 177
teacher reflection tool: my area of focus matrix, 166–167
teacher reflection tool: the ideal state of mattering, 167–168
teacher reflection tool: what is most important to me, 166
teacher retention, 7–9
teacher shortages, 7–9, 25
teacher stress, 25
teacher wage penalty, 112
teachers
about teacher needs, 1–2
assimilation and implications for, 100–102
authenticity and implications for teachers, 46–48
community and implications for, 28–30
compensation and implications for, 118–119
contemporary challenges for teachers, 7–9
flow and implications for, 64–65
foundational elements of mattering for K–12 teachers, 9–10
job crafting and implications for, 152–153
public perception of teaching, 113–115
purpose and implications for, 80–82
role of teachers in mattering, 11–12
stability and implications for, 135–136
when and where of teacher job crafting, 150–151
team synchronization, 81
technology and job crafting, 155. *See also* job crafting
tolerable stress, 99. *See also* stress
toxic positivity, 96, 97, 103
toxic stress, 99. *See also* stress
Trespicio, T., 77
Trudel, L., 96–97
Tsukayama, E., 99
tuition reimbursement programs, 121

U

unemployment rate, 129. *See also* stability

V

validation, 116

W

why, the, 61, 76, 96, 119, 149. *See also* purpose
work
from belonging to workplace health in adults and, 25–26
purpose and, 77–79
stability and working a second job, 130–131
workplace friends, 27–28. *See also* community

Z

zone of proximal development, 121

All Other Duties as Assigned
Ryan Donlan
Explore the wide range of duties inherent in being an assistant principal and gain strategies to achieve success and happiness in this position. This complete guide will equip you with research-informed ways to excel in this critical role for fostering student success.
BKG026

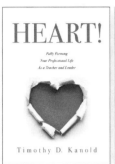

HEART! and SOUL!
Timothy D. Kanold
A highly anticipated companion to the wildly popular HEART!, SOUL! empowers educators to take another giant leap toward fulfilling their professional promise.
BKF982, BKF749

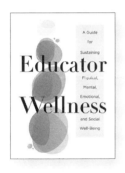

Educator Wellness
Timothy D. Kanold; Tina H. Boogren
How do we bring our best selves to our students and colleagues each day? Designed as a reflective journal and guidebook, *Educator Wellness* will take you on a deep exploration where you will uncover profound answers that ring true for you.
BKG053

From Burnt Out to Fired Up
Morgane Michael
Overwhelmed teachers, this book is for you. The truth is that you can be remarkable without burning out. Drawing from the latest research and her own teaching experiences, author Morgane Michael delivers research-backed strategies to replenish your well-being and reignite your passion for your purpose.
BKG027

Benches in the Bathroom
Evisha Ford
Benches in the Bathroom offers K–12 leadership a wealth of field-tested, research-supported guidance to construct a school culture that values teacher contributions, operates on a framework of emotional wellness, and implements trauma-compassionate organizational strategies to ensure educator success and well-being.
BKG094

Visit SolutionTree.com or call 800.733.6786 to order.

Quality team learning **from authors you trust**

Global PD Teams is the first-ever **online professional development resource designed to support your entire faculty on your learning journey.** This convenient tool offers daily access to videos, mini-courses, eBooks, articles, and more packed with insights and research-backed strategies you can use immediately.

GET STARTED
SolutionTree.com/**GlobalPDTeams**
800.733.6786